Harlots
WHORES
& HACKABOUTS

A HISTORY

OF

SEX

FOR

SALE

KATE LISTER

Contents

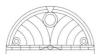

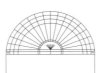

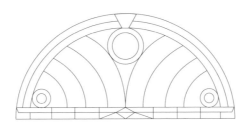

Introduction

TALES FROM
Gropecunt
LANE

TO SEX WORKERS EVERYWHERE,
PAST, PRESENT AND FUTURE.

In the autumn of 1888, five women were brutally murdered in the Whitechapel district of London, England. Despite the best efforts of Scotland Yard, their attacker was never caught. Mary Ann 'Polly' Nichols, Annie Chapman, Elizabeth Stride, Catherine Eddowes and Mary Jane Kelly are now known as the 'canonical five' victims of the serial killer the British press nicknamed Jack the Ripper. Their murders were reported around the world and birthed an international obsession with their killer. In life, Polly, Annie, Elizabeth, Catherine and Mary were unremarkable. Like thousands of Londoners living in desperate poverty, they eked out an existence on the margins of society, but, in death, they attained an almost cult-like status in popular history, as countless historians, authors and amateur 'Ripperologists' have tried to unmask their killer. Every year, tourists still flock to Whitechapel to walk the same streets as the killer once did, take in a Ripper tour or visit the Jack the Ripper Museum. The Ripper is now part of British folklore and continues to evoke hackneyed images of dimly lit streets, swirling smog, a shadowy figure and, of course, the 'prostitutes' that he preyed upon.

The impoverished women who sold sex in the slums of Whitechapel are as much a part of the Ripper mythology as the killer himself. The canonical five may be infamous, but they have never been 'real' women to us. As the Ripper became legendary, his victims became little more than a sensationalist plot device in the story of their murderer. Despite hundreds of books, documentaries and websites dedicated to uncovering the identity of Jack the Ripper, the identity of his victims has never extended much beyond the effacing label of 'prostitute'. They too have become caricatures: hiding in doorways, their faces drawn and pale, their lips rouged, hitching their tattered skirts up past their ankles to reveal a flash of cheap stockings, calling out to clients in the broad, Cockney tones of old London town, and offering sex for the price of a jar of gin or maybe a night at the dosshouse.

The narrative demands that these women were 'prostitutes' in the same way it demands that their killer was somehow mysterious and extraordinary. But Hallie Rubenhold's recent research into the lives of the canonical five suggests that only Elizabeth Stride and Mary Kelly had earned their money by selling sex.[1] The others, like many in the slums of Whitechapel, were homeless and earned their money through a combination of odd jobs, begging, borrowing and pawning what few possessions they acquired. Rubenhold's claim fundamentally disturbed the foundations of the Ripper narrative and led to her receiving considerable online abuse from 'Ripperologists' certain that these women were selling sex because of the poverty they endured. This hostility has laid bare an ongoing determination, both in their own time and today, to make these women stereotyped, cartoon 'prostitutes', in order to fit a more salacious narrative.

The stigma surrounding sex work and sex workers has long blinded us to the reality of these women and others like them. Today, sex work is a diverse and complex experience, ranging from full-service sex workers to dancers, sugar babies,

BDSM providers and those selling photos on OnlyFans. All sell a sexual service, but few would call themselves a 'prostitute'. Conversely, many Victorians comfortably labelled anyone selling a sexual service as a prostitute, as well as any woman living with a partner outside of wedlock. What is meant by 'prostitute' can vary considerably but however it is deployed it is tangled in assumptions about a woman's morality and worth. The Ripper myth demands that these women are prostitutes because the label dehumanizes them, makes them complicit in their own murders and allows us to indulge our own interest in the violence inflicted on their bodies.

We have assumed much about these women but known very little. This is the history of sex work. Stereotypes, stigma and sensationalism have obscured the lived experience of people selling sex throughout much of history. The stigma forced, and continues to force, many into silence, meaning the dominant social narrative around sex work has been constructed and deployed by law makers, moralizers, medics and the media. Stereotypes of the unrepentant, titillating whore or the tragic victim in need of rescue have long stifled the voices of those who sold sex.

The very nature of sex work is, and has always been, to sell a fantasy. When we watch porn, for example, we see only the carefully choreographed final product. We see the actors, the set and the make-believe sex. We do not see the camera crew, standing around and eating sandwiches, the multiple takes, the fake cum or the discussions around consent and boundaries. The fantasy is the finished product, but it is never the whole story.

This book invites you to move beyond the headlines, the sensation and the stereotypes of sex work and meet the people who made their money selling sexual services. Names, photographs and historical documents are placed next to the histories of 'harlots, whores and hackabouts' from around the world, to bring together forgotten faces, names and lives lived in the shadows. Sex work is, and has always been, a highly complex experience that resists easy definition. From the temple whores of Babylon and the legendary courtesans of ancient Greece, to the hustling molly boys of Georgian London, the lob-lob girls of Canton, and the Winchester Geese trading on medieval London's Gropecunt Lane, there is no one version of sex work; there are legion. Some made their name trading sex for fabulous sums of money, others occasionally turned to sex work to supplement a low wage: a side hustle once known as 'dollymopping'. Many who sold sex lived, and continue to live, in terrible poverty and choose full bellies over empty platitudes of morality. Then there are those who did not choose at all but lived in sexual slavery. All traded fantasy and sexual favours, and all faced varying levels of abuse and social stigma.

Quite how much stigma various groups have shouldered has historically been dictated by money and class – the wealthier the client, the less stigma involved. The glamorous, diamond-studded courtesans and professional mistresses

OPPOSITE LEFT **Virginia Oldoini, Countess Verasis de Castiglione**, *c.* 1865
La Castiglione became a mistress of Emperor Napoleon III of France.

OPPOSITE RIGHT **Shuzaburo Usui, an** *oiran*, **or high-ranking sex worker**, 1870
This woman likely worked in the *yūkaku*, or red light district, of Yoshiwara in Tokyo.

ABOVE LEFT **Eugène Atget,** *Rue Asselin, c.* 1924–25
Atget photographed brothels in the 1920s for a book called *La femme criminelle*. It was never published.

ABOVE RIGHT **Margaret Bourke-White, Indian sex workers**, *c.* 1946
Women peeking out of the doorways to their brothel in Lahore, Punjab province.

of the medieval and Renaissance European aristocracy, for example, not only commanded respect, but many wielded considerable political influence over their besotted clients. Royal mistresses were so powerful, many were referred to as the 'power behind the throne'.

Agnès Sorel, the mistress to King Charles VII of France in the 15th century, was one such woman. The king officially designated her the royal mistress in 1444, the first woman to be officially recognized as such in France, and heaped her with wealth, castles and lands. However, King Charles also passed laws that required 'girls and women of ill repute' in France to be rounded up and made to work in municipal, state-approved brothels, or face being expelled from their home towns altogether.[2] The women in these brothels lived as virtual prisoners, while the state made a tidy profit from their earnings – money that went to line the coffers of the king, who in turn handed it over to his own woman 'of ill repute'.

Throughout history authorities have fretted about how to best 'deal' with those who want to buy or sell sex, moving through various stages of repression, toleration, legalization, control, moral outrage and abolition, before circling back again. History is littered with various efforts to prevent sexual exploitation by abolishing sex work. None of them have worked. Torture, mutilation, fines, imprisonment, banishment, excommunication and even the death penalty have all been deployed at various points, and none have succeeded in abolishing the sale of sex. Nor have these punitive measures ended sexual abuse. All that happens is consenting sex workers are forced to work in dangerous conditions and are further stigmatized for what they do, and those who are abused become even harder to find.

One of the central mantras of the modern-day sex worker rights movement is 'Stigma Kills', and with good reason. In 2000, Canadian professor John Lowman analysed descriptions in the media of efforts to abolish sex work by politicians, police and local residents, and identified a 'discourse of disposability'.[3] Lowman linked this with a sharp increase in the murders of street sex

workers in British Columbia, Canada, after 1980. He argued that, 'It appears that the discourse on prostitution of the early 1980s was dominated by demands to get rid of prostitutes from the streets, creating a social milieu in which violence against prostitutes could flourish.'[4] This is how stigma works. Once the sex worker is stigmatized as 'less than', or 'disposable', a message formed, shaped and deployed in debates around morality and abolition, this discourse then influences how sex workers are treated. We can see this rhetoric at work throughout history. Draconian laws and harsh punishments against those selling sex reinforce social stigma which enables violence to flourish. This book uncovers the history of people who have bought and sold sex, but abolishing the ongoing stigma around sex work is everyone's responsibility.

It is said that sex work is the world's oldest profession, but this is not true. In cultures without money, there were no professions at all and little evidence of prostitution – though doubtless, sex has always been a useful commodity in one way or another. It was Rudyard Kipling who first coined the phrase 'the world's oldest profession' in his short story On the City Wall (1898). The tale opens with the immortal line 'Lalun is a member of the most ancient profession in the world.' The expression has since fallen into common parlance as a historical truth. But, perhaps what Kipling wrote after those words offers even more insight into what is, at least, a very ancient profession indeed: 'In the West, people say rude things about Lalun's profession, and write lectures about it, and distribute the lectures to young persons in order that Morality may be preserved.'[5]

How we write about sex work, indeed how we think and talk about it, matters. It might not be the 'oldest', but as this book, and many others, show, it is a very ancient one. Its workers are deserving of rights and respect, of being genuinely heard and seen, rather than stereotyped and silenced.

It is time to move beyond the fantasy. It is time to look, listen and learn.

TOP **Police raid Anna Swift's infamous 'Institute of Massage' in New York,** *c.* **1936**
In her 1934 application for a massage parlour licence Swift styled herself as 'Dr Swift'.

BOTTOM **Sex workers following a police raid,** *c.* **1943**
Sex workers in a police wagon, following a police raid on an upscale midtown apartment in New York.

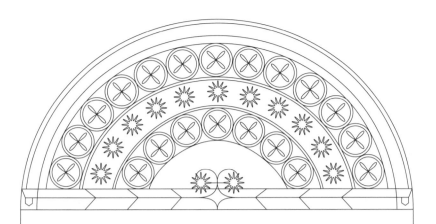

1

Sex in the
ANCIENT WORLD

OF THE GODS

WHEN SHE HAS HAD INTERCOURSE, SHE HAS FULFILLED
HER RELIGIOUS OBLIGATION TO THE GODDESS
AND WILL RETURN HOME. AFTER THIS YOU WILL NOT BE
ABLE TO GIVE HER ANY AMOUNT OF MONEY, HOWEVER
GREAT, WITH THE INTENTION OF SEDUCING HER.

Herodotus, *Histories*, 426–15 BCE

THE WOMAN
WAS DRESSED
IN PURPLE AND
SCARLET
AND GLITTERED
WITH GOLD
AND JEWELS AND
PEARLS, AND SHE
WAS HOLDING
A GOLD WINECUP
FILLED WITH
THE DISGUSTING
FILTH OF HER
PROSTITUTION.

Revelation 17:4

The British people are no strangers to bad weather, but even by their standards 1872 was a very wet year. It was, and remains, one of the wettest years since weather records began in 1766. Rivers burst their banks, chalk cliffs in Dover gave way, crushing the houses below, and ships were wrecked in the ports of Liverpool, Plymouth, Swansea and Portland. Throughout November, heavy thunderstorms pealed above the city of London. To those sheltering in the capital's doorways and public buildings, it must have seemed as if the second flood had come. And for one unassuming man watching the rain fall over Russell Square from the second floor of the British Museum, in a manner of speaking, it had.

Thirty-two-year-old George Smith spent much of 1872 indoors, hunched over thousands of shattered clay tablets that archaeologists had sent back to London from Nineveh in modern-day Iraq some twenty-five years earlier. Carved into the clay fragments was cuneiform script dating back to 1800 BCE, and Smith was one of a handful of scholars who could decipher its meaning. Piecing the ancient fragments back together, Smith had found forgotten Hebrew monarchs, ancient prayers and Assyrian laws, but that November, as the rain beat down, an astonished Smith deciphered a story about a flood, of a boat stranded on a mountain and of a bird sent to find dry land. It seemed to Smith, and many others, that this was an independent account of the biblical flood found in Genesis.

Overwhelmed at his discovery, the usually reserved Smith began shouting, whooping and running around the room. Later accounts claimed he was so beside himself that he started to take his clothes off. Smith had unearthed what would become known as *The Epic of Gilgamesh* (c. 1800 BCE), one of the oldest works of literature in the world. Of course, he did not know this as he danced around the second floor of the British Museum. Nor could he have known that the flood tablet was but one of twelve that contained the legend of Gilgamesh, King of Uruk. Smith would go on to piece all the fractured legends back together and translate them for a new audience – all except for one. The legend of Shamhat the harlot is the earliest surviving story of transactional sex in the world, and Smith simply could not bring himself to tell it. Instead, when he published his seminal *The Chaldean Account of Genesis* in 1876, Smith discreetly omitted the nineteen lines of the poem that describe Shamhat's sexual encounter with the wild man, Enkidu.[1]

OPPOSITE **Plaque depicting the goddess Ishtar,** *c.* **1800–1750** BCE This Babylonian plaque, found in southern Iraq, probably stood in a shrine. The horned crown the figure wears is a symbol of deity in Mesopotamian art, and lions were associated with the goddess Ishtar.

The story Smith tried to hush up tells of how the great goddess Aruru created Enkidu to equal King Gilgamesh. Enkidu lived in the wild, among the beasts. His body was covered in long hair, he grazed on grass with gazelles and he drank at the waterhole, 'his heart delighting with the beasts in the water'. Upon learning of a man 'as mighty as a rock from the sky', Gilgamesh ordered that Shamhat the harlot find Enkidu at the waterhole, 'strip off her raiment to reveal her charms' and 'do for the man the work of a woman!'[2] Obediently, Shamhat goes to meet the wild man and she does as her king bid her to do.

'SHAMHAT UNFASTENED THE CLOTH OF HER LOINS, SHE BARED HER SEX AND HE TOOK IN HER CHARMS. SHE DID NOT RECOIL, SHE TOOK IN HIS SCENT:

ABOVE LEFT **Clay plaque depicting a copulating couple, 2nd millennium** BCE
This Babylonian relief portrays a couple drinking beer as well as having sex.

ABOVE CENTRE **Clay plaque depicting a copulating couple, 2nd millennium** BCE
Victorian archaeologists were shocked at the frank depictions of sex they found when excavating ancient Mesopotamian sites.

ABOVE RIGHT **Erotic carving from the Khajuraho temples, India, c. 600–800** CE
Sexual practices are depicted in sculptures adorning the Khajuraho temples, alongside other scenes from everyday life and mythical stories.

SHE SPREAD HER CLOTHING AND HE LAY UPON HER. SHE DID FOR THE MAN THE WORK OF A WOMAN, HIS PASSION CARESSED AND EMBRACED HER. FOR SIX DAYS AND SEVEN NIGHTS ENKIDU WAS ERECT, AS HE COUPLED WITH SHAMHAT.'[3]

After their week of frenzied lovemaking, Enkidu finds that he is no longer wild. He has reason and understanding, but the animals now fear him, and his strength is greatly reduced. Shamhat has civilized Enkidu through sex. This part of the Gilgamesh epic was not fully translated into modern language until German scholar Arthur Ungnad did so in 1911.

The question of what Shamhat can tell us about the buying and selling of sexual services in ancient Mesopotamia continues to fascinate scholars. George Smith and his conservative contemporaries may have been aghast at Shamhat, but that is evidently not how she was intended to be read. Shamhat is powerful, respected, magical, and may even have been considered sacred. This possibility opens up one of the most contentious areas of historical research, the practice of so-called 'sacred prostitution' in the ancient world.

Sex work is indeed one of the oldest professions and there is ample evidence of a thriving sex trade in ancient Mesopotamia. *The Code of Hammurabi* dates to 1754 BCE and contains several laws pertaining to the regulation and protection of sex workers.

ABOVE LEFT **Ring stone,**
c. **late 2nd–3rd century** BCE
The women and fruiting trees
that decorate this ring stone from
India are suggestive of fertility.

ABOVE RIGHT **Fragment of a
ring stone,** *c.* **1st–2nd century** BCE
This Indian ring stone is decorated
with a female figure. Ring stones
such as these may have been
used as moulds by jewelers.

'IF A MAN'S WIFE DOES NOT BEAR HIM A CHILD BUT A PROSTITUTE *(KAR.KID)* FROM THE STREET DOES BEAR HIM A CHILD, HE SHALL PROVIDE GRAIN, OIL AND CLOTHING RATIONS FOR THE PROSTITUTE, AND THE CHILD WHOM THE PROSTITUTE BORE TO HIM SHALL BE HIS HEIR; AS LONG AS HIS WIFE IS ALIVE, THE PROSTITUTE WILL NOT RESIDE IN THE HOUSE WITH HIS FIRST-RANKING WIFE.'[4]

Legal protection and state regulation of sex work is found throughout the ancient world. The *Arthaśāstra of Kautilya* is an Indian text on politics that was composed sometime between the 2nd century BCE and the 3rd century CE. The *Arthaśāstra* devotes a chapter to discussing the duties of the *ganikadhyaksa*, the 'superintendent of courtesans', and details rules for women in this profession. Sex work was regulated by the state and sex workers paid taxes each month. A *ganika* was appointed by the state to attend the king and received a salary of 1,000 *panas* every year, whereas *bandhaki* worked in brothels and *pumscali* worked on the streets. The *Arthaśāstra* uses the word 'rupjiva' to describe a woman selling sex, which translates to 'one who makes a living out of her beauty'.[5] Clearly, then, as now, sex work was a complex and densely layered experience, ranging from the destitute to wealthy courtesans. But were those who sold sex ever regarded as holy? Did women like Shamhat sell sex in service of the gods of ancient Mesopotamia?

The character of Shamhat is central to this debate and there are many who argue that she is a sexual priestess as she is associated with the goddess Ishtar throughout the epic. After spending a week making love to Shamhat, Enkidu turns to her and says, 'Come, Shamhat, take me along/to the sacred temple, the holy dwelling of Anu and Ishtar,/where Gilgamesh is perfect in strength.'[6] But what did Shamhat and her fellow harlots do in Ishtar's temple? How did they worship this powerful goddess? Did they pray? Were they temple priestesses who sold sex to Ishtar's devoted disciples? Or did they simply solicit for clients at the bustling temple?

Ishtar, or Inanna in Sumerian sources, was an extraordinarily powerful goddess, associated with war, fertility and sex. Many scholars have linked Ishtar to sacred sex, and there is some evidence to support this. The Akkadian word used to describe Shamhat in the original story is 'harimtu', the Sumerian equivalent is 'kar.kid' and both have been translated to mean 'harlot' or 'prostitute'. But these are modern labels and they bring with them layers of meaning that speak more to our own time than to that of ancient Mesopotamia. Precisely what *harimtu/kar.kid* meant to those who once worshipped in the temples of Ishtar is far less clear. On one ancient clay tablet, Ishtar identifies herself as 'a loving *harimtu*', while another surviving tablet from the ancient city of Nuzi describes a woman, Utubalti, being pledged to the temple and service of Ishtar.[7] *Kar.kid* has even been translated by some scholars to mean 'one who knows the penis'.[8] But all this really tells us is that Ishtar and her followers were associated with sex. Whether or not goddesses like Ishtar were once worshipped through transactional sex will continue to draw intense debate, but what is beyond doubt is that many of history's most prominent scholars believed that this did happen and were suitably shocked at the very thought.

OPPOSITE **Reliefs of the goddess Ishtar,** *c.* 2000 BCE–300 CE These sculptures are from ancient Babylonia (a, b, c, f and i) and Mesopotamia (d, e, g and h). Most are made of terracotta or clay, although (g) is made of alabaster. Ishtar was the great goddess of fertility, motherhood and war. Fragmentary sources suggest that she was worshipped with sex in her temples and that her priestesses may have sold sex. Whether or not this is true will continue to be debated.

Over 2,300 years before George Smith bowdlerized the *harimtu* from *The Epic of Gilgamesh*, and some 2,333 miles away from the British Museum, another historian recoiled in horror at the prospect of sacred sex in Mesopotamia. When Herodotus wrote his magnum opus, *Histories*, between 426 and 415 BCE, he intended to tell the story of the Greco-Persian wars of 481–79 BCE. What he produced was an epic nine-book overview of the entire history of Persia: its people, its practices and its prostitutes. Cicero called Herodotus the 'father of history', and like many fathers, Herodotus could be judgemental, stern and rather prone to exaggeration.

Herodotus travelled widely throughout his lifetime and writes with the authority of an eyewitness. His account of Babylon, the cultural capital of ancient Mesopotamia, certainly carries all the gravitas and certainty of a man who has been there. So, when Herodotus claimed Babylonian women sold sex to worshippers in the temple of Aphrodite, his words were accepted as fact. He writes,

ABOVE **Lawrence Alma-Tadema,** *The Women of Amphissa*, 1887
In this painting followers of Bacchus, the god of wine, awake in the marketplace of Amphissa, Greece, following a night of debauched, but devotional, revelries.

'MANY WOMEN WHO ARE RICH AND PROUD AND DISDAIN TO MINGLE WITH THE REST, DRIVE TO THE TEMPLE IN COVERED CARRIAGES DRAWN BY TEAMS, AND STAND THERE WITH A GREAT RETINUE OF ATTENDANTS. BUT MOST SIT DOWN IN THE SACRED PLOT OF APHRODITE, WITH CROWNS OF CORD ON THEIR HEADS; ... PASSAGES MARKED BY LINE RUN EVERY WAY THROUGH THE CROWD, BY WHICH THE MEN PASS AND MAKE THEIR CHOICE. ONCE A WOMAN

HAS TAKEN HER PLACE THERE, SHE DOES NOT GO
AWAY TO HER HOME BEFORE SOME STRANGER HAS
CAST MONEY INTO HER LAP, AND HAD INTERCOURSE
WITH HER OUTSIDE THE TEMPLE; BUT WHILE HE
CASTS THE MONEY, HE MUST SAY, "I INVITE YOU IN
THE NAME OF MYLITTA." IT DOES NOT MATTER WHAT
SUM THE MONEY IS; THE WOMAN WILL NEVER REFUSE,
FOR THAT WOULD BE A SIN, THE MONEY BEING BY
THIS ACT MADE SACRED. SO SHE FOLLOWS THE
FIRST MAN WHO CASTS IT AND REJECTS NO ONE.
AFTER THEIR INTERCOURSE, HAVING DISCHARGED
HER SACRED DUTY TO THE GODDESS, SHE GOES
AWAY TO HER HOME."⁹

ABOVE **Edwin Long,**
The Babylonian Marriage
Market, 1875
British painter Edwin Long was
inspired by the description of
women being auctioned for marriage
in Herodotus's *Histories* (426–15 BCE)
for this painting, which depicts
the sale of Babylonian women
at the temple.

We owe the first extant description of Babylon to Herodotus
and for centuries his work was the authority on Babylonian
history. It was not until the early 20th-century excavations
of Babylon, led by German archaeologist Robert Koldewey,
that Herodotus's account was called into question. In fact,
there are so many errors in his description of Babylon that
many modern scholars have concluded that he could never
have been there. For example, Herodotus claimed the city
had one hundred bronze gates and a wall that was 100 metres
(328 ft) high and 25 metres (82 ft) thick, but no evidence
of this could be found in the city itself. Likewise, his
claims about sacred sex in the Babylonian temple of
Aphrodite could not be corroborated by any archaeological
finds. But a good story is a good story and Herodotus's
description of Babylonian women selling sex to anyone
with a *shekel* in service of the goddess of love proved to
be extraordinarily influential.

Four hundred years after Herodotus, the historian Strabo describes ritual sex practised at Acilisene in Armenia. Here, citizens honoured the Persian goddess Anaïtis by instructing their daughters to sell sex in her temple before they were married.[10] In *De Dea Syria* (2nd century CE), the Greek writer Lucian of Samosata describes a ritual practised in Syria where young women had sex with strangers as an offering of worship to the goddess Aphrodite.[11] The Augustan historian Gnaeus Pompeius Trogus wrote, 'There was a custom among Cyprians to send their virgins to the sea-shore before marriage on fixed days, for employment in order to get dowry money, and to make a first-fruit offering to Aphrodite, a dedication to preserve their virtue in the future.'[12]

Stories of the sacred harlot of Babylon can be found scattered throughout ancient texts. There are rumours and flashes of her everywhere, but she wriggles free from the historian's grasp as soon as anyone feels they have her. But maybe what we have been looking for never existed to begin with. When George Smith silenced Shamhat in the Gilgamesh epic he did so because his culture viewed transactional sex as immoral. Smith lived at a time when prostitution was euphemistically referred to as the 'great social evil'. His understanding of what a 'prostitute' was was dictated by specific social scripts that framed her as wretched, fallen and outcast. Little wonder then that Smith simply could not accept this pathetic figure as sacred and revered. Likewise, when Herodotus writes about temple sex, he is expressing cultural bias, rather than simply reporting. The stigma around transactional sex continues to shape public opinion and modern narratives surrounding sex work continue to draw on discourses of disposability, victimhood, rescue and contagion. So pervasive is this narrative that many people simply cannot believe that anyone could choose to sell sex. The very word 'prostitute' is burdened with the weight of stigma that limits our understanding of those who sell sex. How then can we begin to understand the religious and sexual practices of the *harimtu* in the temples of Ishtar when our own views of those who sell sex are so stigmatized?

The most tangible evidence of sacred prostitution is the 800-year-old Hindu tradition of the *devadasi* in India. *Devadasi* means 'female servant of God', and in southern India they are women dedicated to serve the goddess Yellamma, as they have done for hundreds of years. The earliest written records of dancing temple girls called *devadasi* date to

OPPOSITE **Horace Vernet,** *Judah and Tamar,* 1840
In this representation of the story of Tamar from the Book of Genesis, Tamar is disguised as a sex worker and Judah, her father-in-law, is trying to buy her services.

1230–40 CE, from the time of Raja Raya III in Maharashtra.[13]
A 1,000-year-old inscription in Tanjore temple lists
400 *devadasis* in Tanjore, 450 in Brahideswara temple and
another 500 in Somnath temple. *Devadasi* looked after the
temples, sang and danced in devotion to the deities. They
were also courtesans and supported by wealthy patrons who
sought out the *devadasi* because they were sacred women.
They dazzled the courts with their poetry, music and devotion
to the goddess. Sex was a part of their world, but it was
incidental; they celebrated art, beauty, love and the divine.
When the British colonized India, they brought with them
their rigid world view and were unable to see the *devadasi*
as anything but 'prostitutes'. So repulsed were they by what
they saw, the British set about shaming and dismantling
the *devadasi* institution.

In 1892, the Hindu Social Reform Association petitioned the
Governor General of India and the Governor of Madras to erase
the *devadasi*: 'There exists in the Indian community a class of
women commonly known as nautch girls. And these women are
invariably prostitutes.'[14] The British missionaries taught India
what a 'prostitute' was and why it was so shameful. Support
for the *devadasi* disappeared; they were socially shunned and
stigmatized. Cut off from patrons and the temple, they tried
to earn money by dancing at private events and selling sexual
services. Eventually, the *devadasi* institution was outlawed
throughout India in 1988. The tradition continues in southern
India, but the women are no longer respected. Now that they
are criminalized, stigmatized and without protection, many
abuses occur, but many impoverished parents continue to
dedicate young daughters to the service of the goddess.

We cannot ever know for certain if priestesses sold sex to
worshippers in the temples of Ishtar, but if this practice
did exist it is evidently far more nuanced than the label of
'prostitute' allows for. It is unlikely that priestesses sold sex
to anyone with a few coins, but, like the *devadasi*, perhaps
they were supported by patrons with whom they may have
also had a sexual relationship. Shamhat does not trade sex
for money, but sex with her is clearly a sacred act and one
she bestows at the behest of a king. Sex with her, or indeed
any priestess, is a rare gift indeed. After all, who would
not want to make love to the gods?

OPPOSITE **Photographs depicting**
***devadasi* and nautch girls, *c*. 1860–80**
In southern India, the *devadasi*
are women dedicated to serve the
goddess Yellamma. The tradition
is over eight hundred years old and
the *devadasi* were once revered as
courtesans, artists and priestesses.
Nautch girls were dancers who rose
to prominence in the Imperial courts
of the Mughals (1526–1857). From
the mid-19th century the influence
of Christian missionaries and British
colonialism meant that nautch girls
acquired derogatory connotations,
and once abandoned by their
patrons many women had to
turn to prostitution for survival.

2

Selling Sex in the
CLASSICAL WORLD

~~~~~~~~

Toads

AND

SHE-WOLVES

~~~~~~~~

NAKED SHE STOOD ON THE SHORE, AT THE PLEASURE
OF THE PURCHASER; EVERY PART OF HER BODY WAS
EXAMINED AND FELT. WOULD YOU HEAR THE RESULT
OF THE SALE? THE PIRATE SOLD; THE PIMP BOUGHT,
THAT HE MIGHT EMPLOY HER AS A PROSTITUTE.

Seneca, *Controversiae, c.* 1st century CE

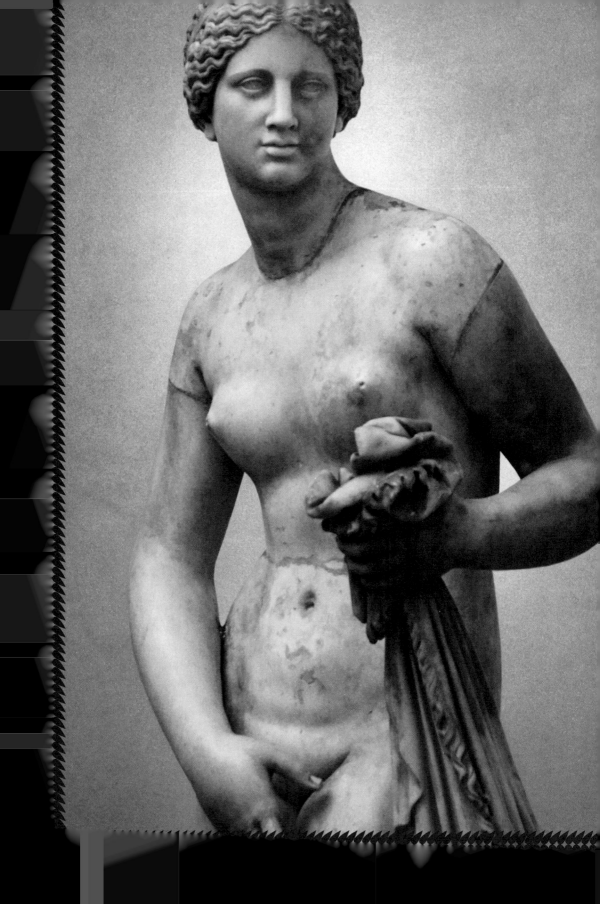

BUT HYPEREIDES, WHEN PLEADING PHRYNE'S CAUSE ...BROUGHT HER FORTH INTO THE MIDDLE OF THE COURT, AND, TEARING OPEN HER TUNIC AND DISPLAYING HER NAKED BOSOM... INSPIRED THE JUDGES WITH A SUPERSTITIOUS FEAR.

Athenaeus, *Deipnosophistae*, 3rd century CE

OPPOSITE **A Roman copy of Praxiteles's *Aphrodite of Knidos*, restored by Ippolito Buzzi, 17th century**
The original statue was said to be modelled on the famous Greek courtesan Phryne, the most beautiful woman in the known world. Praxiteles's original statue has not survived, however many copies were made.

When the great Athenian artist Praxiteles was commissioned in the 4th century BCE to create a sculpture of Aphrodite for the island of Kos he knew that there was only one earthly woman who could be his model for the goddess of love: his mistress and muse, the fabled courtesan Phryne. Or, at least, that is the story the Greek rhetorician Athenaeus liked to tell. But then again, Phryne was the kind of woman that men like to tell stories about.

The legends spun around Phryne have entranced poets and artists for centuries, but we know very little about who she really was. We know she was a *hetaira*, a word that is translated to 'courtesan', but in Greek means 'man's companion', the feminine form of *hetaíros*, the name for a man's war companion, or someone you go into battle with. According to Plutarch, writing in the 1st century CE, her name was not really Phryne, but Mnesarete; or maybe Plutarch was making a joke as Mnesarete means 'remembering virtue'. 'Phryne', meaning 'toad', was either a stage name, a nickname or both, and is said to refer to her 'yellow skin'.[1] Another joke perhaps, as Phryne was said to be one of the most beautiful women in the world.

The statue Praxiteles modelled on Phryne came to be known as the *Aphrodite of Knidos*. It was one of the first life-size depictions of the naked female form in Greek history, and it caused a sensation. The 2nd-century poet Lucian of Samosata told of one man who fell in love with the marble rendering and stole into the temple in the dead of night to 'quench his passion'. The next morning 'signs of his amorous embraces' were discovered on Aphrodite's thighs. Finding he had permanently stained the goddess, the man threw himself into the sea for shame.[2]

Not only was Phryne extraordinarily beautiful, but she was an astute businesswoman who knew her worth. The poet Machon told stories about how much she charged her companions to go into battle. He wrote:

'MOIRICHOS WAS TRYING TO GET PHRYNE OF THESPIAE INTO BED. AND WHEN SHE ASKED HIM FOR A WHOLE MNA, MOIRICHOS SAID, 'THAT'S A LOT. DIDN'T YOU JUST YESTERDAY ACCEPT 40 DRACHMAS OF GOLD TO BE WITH SOME FOREIGNER?' AND SHE SAID, 'WELL THEN, YOU TOO WAIT AROUND, TILL I WANT A FUCK AND THEN I'LL ACCEPT [ONLY] SO MUCH.'[3]

The 4th-century poets Callistratus, Timocles and Amphis all told of Phryne's vast wealth. It is said that she earned so much money she offered to rebuild the walls of Thebes, which had been destroyed by Alexander the Great – but only if the Thebans would inscribe upon them, 'Alexander destroyed this wall, but Phryne the courtesan restored it.'[4] The city refused.

The most famous story about Phryne is that she was acquitted on capital charges of impiety by exposing her breasts to the jury. The specific charges are not known, but they may have arisen following her posing as the goddess Aphrodite for

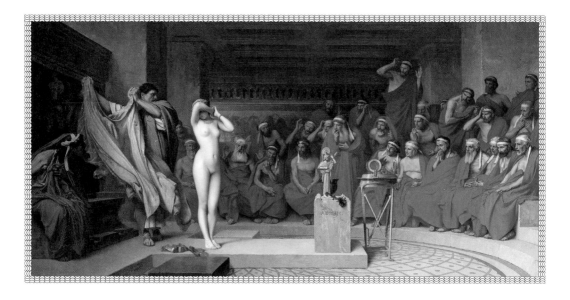

ABOVE **Jean-Léon Gérôme,** *Phryne Before the Areopagus,* **1861** When the great courtesan Phryne was put on trial for impiety, it is said that her lawyer pulled off her robe in order to convince the jury to spare her life. The alleged moment has been a source of inspiration for artists throughout history.

Praxiteles. Athenaeus wrote that Phryne was defended by one of her lovers, the famous orator Hypereides. The trial did not go well, but just as the death sentence seemed inevitable, Hypereides played his trump card. The author known as Pseudo-Plutarch wrote, 'It is said, that when sentence was just ready to be passed upon her, he produced her in court, opened her clothes before, and revealed her naked breasts, which were so very white, that for her beauty's sake the judges acquitted her.'[5] It is a moment that has fascinated artists ever since, but it almost certainly did not happen. Like most of the stories spun around Phryne, the truth has been embellished to titillate and tease. It speaks more to the imagination of men than it does to the facts. But that was the hustle of the *hetaira*, and Phryne was one of the best.

Sex work was entirely legal throughout most of ancient
Greece. It was regulated and taxed, providing an important
source of revenue to the state. The Greek language has over
two hundred words to delineate between various types
of sex work, and the *hetaira* were at the very top of their
game. Generally, these were educated and cultured women
who worked independently and secured wealthy patrons.
But language is slippery, and much has been made of the
various classifications of sex work in ancient Greece.
The more common term for someone who sold sex was
pornē, which comes from the verb *pernanai*, meaning
simply 'to sell'.

ABOVE LEFT **Jean-Jacques Pradier,**
Phryne, c. 1845
Here Phryne is shown with her
breasts exposed, as she was in court.
Pradier's statue was photographed
by Claude-Marie Ferrier in 1881.

ABOVE CENTRE **Francesco Barzaghi,**
Phryne Before the Judges, 1868
A chromolithograph made by
Cosack & Co. of a sculpture by
Francesco Barzaghi.

ABOVE RIGHT ***Phryne, c. 1788***
An engraving of Phryne taken from
Jean-Jacques Barthélemy's *Voyage
du jeune Anacharsis en Grèce* (1788),
a fictional account of the travels
of the philosopher Anacharsis.

Then, as today, the words used to discuss sex work conveyed
layers of meaning. Linguistic distinctions were able to
imply a difference of class. The closest modern equivalent
to *pornē* is 'prostitute', and like 'prostitute' *pornē* could
be applied to anyone selling sex, but it generally referred
to sex workers at the lower end of the economic scale: the
brothel workers, street walkers, dancing girls and slaves.
The gradation in sexual services was quite clear to the
Athenian politician Apollodorus of Acharnae when he spoke
against the former *hetaira* Neaera between 343 and 340 BCE.
'We have courtesans for pleasure, concubines for the daily
tending of the body and wives in order to beget legitimate
children and have a trustworthy guardian of what is
at home.'[6]

A MAN SOLICITING
A BOY FOR SEX
Tondo of an Attic kylix, 5th century BCE.

A *HETAIRA* URINATING
INTO A *SKYPHOS*
Tondo of a kylix, *c.* 480 BCE.

A *HETAIRA* HAVING SEX
WITH A MAN
Tondo of a cup, *c.* 480 BCE.

A *HETAIRA* AT A BANQUET
Tondo of a cup, attributed
to Makron, *c.* 490 BCE.

A *HETAIRA*
FASTENING HER ROBE
Tondo of an Attic cup, *c.* 490 BCE.

A *HETAIRA* PLAYING
DRINKING GAMES
Tondo of a cup, *c.* 500 BCE.

TWO MEN EMBRACE
Tondo of an Attic cup, attributed
to the Briseis Painter, *c.* 480 BCE.

A *HETAIRA* AT A PARTY
Tondo of a cup, attributed to
the Brygos Painter, *c.* 490–80 BCE.

**A *HETAIRA* ATTENDS TO A
VOMITING CLIENT AT A PARTY**
Tondo of attic kylix by Douris, *c.* 480 BCE.

A MAN FLIRTS WITH A *HETAIRA*
Tondo of an Attic cup, attributed to
the Briseis Painter, *c.* 470–80 BCE.

**A *HETAIRA* HAVING SEX
WITH A MAN**
Tondo of an Attic cup, 5th century BCE.

**A *HETAIRA* HAVING SEX
WITH A MAN**
Tondo of a cup, *c.* 490–80 BCE.

The story of Neaera offers a valuable insight into the
turbulent and often cruel life of a sex worker in ancient
Greece that moves beyond the glamorous stories of the
hetaira. Neaera was a contemporary of Phryne and she too
found herself on trial in a court of men. She was accused
of illegally living as the wife of an Athenian citizen called
Stephanus. Athenians were only permitted to marry other
Athenians, and Neaera was a former slave from Corinth. The
case was the result of an ongoing feud between Stephanus and
Apollodoros, the politician whose case for the prosecution was
recorded in the speeches of Demosthenes. In order to prove
that Neaera was a foreigner and to ensure maximum damage
to her partner's reputation, her history as a sex slave and
eventual *hetaira* was described in lurid detail. The speaker

ABOVE LEFT **An *oinochoe* (wine
vessel) depicting two women
in festive dress, *c.* 420–10 BCE**
As a former slave, and Corinthian,
Neaera was excluded from
respectable Athenian society.

ABOVE CENTRE **Attributed to
the Amasis Painter, a *lekythos*
(oil vessel) depicting a wedding
procession, *c.* 550–30 BCE**
For Athenian wives, marital life
meant running the household and
bearing children, a very different
existence from that of the *hetaira*.

ABOVE RIGHT **A *hydria* (water
vessel) depicting women talking at
the water fountain, *c.* 510–500 BCE**
The ideal Athenian wife only left the
house to complete domestic chores,
and was not allowed to interact
with men she was not related to.

tells us that Neaera was one of seven 'small children' who
were purchased by Nicaretê, a brothel keeper in Elis, southern
Greece. Nicaretê 'got her livelihood from the girls' by
'bring[ing] them up and train[ing] them artfully'. We are not
told at what age Neaera was put to work, but once Nicaretê
'had reaped the profit of the youthful prime of each, she sold
them, all seven'. While she was a slave in Nicaretê's brothel,
Neaera was pimped out to influential clients, such as the
poet Xenocleides and the actor Hipparchus. Although still a
slave, we are told Neaera 'plied her trade openly in Corinth
and was quite a celebrity'. Celebrity or not, all clients had to
go through Nicaretê, who charged them vast sums of money.
Eventually, Timanoridas the Corinthian and Eucrates the
Leucadian bought Neaera from the brothel to be their slave,
and 'kept her and made use of her as long a time as they pleased'.
With the help of another client, Phrynion of Paeania, Neaera

was able to raise enough money to buy her freedom from Timanoridas and Eucrates. She may have been free, but Neaera was now beholden to Phrynion, who we are told treated her appallingly and enjoyed passing her around his friends. Eventually, Neaera fled with two servants and as much jewellery as she could carry. By the time Phrynion tracked her down, she was living in Athens with Stephanus. After he failed to take her back by force, an out-of-court settlement forced Neaera to return what she had stolen from Phrynion and live with both men on alternate days.[7]

Neaera's experiences of sexual enslavement and brothel work, and her eventual position as a free, albeit kept, mistress, cannot be said to be representative of all sex work in ancient

ABOVE LEFT **Statuette of a woman, 3rd century** BCE
The woman is depicted elegantly draped in a *himatia*, or thin cloak.

ABOVE CENTRE **Statuette of a woman, late 4th–early 3rd century** BCE
Many figures such as these have been found in private dwellings, where they likely had a devotional purpose. The religious sphere was the area of civic life in which Athenian women were most free to participate.

ABOVE RIGHT **Statuette of a girl, c. 300** BCE
The childlike proportions and features on this statuette indicate that it is a young girl. Many ancient Greek women were married by the age of 14.

Greece. In her story we can see something of the precarity and complexity of sex work at that time. Even when she bought her freedom, she was still dependent on wealthy patrons, but she was also a free woman and a 'celebrity'. Women like Neaera and Phryne acquired money and an independence denied to many wives, who were expected to stay at home and dutifully bear children to their philandering husbands. Sex work in ancient Greece existed within a deeply patriarchal and exploitative world, but it was not seen as inherently wrong. The stigma was primarily attached to class, rather than sex. Whereas in ancient Rome, sex work was viewed as shameful and the sex workers themselves were legally classed as *infames*, meaning 'of no reputation'.

The Roman legal system was rooted in notions of shame and honour. The legal status *infamia* barred certain

ABOVE **Jean-Léon Gérôme,**
The Slave Market in Rome, 1884
Gérôme's work invites viewers to
condemn the slave trade, whilst
admiring a sensuous female nude.

ABOVE **Jean-Léon Gérôme,**
A Roman Slave Market, 1884
Gérôme painted multiple slave
market scenes, set in either ancient
Rome or 19th-century Istanbul.

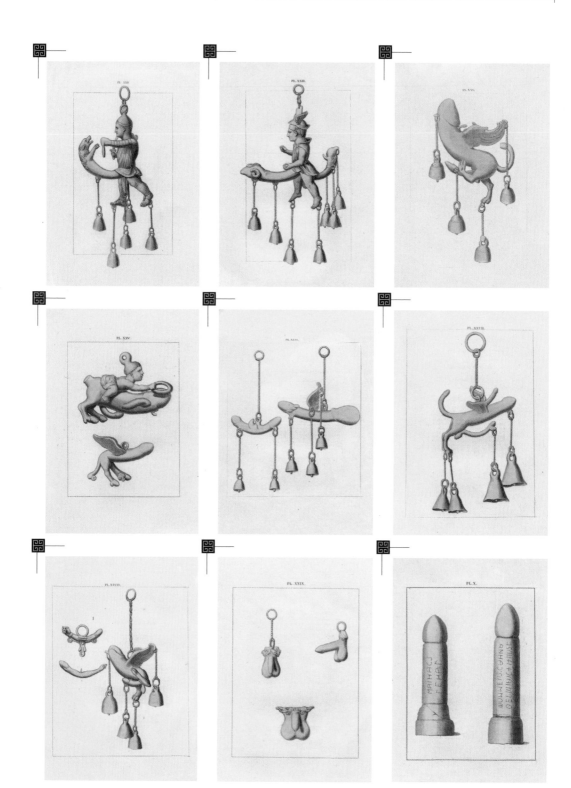

'dishonourable' professions from full citizenship and the legal rights that came with it. Sex workers were regarded as *infames*, as were actors, gladiators, certain musicians, pimps and procurers. Workers in any profession using their body to entertain the public were *infames*. As such, they could not vote or provide testimony in court, and they could be publicly beaten if they committed a crime. The infamy belonged entirely to the sex worker, of course. As long as the client was a man, there was no shame in paying for sex. In the Roman social hierarchy, the *infames* were one rung above slaves, if they were not slaves already.

But, Roman attitudes to sex work were deeply ambivalent. Those who sold sex were socially stigmatized, but that did not mean they were socially banished. Sex workers were at once shameful but essential. The status of *infamia* denied people full citizenship, but many *infames* were adored by Roman citizens. They were regarded as inferior but could wield enormous power and influence. For example, in the 6th century the wife of Justinian the Great, Theodora, ruled the Roman Byzantine Empire alongside her husband until her death, but began her career working in brothels and performing nude on stage. Theodora had come a long way by the time she caught Justinian's eye, but he still had to have the law changed to allow the emperor to marry an *infamis*; and to her enemies, she was always 'Theodora from the brothel'.

Despite the obvious stigma, sex work was as much a part of the Roman world as the roads and the wine. It even played a part in Rome's creation myth. The city is famously said to have been founded by the twins Romulus and Remus, who were raised and suckled by a she-wolf, or *lupa*. A less well-known part of that story is that the twins were adopted by a woman called Acca Larentia. In some variations Acca Larentia is the wife of a shepherd called Faustulus, in others she is one of Hercules's lovers, but according to several writers, including Plutarch, Acca was a sex worker. The Latin equivalent of the Greek *hetaira* was *meretrice*, but *lupa* was also common Roman slang for a woman who sold sex. Given the dual meaning of *lupa*, it is entirely possible that the she-wolf of legend and Acca are one and the same. In his commentaries on the works of Virgil, published in the 4th century, Maurus Servius Honoratus claimed this myth was wilfully misinterpreted to conceal the truth.

OPPOSITE **César Famin, *Royal Museum of Naples, Paintings, Bronzes and Erotic Statues from the Secret Cabinet*, 1836** These illustrations show objects inside the so-called 'secret cabinet' of the National Archaeological Museum, Naples. The room contains erotic art collected from Pompeii and Herculaneum during the Enlightenment, which was locked away after being deemed too obscene for public consumption in 1821.

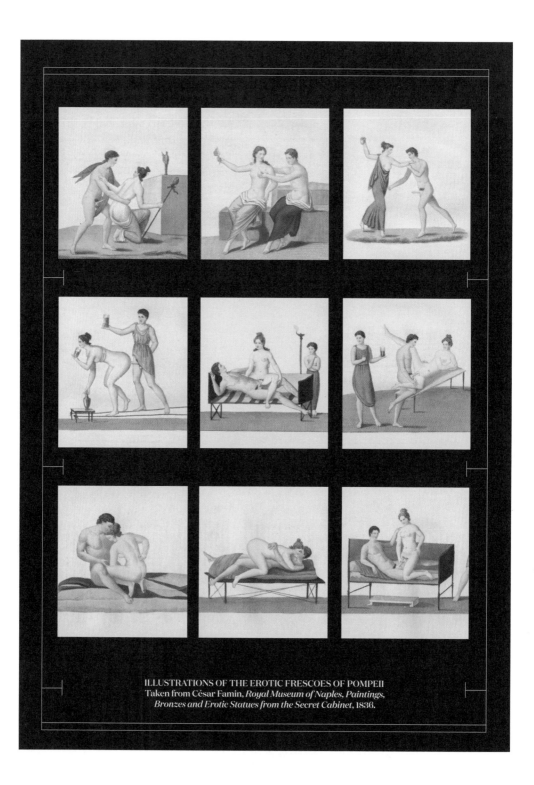

ILLUSTRATIONS OF THE EROTIC FRESCOES OF POMPEII
Taken from César Famin, *Royal Museum of Naples, Paintings,
Bronzes and Erotic Statues from the Secret Cabinet*, 1836.

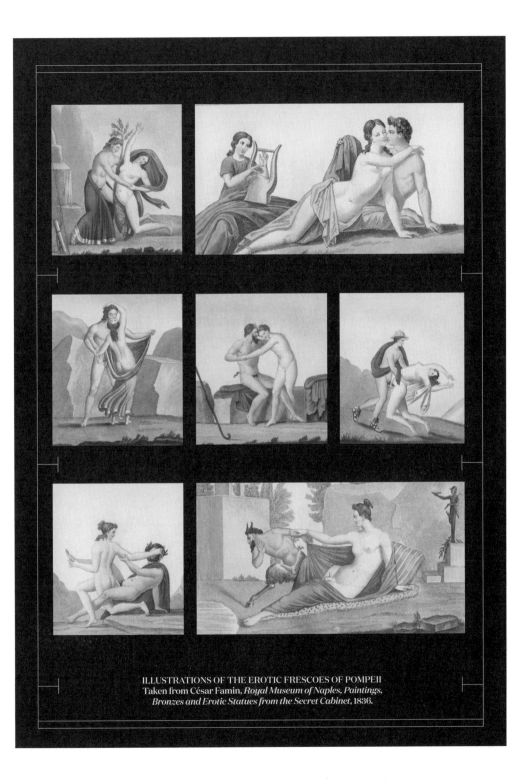

ILLUSTRATIONS OF THE EROTIC FRESCOES OF POMPEII
Taken from César Famin, *Royal Museum of Naples, Paintings,
Bronzes and Erotic Statues from the Secret Cabinet,* 1836.

'THE STORY THAT THEY WERE BROUGHT UP BY A
SHE-WOLF *(LUPA)* IS A FICTIONAL TALE INTENDED TO
HIDE THE SHAME OF THE FOUNDERS OF THE ROMAN
NATION. AND IT IS NICELY DONE TOO BECAUSE WE
ALSO CALL THE MERETRICES "WOLVES" (LUPAS),
HENCE THE TERM LUPANARIA FOR BROTHELS.'[8]

There were remarkably few laws directly pertaining
to sex work. Most laws passed that did concern sex work
were those dealing with the wider legality of the *infames*.
It was not until Emperor Augustus passed laws in 17 and
18 BCE intended to reform marriage and prevent sex workers
marrying that prostitution was specifically addressed.
That sex work did not merit specific regulation because
it was covered by labour laws perhaps tells us something
of just how everyday it was.

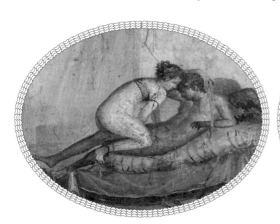 

ABOVE LEFT **An erotic fresco
from the House of the Centenary,
Pompeii, 1st century CE**
The House of the Centenary
is the name given to the house
of a wealthy resident of ancient
Pompeii discovered in 1879,
the 18th centenary of the
eruption of Mount Vesuvius.

ABOVE RIGHT **An erotic fresco
from the Pompeii *lupanar* (brothel)
depicting group sex, 1st century CE**
It has been suggested that these
images functioned as a menu for
clients, though it is more likely
that they were simply designed
to arouse the punters.

The Romans' casual attitude to sex and sex work shocked
the archaeologists who started excavating the buried cities
of Pompeii and Herculaneum in 1748. The erotic frescoes,
statues, mosaics and carvings that were uncovered caused
considerable embarrassment for many great men of learning
who held up Classical Rome as the pinnacle of civilization.
When King Francis I of Naples took his family to see the
exhibits on display in the National Archaeological Museum
in 1819, he was so upset that he ordered the collection to be
locked away and made accessible to only 'people of mature
age and respected morals'.[9] But for the citizens who had
once lived in Pompeii, sex was very much on display.

Sex was on sale throughout the town. The erotic frescoes
adorning the public bathhouse have led historians to suggest

extra services were on offer. Graffiti scratched into the walls around taverns have left us records of sexual commerce in the streets, including the prices: 'Felicla the slave' cost '2 asses', and 'Acria 4 asses, Epafra 10 asses, Firma 3 asses'.[10] The rich had sexual access to their slaves, but for the less well off, or those passing through the town, there were the brothels.

In 1995, historian Andrew Wallace-Hadrill proposed the following criteria for archaeologists determining whether a building was primarily used to sell sex:

1. Stone beds in a small room that was easily accessible to the public.
2. Sexually explicit frescoes on the wall.
3. The presence of sexually explicit graffiti, boasting about sexual prowess.[11]

ABOVE LEFT **An erotic fresco from the Pompeii *Terme Suburbane* (Suburban Baths), 1st century** CE The presence of these images in a public bathhouse suggests that they may have been viewed as humorous, rather than offensive, by Roman audiences.

ABOVE RIGHT **An erotic fresco from the Pompeii *Terme Suburbane* (Suburban Baths), 1st century** CE This fresco depicts a man performing cunnilingus on a reclining woman. Some historians believe that these depictions suggest that sexual services could be purchased at the baths.

No doubt many of the taverns, bathhouses, theatres and private residences also operated as brothels, and met one or two of Wallace-Hadrill's markers, but there is only one known building in Pompeii that meets all three. Just behind the Stabian Baths is the famous Pompeiian brothel, the *lupanar,* or 'wolf-den'.

The five rooms are dark and cramped, with barely enough space for each of the narrow stone beds. If curtains once hung in the doorways, they have long since been lost. The walls, which would once have been painted white, still display the faded erotic paintings of various sex acts, and obscene graffiti, etched by clients and she-wolves. Perhaps one of the most surprising things about the *lupanar* is that it was not only slaves who worked there.

Amongst the 150 surviving incidents of graffiti on the walls are the names of people who worked in those rooms. One out of every five names on the walls is *gentilicia*, meaning a family name not given to slaves.[12] Mola is described as a 'fucktress', while Murtis is a *felatris*, or 'sucker'. The name Victoria appears several times, as does Phoebus, who is described as a 'good fucker'. There is a great deal of boasting from clients too, such as 'when I came here, I fucked, and then I returned home', and 'here I fucked many girls'. The sex workers even left jokes for one another. One piece of graffiti reads 'Scordopordonicus fucked well here who he wished'. Scordopordonicus translates roughly to 'mister garlic farts'.[13]

Paris and Castrensis are men who once worked there and are described on the walls as being 'beautiful'. They may have served female clients, but it is more likely they served men. Men paying men for sex was very common throughout pre-Christian Rome, but the Church's condemnation of non-procreative sex brought with it widespread persecution of homosexuality. In 390 CE, an edict of Emperor Theodosius I made forcing or selling men into prostitution a capital offence, but his orders made male sex workers an obvious target, and jeering mobs dragged sex workers out of male brothels and burned them in the streets. Such efforts were not successful in abolishing men either selling or buying sex. In the reign of Constantine I, a tax was imposed to discourage men from selling sex. Despite the considerable shame the authorities heaped on the practice, in his *Ecclesiastical History* (593 CE) Evagrius Scholasticus notes that every single emperor made sure to collect that tax.

The selling and buying of sex was woven into the very fabric of Greek and Roman society. These were deeply patriarchal cultures that ran on slavery and exploitation, and the experience of those selling sex no doubt reflected that. But, in trying to untangle the various threads that knot around the complexity of sex work, it becomes obvious that binary identities of slave and courtesan do nothing to capture the nuance at work. Stories like those of Phryne, or Paris and Castrensis, show us the experience of sex work can accommodate many narratives. Behind the glamorous legends of the courtesans are myriad lives lived on the margins of society. Infamous they may have been, but sex work lay at the very heart of Classical civilization.

ABOVE **Erotic fresco of the god Priapus weighing his penis, 1st century** CE
This fresco was found in the House of the Vettii, Pompeii.

3

Sex Work in
MEDIEVAL LONDON

~~~~~~~~~~~~~~~~~~~~~~~~

The Geese
THAT LAID
THE GOLDEN EGG

~~~~~~~~~~~~~~~~~~~~~~~~

THE PUBLIC WOMAN IS IN SOCIETY WHAT BILGE
IS IN A SHIP AT SEA AND THE SEWER PIT IS IN
A PALACE. REMOVE THIS SEWER AND THE
ENTIRE PALACE WILL BE CONTAMINATED.

St Augustine, *De Ordine*, 386 CE

THE DISSOLUTE AND MISERABLE PERSONS WHO HAVE BEEN SUFFERED TO DWELL BESIDE LONDON IN PLACES CALLED THE STEWES HAVE LATELY SO INCREASED AND ENGENDER SUCH CORRUPTION AMONG THE PEOPLE AS TO BE AN INTOLERABLE ANNOYANCE TO THE COMMON WEALTH.

Suppression of the Stews, 1546

On 27 July 1385, Elizabeth Moryng, wife of Henry Moryng, was brought from her jail cell to London's Guildhall to stand trial on charges of being 'a common harlot and a procuress'. The records tell us that the men assembled to preside over Elizabeth's fate were 'Nicholas Brembre, knight, the mayor, the aldermen, and the sheriffs of London'.[1] To a poor woman with little social standing, these important men must have seemed impossibly grand. To a prisoner on trial for her freedom, they must have been terrifying. Accusations of harlotry and whoring were not usually heard in the mayor's court, and while Elizabeth could never have inspired the same levels of fear in her judges as she must have felt, they may, at the very least, have been surprised to see her. Although, considering just how prolific a harlot and whoremonger Elizabeth turned out to be, it is entirely possible that she had met her accusers before.

The sex trade thrived in London long before Elizabeth Moryng was dragged to the dock, and its history is one of regulation, suppression and failed attempts at abolition. It is testament to the sheer resilience of the sex trade that the London authorities have yet to find a way to stamp it out despite over a thousand years of trying. Prostitution was not illegal in medieval London, but it was very heavily regulated, and the tactics deployed to control it were stigma and zoning.

As early as 1277, the London courts passed a law banning any 'whore from a brothel' living within the city walls. Similar ordinances were passed in the medieval cities of York, Coventry, Leicester and Bristol, but proved ineffective and difficult to enforce. The city's failure in prohibiting the buying and selling of sex is evident in the host of bluntly named streets where one could do just that. As historian Ephraim J. Burford explained in *The Orrible Synne: A Look at London Lechery from Roman to Cromwellian Times* (1973):

'WHEN LONDON WAS COMPARATIVELY RURAL, SANITATION WAS A SIMPLER MATTER. THE PEOPLE DEFECATED OR URINATED IN THEIR GARDENS AND THOUGHT NOTHING OF IT: BUT AFTER THE NORMAN CONQUEST WHEN THE TOWNSHIP BEGAN TO DEVELOP MIGHTILY, PROBLEMS OF SANITATION AROSE THAT NEVER EXISTED BEFORE. NATURALLY OLD HABITS WERE HARD TO BREAK, AND WHEN GARDENS WERE FEWER, EASEMENTS WERE DONE IN THE LANES AND ALLEYS. THE CONSEQUENT

OPPOSITE **An old man caressing a young woman,** *c.* 1500–20
In this German engraving, an old man is depicted stroking the breast of a younger woman, while she passes coins from his purse to another man. The old woman in the background may represent a procuress.

STENCH AND OBSTRUCTIONS WERE CASUALLY REFERRED TO AS PISSING LANE, STYNKYNG ALLEY, SHITEBURN LANE OR FOUL LANE. IF THE LANE WERE ADDITIONALLY USED FOR FORNICATION IT MIGHT ALSO BEAR A SUITABLE TITLE SUCH AS GROPECUNT LANE – ASSUREDLY A HARK-BACK TO SAXON TIMES – OR CODPIECE ALLEY, OR EVEN WHORES LIE DOWN. THESE PLACES, AS MAY BE EXPECTED, EVENTUALLY WERE DEODORIZED INTO GRAPE LANE, COPPICE ALLEY AND HORSLEYDOWN. WHERE THERE WERE WHOREHOUSES, THE STREETS WOULD BEAR NAMES LIKE WHORES' NEST OR SLUTS' HOLE OR MAYDEN LANE (IN WHICH THERE WERE NO MAIDENS AT ALL) OR ROSE ALLEY (TO PLUCK THE ROSES OF MAIDENHEADS) OR GOLDEN LANE, WHENCE GOLD COULD BE SO EARNED.'[2]

ABOVE LEFT **Book of Hours, Use of Sarum, known as *The Taymouth Hours*, 14th century**
This illumination shows a monk and a woman in the stocks. The stocks were both a physical punishment and a public humiliation.

ABOVE CENTRE **Rabano Mauro, *De Universo*, 1023**
This miniature is entitled 'Sentencing to Pillory'. The pillory was a common punishment for men and women accused of 'whoremongering' (pimping).

ABOVE RIGHT **Customs of Toulouse, 1295–97**
This miniature depicts a figure in the pillory. This public punishment was utilized across Europe in the Middle Ages.

By 1393, the London authorities had confined brothels to the territory of the Bishop of Winchester in Southwark, which lay outside city jurisdiction, and just one street within the city walls, Cock Lane.[3] In an effort to identify and control the women who sold sex, laws were passed to prevent harlots from dressing like 'good and noble dames and damsels'.[4] In 1351, the 'Ordinance for Sumptuary Regulation' forbade 'common lewd women' wearing fur or 'any other noble lining'. Instead, they were to 'go openly with a hood of cloth of ray, single, and with vestments neither trimmed in fur nor yet lined with lining... that so all folks, natives and strangers, may have knowledge of what rank they are'.[5] Sumptuary laws demanding 'common women' identify themselves by wearing a striped, or 'rayed', hood were also passed in Bristol, Great Yarmouth, Exeter and Gloucester.[6] Such measures were designed to stigmatize and shame, but they also brought about an uneasy truce between the authorities and 'lewd women'. As long as people followed the rules, the city of London was prepared to tolerate the sex trade. However, as Elizabeth Moryng was about to discover, the punishments meted out to those who did not comply were severe indeed.

The *Liber Albus* is a book of London laws, compiled in 1419, and it is a treasure trove of information about justice in medieval London. It outlines the various punishments for harlotry, whoremongering and harbouring 'women of evil life' in considerable detail. Men found guilty of whoremongering (pimping) had their heads and beards shaved and were sentenced to be pilloried for a time determined by the court. The pillory was a variation on the stocks where the victim had to stand, bent over, with their head and hands locked into a wooden frame. This would have been carried out in a public place, while drums were banged, minstrels sang and their crimes were proclaimed to a baying mob.

ABOVE LEFT *Des cleres et nobles femmes*, an anonymous French translation of Giovanni Boccaccio's *De claris mulieribus*, 15th century
This is an illustration of Leontion, a female Epicurean philosopher and possible courtesan.

ABOVE CENTRE *Des cleres et nobles femmes*, an anonymous French translation of Giovanni Boccaccio's *De claris mulieribus*, 15th century
Here a sex worker is shown with a client at the Floralia festival in ancient Rome. The Floralia, held in honour of the goddess Flora, is said to have included performances from prostitutes.

ABOVE RIGHT **Martial d'Auvergne, *Vigils of King Charles VII*, c. 1484**
This illustration shows Joan of Arc driving sex workers out of her army's camp.

Women accused of 'common harlotry' or bawdry (pimping) as a first offence had their heads shaved and then were paraded about the town centre, holding a white rod and wearing a striped hood, while minstrels played and their crimes were read aloud. They would eventually be led to Cock Lane where they would be made to sit in the thewe, a pillory specifically for women. When the punishment was complete, they would be left at Cock Lane and expected to 'remain there'. If the harlot had not learned her lesson and was convicted a second time, she could expect the same punishment and up to ten days in prison. Should she be caught for a third time, not only would she be subjected to the same public humiliation, but she would also be banished from the City of London, which brings us back to Elizabeth Moryng.[7]

Elizabeth stood accused of being a 'common harlot and procuress', though a hearing before the mayor himself is testament to the uncommon seriousness of her crimes. She claimed to work as an embroiderer in the parish of

All Hallows and would regularly recruit young female apprentices to train in the art; at least, this was the story Elizabeth told to her prospective trainees. Johanna was one such recruit and after she had broken free from Elizabeth's clutches, she had a very different tale to tell.

Johanna testified that on 4 May 1385 Elizabeth ordered her to accompany a chaplain to his house at night, 'that she might carry a lantern before him to his chamber'. Unbeknown to her, Elizabeth and the chaplain had contrived that she should 'stay the night there'. The next morning, Johanna returned to her mistress, who asked her if she had 'brought anything with her for her trouble that night'. When she said she had not, an enraged Elizabeth berated her and made her return to the chaplain that night, where she was to steal anything of value and bring it back. The court records that 'many other times this Elizabeth received the like base gains from the same Johanna, and her other serving-women, and retained the same for her own use; living thus abominably and damnably, and inciting other women to live in the like manner; she herself being a common harlot and a procuress.'[8] Although Johanna was the only woman to testify against Elizabeth, there were clearly many more victims who she had similarly coerced, deceived and forced into prostitution.

Despite protestations of innocence, Elizabeth was confined to jail until the following day when 'twelve good men' found her guilty of all the offences laid against her. Given the scale and nature of Elizabeth's crimes, the courts were not inclined to be merciful.

OPPOSITE **16th-century representations of harlots and courtesans**
During the 16th century illustrations of sex workers were often overlaid with a moral lesson, whether it was through cautionary depictions of their lifestyle, works inspired by the biblical tale of the prodigal son or engravings showing old men being taken for fools. Shown here are (top left) Urs Graf, *A Courtesan Drinking and Gambling in the Presence of Death*, c. 1511, (top right) *The Prodigal Son with the Harlots*, 1512–83, (bottom left) Cornelis Anthonisz, *The Prodigal Son Wastes his Inheritance*, 1535–45 and (bottom right) *The Old Man and the Courtesan*, c. 1520–50.

'IT WAS ADJUDGED THAT THE SAID ELIZABETH SHOULD BE TAKEN FROM THE GUILDHALL AFORESAID TO CORNHULLE, AND BE PUT UPON THE THEWE, THERE TO REMAIN FOR ONE HOUR OF THE DAY, THE CAUSE THEREOF BEING PUBLICLY PROCLAIMED. AND AFTERWARDS, SHE WAS TO BE TAKEN TO SOME GATE OF THE CITY, AND THERE BE MADE TO FORSWEAR THE CITY, AND THE LIBERTY THEREOF, TO THE EFFECT THAT SHE WOULD NEVER AGAIN ENTER THE SAME; ON PAIN OF IMPRISONMENT FOR THREE YEARS, AND THE SAID PUNISHMENT OF THE THEWE, AT THE DISCRETION OF THE MAYOR AND ALDERMEN FOR THE TIME BEING, SO OFTEN AS IT SHOULD PLEASE THEM THAT SHE SHOULD SUFFER SUCH PUNISHMENT.'[9]

After this, all trace of Elizabeth vanishes from the records. Perhaps she relocated to a new town and reinvented herself, or joined a nunnery and lived out her days atoning for her many sins; or maybe, just maybe, she took the short ferry ride across the Thames to Southwark and joined the flock of 'Winchester Geese', who kept the Church's bed well-feathered with the money they earned in their own.

In 1107 Bishop William Giffard of Winchester rented land in Southwark from Bermondsey Priory to build a manor house. By 1329, the office of Bishop of Winchester came with ninety acres of land, known as the 'Liberty of the Clink', the spiritual responsibility for all souls residing there and control over the

ABOVE **Illuminations of bathhouses and brothels, 15th century**
In these illustrations the bathhouse is shown as a place to socialize, eat and drink, however, its sexual connection is also made clear.

rents, borough courts and bylaws. Lying outside the city walls and beyond the sheriff's jurisdiction, Southwark was home to all manner of outcasts and villains who found sanctuary within the mass of crooked streets. The banks of the Thames were cluttered with brothels and exiled strumpets who had been banished beyond the walls. In his 1598 *A Survey of London*, John Stow described eighteen 'stew houses' that once perched along the banks of the Thames. 'These allowed stew houses had signs on their fronts, towards the Thames, not hanged out, but painted on the walls, as a Boar's Head, the Cross Keys, the Gun, the Castle, the Crane, the Cardinal's Hat, the Bell, the Swan, etc.'[10] On the west bank, there were two bear gardens where bears, bulls and mastiff dogs tore each other apart for the amusement of paying crowds. Southwark was also home to several jails, including the infamous 'Clink' on the banks, the White Lion and the King's Bench. Taverns, townhouses, bordellos and bearpits: the Bishop of Winchester was lord and master of all. While the medieval ecclesiastical courts continued to punish people for selling sexual services across London, the Liberty of the Clink decided to turn a profit instead.

Considerable evidence survives about life in the Southwark stews because of a remarkable document, drawn up in the 15th century, that allowed the Bishop of Winchester to sanction and profit from sex work in his jurisdiction. The 'Ordinances Touching the Government of the Stewholders in Southwark under the Direction of the Bishop of Winchester'

sets out thirty-six regulations for those working in the stews, and the fine each infraction would incur.[11]

The Ordinances cover everything from what a 'single woman' could wear to her sleeping arrangements, and from working on religious holidays to selling food to boost trade. Many of the regulations were designed to protect sex workers from being exploited by nefarious stew owners such as Elizabeth Moryng. For example, item (A3) stipulates that a stewholder cannot 'keep any of their women within the houses against their will, upon pain of a hundred shillings'. While (B10) states that no stewholder can 'hold any woman that lives by her body to board, but that they go to board elsewhere they wish, upon pain of twenty shillings at every time that this ordinance is broke'. And item (B4) rules that 'religious women and

ABOVE **Illuminations of bathhouses, 15th century** Medieval bathhouses, or stew houses, were known as places where sex workers solicited for clients. By the early 1400s, all stews were banned from the City of London.

wives are not to be received in the stew houses…under pain of twelve pence'. One of the harshest punishments was reserved for any woman who had a lover that she supported financially, which was intended to prevent pimping. 'If any woman that lives by her body holds any paramour against the use and custom of the manor she shall be three weeks in the prison and make a fine of six shillings eightpence and then be set once on the cucking-stool and forswear the lordship.'

There are also regulations to protect customers from being fleeced by the wily Geese. Item (B2), for example, prohibits

brothel owners holding 'any man against his will within his house as prisoner for any debt that he owes'. No woman with 'sickness of burning' was allowed to work in the stews and item (B7) prohibits women physically dragging men in from the street. There is also a list of questions to be asked of common women during the mandatory inspections, which include: 'Does she draw any man by his clothes against his will? Does she hinder any officer from making his due search? Does she not keep her hours on the Holy days? Does she hold or keep any paramour, against the Ordinance? Does she spin or card with any stewholder? Does she chide with any person, or cast stones? Is she absent in the parliament and council time? Does she take any money to lie with men, and not perform it? Is she single and keeps a stew house?'[12]

ABOVE LEFT **Brunswick Monogrammist,** *Merry Company,* **1537**
This rowdy brothel scene includes cuddling couples and fighting women.

ABOVE RIGHT **Brunswick Monogrammist,** *Brothel Scene,* **1540**
This similarly disorderly scene shows one couple heading up the stairs to a bedroom, while others carouse below.

The voices and experiences of the sex workers themselves are frustratingly absent from surviving records, and we have no way of knowing how the Geese themselves felt about the Ordinances, or indeed about handing over a share of their earnings to the Church. We are left with only the laws to which they were subjected to try and understand the experience of being a sex worker in medieval London. The extensive regulations governing life in the stews were intended to control the sex trade, rather than stamp it out. They are suggestive of a society that viewed prostitution as a social issue rather than purely a moral one, but they can tell us little about the Geese themselves.

When King Henry VIII broke with Rome in 1533, the Crown assumed all previously church-owned lands and property – including the lands belonging to the Bishop of Winchester.

ABOVE LEFT **Joachim Beuckelaer,**
Brothel, 1562
This depiction of a brothel includes a drunkard performing a handstand, providing a moralizing message that excess leads to foolishness.

ABOVE RIGHT **Pieter Bruegel the Elder,**
The Peasant Dance, 1568
The red flag in the background of this merry scene signals that the building is a brothel.

In 1546, Henry VIII ordered the Bankside stews be closed by a royal proclamation accompanied by trumpeters and a herald-at-arms. The 'dissolute and miserable' who abused their bodies in the stews were given only eleven days to move out.[13] Southwark was now within the jurisdiction of London and subject to its laws. The Church no longer licensed the brothels and the rise of Protestantism brought with it renewed zeal to rid the city of sin. Of course, this did not abolish the sex trade. The Geese simply packed up and moved to new areas of the city, including Cock Lane, Petticoat Lane and Gropecunt Lane in Cheapside. The Crown's failure to abolish the sex trade by suppressing brothels in Southwark had not escaped the notice of Hugh Latimer, Chaplain to Edward VI. In 1549, Latimer delivered a sermon before the King that announced the effort a failure: 'My Lords, you have put down the stews, but I pray you, how is that matter amended? What availeth that? You have but changed the place, and not taken the whoredom away... I hear say there is now in London more than ever there was on the Bank'.[14]

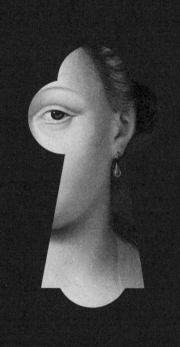

4

Selling Sex in
RENAISSANCE EUROPE

〰〰〰

THE

HONEST

Courtesans

〰〰〰

THERE IS A CUSTOM IN VENICE...NAMELY THAT A
COURTESAN TAKES SIX OR SEVEN LOVERS, ASSIGNING
TO EACH A CERTAIN NIGHT OF THE WEEK WHEN SHE
DINES AND SLEEPS WITH HIM. DURING THE DAY SHE
IS FREE TO ENTERTAIN WHOMEVER SHE WISHES SO
THAT HER MILL NEVER LIES IDLE AND DOES NOT RUST
FROM THE LACK OF OPPORTUNITY TO GRIND GRAIN.

Matteo Bandello, *Novelle* [Tales], 1554–73

THE STATUTE SERVES TO EXTIRPATE THE EVILS AND SINS WHICH MIGHT ENTER THE CITY OF FLORENCE STEMMING FROM THE INDECENCY OF WHORING WOMEN WHO CIRCULATE CONTINUOUSLY THROUGH THE CITY.

Statutes of the Podestá, 1355

The Ponte delle Tette is one of many small bridges that traverse the iconic waterways of Venice. Tucked away on the Rio di San Canciano and within the shadow of San Cassiano church, the Ponte delle Tette is an unimpressive sight. Humped and squat, it lacks the splendour of the Ponte di Rialto or the Ponte dell'Accademia. It offers none of the mystery of the Ponte dei Sospiri or the Ponte dei Pugni, and yet every year tourists flock to see it. The appeal lies not so much in its design as its name; Ponte delle Tette can be translated to 'Bridge of Breasts', though a more accurate translation would be the 'Bridge of Tits', or 'Tit Bridge'.

Legend has it that in the 16th century, the 'common prostitutes' (or *meretrice*) of Venice stood atop the bridge and exposed their breasts to attract customers and to help rid the city of homosexuality. It was this display that gave the Ponte delle Tette its iconic name. How much of this is true and how much should be ascribed to folklore is unclear, but the bridge itself is an apt symbol of how sex work was understood in Renaissance Italy: ugly, but necessary.

Shortly after his religious conversion, St Augustine of Hippo set about addressing social and moral disorder in his work *De ordine* (386). When it came to sex work, although Augustine thought it immoral, he argued that prostitution was an essential outlet for men's lust, without which they may indulge in even worse behaviour. He wrote:

> 'WHAT CAN ONE FIND THAT IS MORE IGNOBLE, MORE DEPRIVED OF HONOUR, MORE CHARGED WITH TURPITUDE, THAN COMMERCIAL WOMEN, PROCURERS AND ALL SUCH SCOURGES. IF ONE SUPPRESSES PROSTITUTES, THE PASSIONS WILL CONVULSE SOCIETY; IF ONE GIVES THEM THE PLACE THAT IS RESERVED FOR HONEST WOMEN EVERYTHING BECOMES DEGRADED IN DEFILEMENT AND IGNOMINY. THUS, THIS TYPE OF HUMAN BEING, WHOSE MORALS CARRY IMPURITY TO ITS LOWEST DEPTHS, OCCUPIES, ACCORDING TO THE LAWS OF GENERAL ORDER, A PLACE, ALTHOUGH CERTAINLY THE MOST VILE PLACE, AT THE HEART OF SOCIETY'.[1]

OPPOSITE **Bartolomeo Veneto,** *Portrait of a Lady in a Green Dress,* 1530
In Bartolomeo Veneto's painting the woman wears a saffron yellow bodice, indicating that she is likely a courtesan. In Venice, yellow was associated with the sex trade, as sumptuary laws stipulated that prostitutes wear yellow cloaks.

In his 13th-century *Summa Theologiae* (1265–74), St Thomas Aquinas considered Augustine's words and agreed that such sinners 'may be tolerated, either on account of some good that ensues therefrom, or because of some evil avoided.'[2]

This moral ambivalence underpinned state regulation of sex work throughout much of Christendom in the early modern period. Although many countries were prepared to grudgingly tolerate prostitution, none were willing to forgive it. Nor were governments about to adopt a policy of laissez-faire or turn a blind eye. This uneasy dynamic led to the emergence of state-controlled prostitution across Europe in the 15th and 16th centuries, and it was the Italians leading the way.

Any woman wanting to sell sex in the major cities of Renaissance Italy could expect to be registered with the state, licensed, taxed and restricted to official zones,

ABOVE LEFT **Bartolomeo Grassi,**
Two Prostitutes and an Old Matchmaker, c. 1580
The procuress – usually presented as an old, unpleasant woman in juxtaposition to young and beautiful prostitutes – was a common figure in early modern art.

ABOVE RIGHT **Pietro Bertelli,**
Venetian Courtesan, 1594–96
The plate shows a courtesan with her skirt raised, revealing her *chopins* and breeches underneath.

where she would work in a government brothel and be subjected to laws that governed what she could wear, where she could go and where she could live.

In order to justify profiting from the sale of sex, the Italian authorities took their cue from St Augustine and promoted the idea that prostitution was a necessary buffer against far worse sexual sin. As the Dominican theologian Giordano da Pisa preached in Florence in 1306, 'Do you see that in cities prostitutes are tolerated? This is a great evil, but if it were to be removed a great good would be eliminated, because there would be more adultery, more sodomy, which would be much worse.'[3]

Far from Giordano being a lone voice, the idea that an availability of *disonesta* (women living dishonourably) would curb the sin of homosexuality was not only well-established in Renaissance Italy but actually shaped public policy. Many historians have suggested that Italy's move to legalize the sex trade in the 15th century was largely motivated by homophobia.[4] Indeed, part of the mythology of Venice's 'Tits Bridge' is that the women displayed themselves to 'divert with such incentive the men from sin against nature'.[5] You might be forgiven for thinking this reasoning has long been abandoned by the Church, but you would be wrong. In 2000, the former Bishop of Vicenza, Pietro Nonis, published an article in the *Gazzettino di Venezia* supporting the legalization of prostitution *'per il male minore'* (for the lesser evil).[6]

ABOVE LEFT **Pietro Bertelli,**
The Roman Courtesan, c. 1580
In Renaissance Rome sex workers operated as part of a government-regulated system.

ABOVE CENTRE **Pietro Bertelli,**
Roman Courtesan, 1594–96
Bertelli depicted this courtesan as part of a book illustrating the clothes worn by different characters across Europe.

ABOVE RIGHT **Christoph Krieger,**
Venetian Courtesan, 1598
This Venetian sex work wears a surcoat and *fazzuola,* or veil, over her head.

Like most countries in medieval Europe, in Italy the preferred system of regulating the sex trade was suppression and punishment, punctuated with periodic efforts at toleration. Various Italian states had attempted to expel the *disonesta* from their cities, and all had found this to be impossible.

In 1259, the authorities of Bologna passed a statute that banished all sex workers from the city. Any woman caught selling sex was to have her nose cut off.[7] In 1287, Florence passed laws that forced the bordellos to relocate outside the city walls. In 1313, Orvieto exiled its harlots and made the sale of sex illegal throughout the city. Any landlords caught renting to dishonourable women were fined and any woman found holding other women in a brothel was punished with a public beating.[8] And Venice, home of the infamous 'Tits Bridge', exiled all 'women of evil life' in 1266, and then again in 1314.[9]

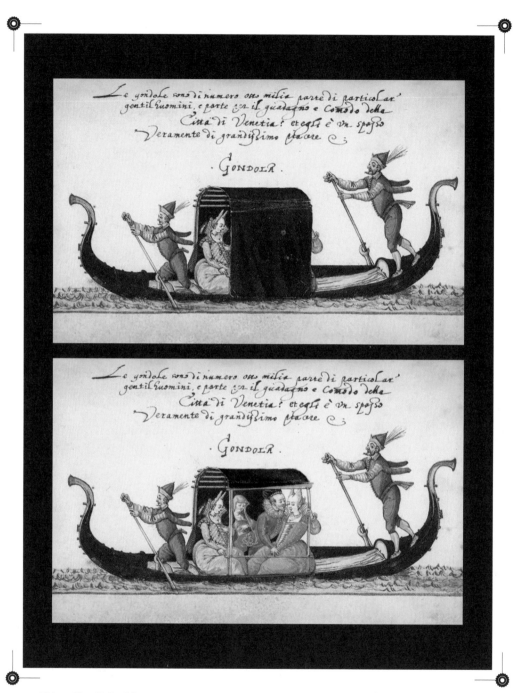

ABOVE **Niclauss Kippell,** *Gondola Ride*, **1588**
This playful illustration features a flap of paper over the gondola cabin, hiding the lovers within.

ABOVE **Niclauss Kippell,** *Book of Italian Costumes,* **1588**
In the top right image a flap of paper allows readers to reveal the *chopins* and breeches beneath the courtesan's skirt.

By the mid-14th century, Italy's enthusiasm to eradicate sex for sale had been replaced with a grudging realization that this was just not going to work. Faced with the futility of abolition, a policy of legalized, municipally regulated prostitution was introduced across Italy. But legalization does not mean acceptance and the rules set down to control these dishonourable women were as restrictive as they were punitive.

In 1384, Florence passed sumptuary laws that required its *meretrici* to wear bells on their heads, gloves and towering platformed shoes (known as *chopins*).[10] In Mantua and Parma, sex workers were ordered to wear a white cloak in public. In Milan, the cloak was black, and in Ferrara, Bergamo and Venice it was yellow.[11] Any woman caught flouting the laws was subject to punishments that ranged in severity from a fine and a night in the cells, to being paraded nude throughout the city streets while the mobs brayed and hurled rotten food.

Being marked out from a *donna onesta* (honourable woman) did little to control where sex was sold, so many cities introduced strict zoning policies and state-owned brothels to regulate where transactional sex could take place. Choosing the location of the area was always problematic. Citizens may have been willing to tolerate prostitution, but they did not want to live next door to it. When Florence introduced the 1355 Statutes of the Podestá to regulate prostitution, a key policy was segregation.[12]

Most of these zones were established in the poorer areas of the city. Rome, Milan, Pavia and Venice went even further to protect their honourable citizens and ordered the designated brothel areas be walled in.[13] In Rome, this district was known as the Ortaccio. In Venice, it was called the Castelletto, or the small castle, and was accessed via 'Tits Bridge'. In order to get there, clients would have to cross the Grand Canal to a ferry point known as the *traghetto del buso*, or 'the crossing of the hole'.[14]

Any women working within these districts were subject to further laws that forbade them from entering taverns, inns and churches. Women might be under a curfew or confined to their rooms during daylight hours or only permitted to walk in the side streets. In Ferrara, strict laws forbade *meretrici* from renting rooms from private citizens and from going to

OPPOSITE *Chopins, c.* 1600
High-platformed *chopins* were very popular with Venetian courtesans in the early modern period. They allowed the wearer to stay above the mud on the streets, and also signified a higher social status. Italian *chopins* could be made of plain materials, or they could be very extravagant, like the silk and velvet styles shown here.

the market on any day other than a Saturday.[15] The brothels and the women who worked in them were licensed, regulated and taxed. In return, the state was obligated to protect and offer legal recourse to the women working within its various jurisdictions. In Florence, this meant the establishment of the Onestà (Office of Decency) in 1403.

The Onestà comprised of a rotating board of eight male citizens of Florence, who would occupy this role for six months. There was also a notary, a treasurer, a secretary and six messengers who carried out arrests, delivered notices, brought offenders before the courts and so forth.[16] The Onestà enforced the law, facilitated the registering and licensing of *meretrici*, collected taxes, maintained existing brothels and built new ones. It also offered legal recourse to any woman who had been abused, as well as protection from creditors outside of Florence.[17]

Women who wished to voluntarily register with the Onestà for a licence to sell sex would have to pay a fee for doing so and then would be immediately escorted to an approved brothel. The police were not allowed to harass any woman carrying a licence, so theoretically at least, they offered the *meretrici* some protection. Should a woman be accused of harlotry, her fate would be decided by the city magistrates who would take a vote on her guilt. If she was found guilty, she too would be issued a licence and taken to a brothel.[18]

By 1436, there were seventy-six sex workers registered with the Onestà. Interestingly, only one was from Florence. Of the other seventy-five, sixteen came from Germany, and the others came from the Low Countries and northern Italy.[19] Today, sex workers regularly go on tour to increase their revenue. It seems this made good financial sense in 15th-century Italy as well. As restrictive as all this was, the *meretrici* still had more rights than other Florentine women. They could, and did, bring cases before the Onestà court. They brought cases against their customers, their employers and each other. In 16th-century Lucca, the Protettori delle Meretrici (Protectors of Prostitutes) dealt with any issues the city's *meretrici* had. Between 1564 and 1571, there were over forty complaints lodged with the Protettori delle Meretrici, the vast majority of which were concerned with large groups wandering around the brothel area, banging on doors, hurling abuse, gawking and generally being a nuisance.[20]

OPPOSITE **Vittore Carpaccio,** *Two Venetian Ladies, c.* 1490 This painting, thought to be a quarter of the original work, shows two unknown Venetian ladies, who some historians believe to be courtesans. Note the *chopins* in the left of the scene.

Cities, like Venice, forbade men from managing the brothels, instead installing older women known as matrons to do the job. A good matron not only looked after her girls, but knew how to keep the customers happy as well. In fact, the iconic Italian dish tiramisu is said to have been invented in the brothels to revive flagging energy levels.[21] Whereas puttanesca, a flavourful sauce served with pasta, literally translates to 'cooked in the whorish fashion' and is said to have been eaten in the brothels when women were between clients.[22] For all the moralizing around sex work, it did allow women to earn their own money, run their own business, and in a few cases, become internationally celebrated celebrities.

ABOVE LEFT **Moretto da Brescia,** *Portrait of Tullia d'Aragona as Salome*, 1537
Tullia was an Italian courtesan, writer and intellectual. She was both celebrated and condemned in her day.

ABOVE CENTRE **After Bonifacio Veronese,** *The Parable of the Rich Man (Dives) and Lazarus*, c. 1540
It is thought that the poet and musician Gaspara Stampa was a model for this painting. Whether or not she was also a courtesan continues to be debated among scholars.

ABOVE RIGHT **Titian,** *The Venus of Urbino*, 1534
It was Titian's biographer Giorgio Vasari who gave the painting its name – Titian himself only called it *la donna nuda* (the nude woman). The model is believed to have been courtesan Angela del Moro.

Today, sex work is a complex experience and subject to social hierarchy, and things were no different in Renaissance Italy. The poorest women were known as *cortigiane di candela* (courtesans of the candle) and the *cortigiane da gelosia e da impannata* (courtesans of jealousy and panic). Then there were the *cortigiane domenicali* (Sunday courtesans) who only worked occasionally. But right at the top were the *cortigiane oneste* (honest courtesans). These women were highly educated, cultured and funded by wealthy and powerful patrons. Tullia d'Aragona and Gaspara Stampa were regarded as being among the most esteemed poets and philosophers of their time, and many believed they were also sexually available to their patrons.

Italy's first celebrity courtesan was Imperia Cognati, also known as Imperia *La Divina*, which means Imperia the Divine, or Queen of Courtesans. Despite her grand title not much is known about Imperia's life. She was said to be the daughter of Diana di Pietro Cognati, herself a 'dishonest woman', and her father was said to be Paris de Grassis, the master of ceremonies of Pope Julius II, but this may be nothing more than rumour. Wherever she came from, by the time she was twenty she had secured Agostino Chigi, a Sienese banker and one of the wealthiest men in Italy, as her patron. Chigi lavished his wealth on Imperia, allowing her to maintain a palace in Rome and a villa in the country. He is also assumed to be the father of Imperia's two daughters, Lucrezia and Margherita. Being a savvy businesswoman, Imperia diversified her income streams. Her other clients included

ABOVE LEFT **Palma Vecchio**, *Portrait of a Woman*, known as *Portrait of a Courtesan*, 1520
Vecchio painted several seductive half-length portraits of Venice's famous courtesans.

ABOVE CENTRE **Raphael**, *Portrait of Young Woman with Unicorn, c. 1505*
Some historians believe the model for the painting to have been Giulia Farnese, the mistress of Pope Alexander VI.

ABOVE RIGHT **Tintoretto**, *Portrait of a Lady, c. 1574*
The portrait is said to be of the legendary courtesan and poet, Veronica Franco. On the lining of the painting, Franco's name appears in block letters

the banker Angelo di Bufalo, the papal secretary Angelo Colocci and the painter Raphael, who painted Imperia several times. Imperia's end is as unclear as her beginning. She died of suspected poisoning on 15 August 1512, aged just twenty-six. Whether she took her own life or was murdered is not known, but her funeral, paid for by Agostino Chigi, was a very grand affair. The Queen of Courtesans was laid to rest in the church of San Gregorio Magno al Celio, Rome.

Imperia was the first, but the most famous courtesan of Renaissance Italy is undoubtedly Veronica Franco. She was one of the foremost Venetian courtesans of her time, and in 1565 was included in the *Catalogo de tutte le principal et più honorate cortigiane di Venetia* [Catalogue of all the Principal and most Honoured Courtesans of Venice]. Franco was an accomplished writer and poet who counted the King of France among her many lovers. Her work is intensely erotic and

unapologetic about being a courtesan. In *Capitoli in Terze rime* (1575), for example, she wrote:

> 'SO SWEET AND DELICIOUS DO I BECOME,
> WHEN I AM IN BED WITH A MAN
> WHO, I SENSE, LOVES AND ENJOYS ME
> THAT THE PLEASURE I BRING EXCELS ALL DELIGHT,
> SO THE KNOT OF LOVE, HOWEVER TIGHT
> IT SEEMED BEFORE, IS TIED TIGHTER STILL.'[23]

She may have been rich and famous, but Franco was also brutally honest about the life of the courtesan. In *Lettere familiari* (1580) she writes to a mother and daughter about the pain and misery she has had to endure at the hands of men.

> 'IT IS A MOST WRETCHED THING, CONTRARY TO HUMAN
> REASON, TO SUBJECT ONE'S BODY AND LABOUR TO
> A SLAVERY TERRIFYING EVEN TO THINK OF. TO MAKE
> ONESELF PREY TO SO MANY MEN, AT THE RISK OF
> BEING STRIPPED, ROBBED, EVEN KILLED, SO THAT
> ONE MAN, ONE DAY, MAY SNATCH AWAY FROM YOU
> EVERYTHING YOU HAVE ACQUIRED FROM MANY OVER
> SUCH A LONG TIME, ALONG WITH SO MANY OTHER
> DANGERS OF INJURY AND DREADFUL CONTAGIOUS
> DISEASES; ...WHAT WEALTH, WHAT LUXURIES,
> WHAT DELIGHTS CAN OUTWEIGH ALL THIS?'[24]

Franco was right to fear the precarity of male patronage. In October 1580, she was denounced by the Inquisition and tried for witchcraft. The intercession of her patron Domenico Venier saw the charges dropped, but neither her reputation nor her fortune ever recovered. When Venier died in 1582, her fortunes declined further. One year later, Franco was living in the parish of San Samuele in Venice, a short walk from 'Tits Bridge' and her impoverished sisters working in the brothels of the Castelletto. By 1591, she was dead. She was just 45 years old.

Attitudes to sex work began to change dramatically across Europe following the rise of Protestantism. Protestants utterly rejected Augustinian notions that prostitution could curtail far worse sexual sins. Martin Luther called sex workers 'murderers' and suggested they be 'broken on the wheel'.[25] Protestant preachers utterly condemned any toleration and called for state-run brothels to be closed

OPPOSITE **Crispijn van de Passe,**
*The Mirror of the Most Beautiful
Courtesans of Our Time, c.* 1630–32
This book features numerous
portraits of courtesans from England,
France, the Dutch Republic, the
Spanish Low Countries, Denmark,
the German states, Bohemia, Poland,
Spain and Italy.

and for prostitution to be abolished. Catholic attitudes to prostitution were soon viewed as evidence of wider moral corruption. The Vatican responded by ushering in a new era of sexual repression. In 1566, Pope Pius V ordered all harlots to leave the city of Rome within six days and to evacuate the Papal States within twelve days. The Italian authorities may have attempted to justify state-sanctioned prostitution on moral grounds, but there is no denying just how lucrative this system was. Pius V had vastly underestimated just how integral to the Roman economy the sex workers were. Many courtesans lived on credit, they brought trade to the city and they spent their money freely. The mass exodus of thousands of sex workers meant a significant drop in revenue. Faced with this loss of income, the citizens of Rome petitioned the pope and demanded compensation. The uproar was so great that on 17 August Pius repealed his edict and permitted sex workers to reside in certain areas of the city.[26]

Reforming zeal to abolish the sin of sex work was steeped in class prejudice and it was always the poor women who paid the price. The courtesans who sold sex to the aristocracy of Europe were not only protected but powerful. Francis I of France was the first king to confer the title of mistress (maîtresse-en-titre) on his lovers, making the role of mistress an official position at court. Over the next 200 years, the role of maîtresse-en-titre became so established in European courts that royals without one were thought very strange indeed. The pressure to have a mistress was so great that Frederick I of Prussia, who was deeply in love with his wife, appointed Catharina von Wartenberg to the role, but never actually had sex with her.

Many royal mistresses involved themselves in politics and wielded enormous influence over the king. Diane de Poitiers, for example, was mistress of Henri II of France, and was not only a member of the French council but had authority to pass laws and sign official decrees with the King, which they jointly signed as 'HenriDiane'. In England, Charles II entertained a veritable harem of mistresses. The most popular was undoubtedly the actress and former orange-girl Nell Gwyn, but the most powerful was Barbara Villiers, the Countess of Castlemaine. Villiers managed to install her friends and family in positions on the Privy Council and had so much influence over Charles she was referred to as the 'Uncrowned Queen'.

OPPOSITE TOP LEFT **François Clouet,** *A Lady in Her Bath,* **1571** The model's identity is unknown, but it has been suggested that she is supposed to represent Mary Queen of Scots.

OPPOSITE TOP CENTRE **Pierre Mignard,** *Portrait of Olympia Mancini,* **17th century** Olympia Mancini was the mother of Prince Eugene of Savoy and mistress to King Louis XIV of France.

OPPOSITE TOP RIGHT **Portrait painting** of Françoise de Rochechouart, Madame de Montespan, *c.* 1651–1700 Madame de Montespan was the most celebrated and powerful *maîtresse-en-titre* of King Louis XIV of France.

OPPOSITE CENTRE LEFT **Peter Lely,** *Barbara Palmer (née Villiers), Duchess of Cleveland with her son, probably Charles FitzRoy, as the Virgin and Child, c.* 1664 Barbara Villiers was mistress to King Charles II of England, with whom she had five children.

OPPOSITE CENTRE **Peter Lely,** *Portrait of Louise de Kéroualle, Duchess of Portsmouth, c.* 1671–74 Louise de Kéroualle was mistress to King Charles II of England. She was very unpopular with the public, who believed her to be a French spy.

OPPOSITE CENTRE RIGHT **Peter Lely,** *Mary Davis, c.* 1665–70 Mary 'Moll' Davis was an actress, and one of King Charles II of England's many mistresses.

OPPOSITE BOTTOM LEFT **Peter Lely,** *Portrait of a Courtesan, c.* 1670s A courtesan, believed by some to be Nell Gwyn, painted by the court painter of King Charles II of England.

OPPOSITE BOTTOM CENTRE **François Boucher,** *Madame de Pompadour,* **1756** Madame de Pompadour was a *maîtresse-en-titre* of King Louis XV of France.

OPPOSITE BOTTOM RIGHT **Élisabeth Louise Vigée Le Brun,** *Portrait of Madame Du Barry,* **1781** Madame du Barry was the last *maîtresse-en-titre* of King Louis XV of France, and was eventually executed in the French Revolution.

But while Villiers and the other courtesans lived a life of luxury, a wave of violence was unleashed on London's sex workers. The so called 'bawdy house riots' began on Shrove Tuesday 1668. Gangs of men burned and looted brothels across London's East End. Sex workers were assaulted and robbed. The obvious social disparity between courtesans and the women working in brothels and on the street was laid bare in a satirical letter called *The Poor Whores' Petition* (1668), supposedly from the 'poore distressed whores' of London to the Countess of Castlemaine. The letter begs Castlemaine for help following the riots, reasoning that whoring is 'a Trade wherein your Ladyship hath great Experience', and she must surely help 'us poor inferior whores'. Castlemaine was outraged at the letter and the suggestion she was a 'sister' to the poor whores of London. The petition also asks for sex workers to be protected by law and work 'as our sisters do at Rome and Venice to his Holiness the Pope'.[27] This is a not too subtle dig at the perceived corruption of the Catholic Church, but it also suggests Italy's model of legalized sex work was well known.

As moral reform established itself across Europe, state-regulated prostitution was abandoned in favour of abolition, but Italy remained opposed to an outright ban, preferring regulation instead. Italy's system of regulated brothels, or *case chiuse*, was not abolished until 1958 with the passing of the Merlin Law, named after Senator Lina Merlin who was the first signatory. As Pope Pius V had found out in 1566, Italians do not take kindly to the eviction of their *meretrice* and the law was bitterly contested and deeply unpopular. The owners of the brothels, or 'houses of tolerance', banded together to form the APCA (Association of Authorized Home Owners) to fight the Merlin Law but were unsuccessful; so died a system of regulation that had been in place for hundreds of years. Of course, the law failed in abolishing sex work; it simply forced it underground and out of sight. But the legacy of Italy's dishonest women remains in plain sight: in the writings of Veronica Franco, in the paintings of the legendary courtesans, in puttanesca and tiramisu and, of course, in the humble 'Tits Bridge' of Venice.

OPPOSITE **A series of prints giving the names and tariffs of famous sex workers, 19th century**
Some of these illustrations appear to be copied from etchings by Wenceslaus Hollar, a Bohemian printmaker who worked in England during the 17th century.

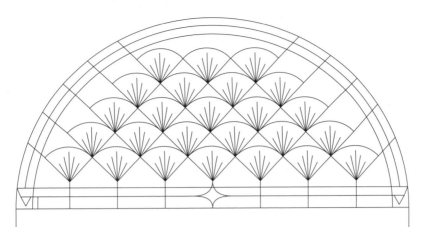

5

The Floating World of
EDO JAPAN

THE
Pleasures
OF THE
MOON

LOOSENING THE SASH OF YOSHINO RIVER,
FORGING A BOND 'TWIXT IMO AND SE MOUNTAINS,
SPREADING THE SKIRTS OF MOUNT TSUKUBA – THUS
DO LOVERS PLIGHT THEIR TROTH. ENVELOPING
THEMSELVES IN A SCREEN OF MIST, SPREADING
A QUILT OF FLOWERS, REACHING FOR A PILLOW.

Utamakura [Poems of the Pillow], 1788

A COURTESAN IS A WOMAN WHO, BY NATURE, ADORNS HERSELF AND TAKES CARE TO MAINTAIN HER APPEARANCE. SHE IS THEREFORE ALLURING AND SEDUCTIVE. THUS, IT IS EASY TO UNDERSTAND HOW A MAN CAN LOSE HIS HEART TO HER.

Asai Ryōi, *Ukiyo Monogatari*
[Tales of the Floating World], 1666

OPPOSITE **Kitagawa Utamaro,**
A Courtesan, **18th century**
Kitagawa Utamaro was one of the
most influential designers of
ukiyo-e woodblock prints and
paintings. He is best known for
his *bijin ōkubi-e,* or 'large-headed
pictures of beautiful women'.

Jōkan-ji is an unassuming Buddhist temple, just a short walk from Minowa station in Tokyo, Japan. It dates to the mid-17th century and the Edo period (1603–1868), its long history now somewhat belied by the concrete tower blocks, fast food restaurants and dilapidated shops that have grown up around it. It is also known as *Nage-komi-dera* (投込寺), meaning the 'throw away temple'. Surveying its urbanized surroundings, it is not hard to see why, but it was once at the heart of Yoshiwara, Tokyo's *yūkaku* (遊廓), or pleasure quarter. The temple's name derives not from its anomalous location, but from the thousands of sex workers who were quietly buried there when no other funeral could be paid for. Legend has it that their bodies were wrapped in straw mats by the brothel owners and left at the back door to be disposed of. There is doubtless some truth to this, but it was the mass burial of hundreds of women from Yoshiwara who died in the 1855 Great Ansei Edo earthquake that gave the temple its name. Today, people burn incense there and leave gifts of hair combs and flowers on the graves to remember the outcast dead. A plaque outside the temple provides a brief history of Yoshiwara and those who were 'thrown away' in its graveyard. It also contains lines penned by Hanamata Hanayoi, a woman who once worked there and a name found only on this memorial. It reads, 'I was born to live in hell and to be buried in Jōkan-ji temple.'

In 1589, Toyotomi Hideyoshi, one of the most powerful rulers in Japan, granted one of his favourites, Hara Saburoemon, permission to open a brothel in the city of Kyoto. With his lord's blessing, Saburoemon opened several brothels and teahouses in a district close to the Emperor's palace, which he walled off from the rest of the city, leaving only a single gate for entry and exit. He staffed his brothels with beautiful, educated and highly trained courtesans and called the area Yanagimachi (Willow Town). It was Japan's first official *yūkaku* and it was a huge success. In 1640, Yanagimachi had become so popular with rowdy pleasure seekers it had to be moved away from the imperial palace to the western suburb of Suzakuno, where it was renamed Shimabara after the Shimabara fortress in Kyushu. There it stayed until it burned down in 1854, just a year before the earthquake claimed Yoshiwara in Tokyo.

Yanagimachi may have been the first *yūkaku* to be recognized by the state, but prostitution had existed in Japan for thousands of years before this. From the fabulously wealthy imperial courtesans to the poor washerwomen trying to supplement their income, Japanese literature and history are full of references to transactional sex. The poet Ōe no Masafusa wrote a short essay, *Yūjoki* [Records on Women of Pleasure], sometime in the late 11th century. He describes poor women selling sex to sailors along the riverbanks and ports of Kyoto and Osaka, and the dancing girls who prayed to the god Hyakudayū at the shrine in Hirota and traded sex for silks and rice. 'They can melt people's hearts,' he wrote, before adding, 'This also, is an old practice.'[1] The everyday nature of sex for sale is reflected in Masafusa's tone, which is neither alarmist nor lurid. In this world, men from every social rank, from ruling warlords to those who tilled the land, paid for sexual services.[2]

The expression 'money talks' is particularly pertinent when studying history, and especially the history of sex work, as it is primarily the voices of the rich and powerful that have been preserved. Masafusa tells us people from all classes and backgrounds bought and sold sex, and this is doubtlessly true, but we know more about the courtesans of the aristocracy than we do about those who lived in poverty. Elite courtesans of the Heian period (794–1185), for example, came from noble families and composed poetry and music for the emperor and his court. The 10th-century poet Shirome was the daughter of the governor of Tango and one of the most famous and influential Heian courtesans. She performed in front of the emperor and her poetry was included in the *Kokin Wakashū* [Collection of Japanese Poems of Ancient and Modern Times], an imperial anthology of poetry commissioned by Emperor Uda and published by his son, Emperor Daigo, around 905 CE.

By the Kamakura period (1185–1333), the *shirabyōshi* (白拍子) had emerged as an influential and revered class of courtesan. They were dancers and musicians who performed in men's clothing in front of the nobility at various celebrations. The *shirabyōshi* were sexually available to their patrons, but sex was incidental as they were primarily artists. The training they received in the arts was considerable and many women willingly left their families to join their ranks. The most famous *shirabyōshi* was Shizuka Gozen, or Lady Shizuka, who was a mistress of the military commander Minamoto no Yoshitsune. Her story is told in several plays and poems, making it difficult to separate fact from fiction. It is said she could summon the rain with her dancing and that she was kidnapped by Yoshitsune's half-brother,

OPPOSITE **Ukiyo-e works of courtesans and actors, 19th century** *Ukiyo-e*, or 'pictures of the floating world', was a popular art form in Japan from the late 17th to 19th centuries. Aimed at the prosperous merchant class, they depicted characters from the floating world, including *kabuki* actors, *geishas* and courtesans. Shown here are (top left) Utagawa Toyokuni I, *The actor Onoe Shoroku I as the Ghost of the Shirabyoshi Hanako, in the play Uruo-ogi Sumizome no Sakura,* c. 1810, (top centre) Mizuno Toshikata, *Shirabyōshi Dancer: Women of the Kenkyū Era,* 1891, (top right) Hokusai, *Shizuka Gozen,* c. 1825, (centre left) Utagawa Kunitomi, *The Courtesan Hanamurasaki from the Tamaya Teahouse,* c. 1830, (centre) Keisai Eisen, *The Courtesan Hanamurasaki from the Tamaya Teahouse with a Fan in her Hand,* c. 1830, (centre right) Keisai Eisen, *Courtesan Under an Umbrella,* c. 1820–30, (bottom left) Ikeda Eisen, *The Courtesan Hanaogi of the Ogiya House,* c. 1825–35, (bottom centre) Utagawa Kuniyasu, *Egawa from the Maruebiya House,* c. 1820s, and (bottom left) Keisai Eisen, *The Courtesan Hanaogi from the Ogiya House at the Courtesans' Spring Parade,* c. 1830.

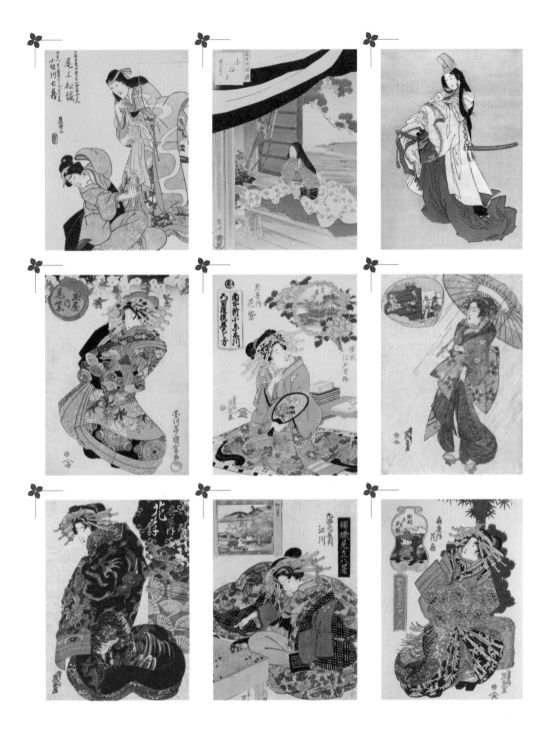

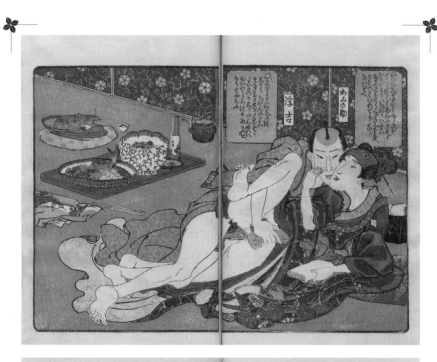

ABOVE **Utagawa Kuniyoshi,** *Chinpen*
Shinkeibai [Plum boudoir], 1839
Chinpen Shinkeibai is a three-volume
album of *shunga,* a type of Japanese
erotic art.

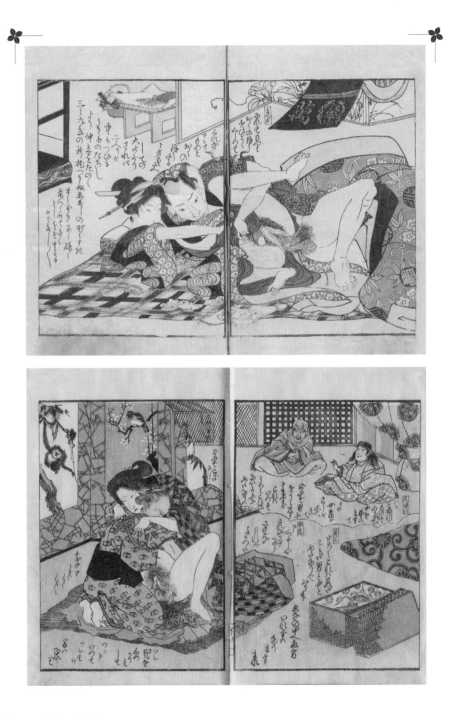

ABOVE **Utagawa Kuniyoshi,** *Chinpen Shinkeibai* **[Plum boudoir], 1839**
These *shunga* artworks offer
a glimpse inside the brothels
of Edo Japan's floating worlds.

Minamoto no Yoritomo. She was heavily pregnant with Yoshitsune's child, and Yoritomo swore if the baby was a boy, he would have it killed. Shizuka gave birth to a boy and depending on which source you read, the child was either murdered immediately, or sent away to his grandmother, but later found and murdered on Yoritomo's orders. Some say Shizuka became a Buddhist nun, others that she drowned herself for grief in a river. Shizuka Gozen is still venerated throughout Japan today, and every year festivals are held in the many towns that lay claim to her exile, death and burial.

Shizuka's story has become part of Japanese folklore, whereas the names of the thousands of men and women selling sex during her lifetime are now lost to history. Legal documents can tell us something of the culture they existed in and how widespread sex work was, but little of who these people were. In 1193, for example, the official post of *keisei betto* (傾城 別当, intendant of courtesans) was established by the shogunate in the city of Kamakura to try and control prostitution, and in particular the sex workers who solicited travellers along the Kewaizaka Pass. '*Kewaizaka*' (仮粧坂) can be roughly translated as 'make up' or 'cosmetics', a legacy of medieval Kamakura's once thriving sex trade.[3]

ABOVE **Chōbunsai Eishi,** *Oiran and Attendants at the Ō Mon, or Great Gate of the Yoshiwara, c.* 1794 The Yoshiwara was the *yūkaku*, or red-light district, of Edo, present-day Tokyo. Sex work could be legally practised in the *yūkaku*, but the area was closed off from the rest of the city behind walls or moats.

An Ashikaga shogun named Ashikaga Yoshiharu ruled over Japan from 1521 to 1546. In order to try and raise funds for the state, his government established a bureau of prostitution and taxed sex workers, a step that officially recognized sex work as a business.[4] However, it was the establishment of designated pleasure quarters in the Edo period that facilitated widespread acceptance of sex work within Japanese culture. This acceptance did not mean however that sex workers had rights, or were able to control their own lives.

The ordering of sexual pleasure into geographical zones strongly appealed to the teachings of Neo-Confucianism, which had been adopted as the primary guiding philosophy of the Tokugawa shogunate (1600–1868) in the early 17th century. Drawing on and developing the principles of ancient

Confucian philosophy, Neo-Confucianism teaches that social harmony is only achieved through strict order, respect and obedience to one's social betters, who, in turn, are expected to be benevolent to those ranked below them. What is more, this rigid class distinction was enshrined in law. Sumptuary laws dictated where people could live, what they could wear, what they could eat, who they could marry and what work they could do. Neo-Confucianism holds that the role of women is defined by 'three submissions': as a young girl she will submit to her father, as a wife she will submit to her husband, and finally as a mother she will submit to the sons she is expected to bear.[5] Wives had to be faithful and obedient and stay at home. Husbands, on the other hand, were expected to take

ABOVE **Utagawa Toyokuni I,**
Courtesans Promenading on the
Nakanochō in Yoshiwara, c. 1795
Nakanochō was a boulevard within the Yoshiwara. The sex workers who lived there were often beautifully dressed and highly educated.

mistresses. As long as he provided for his wife and family, a man could indulge his sexual proclivities with impunity. It was a double standard that was not lost on François Caron, a 17th-century French Huguenot refugee who lived in Japan for twenty years as a merchant and translator.

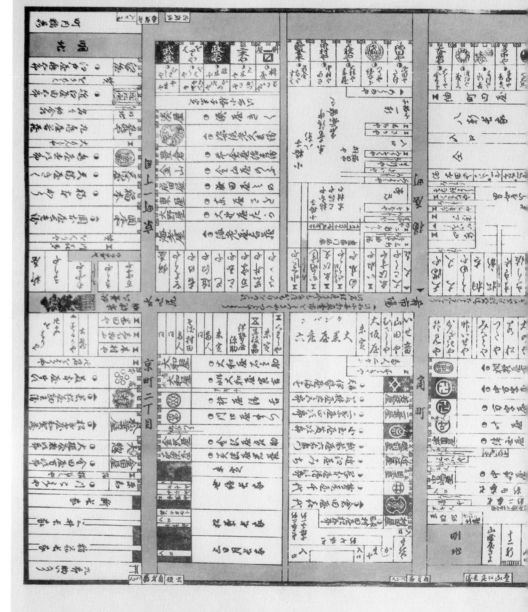

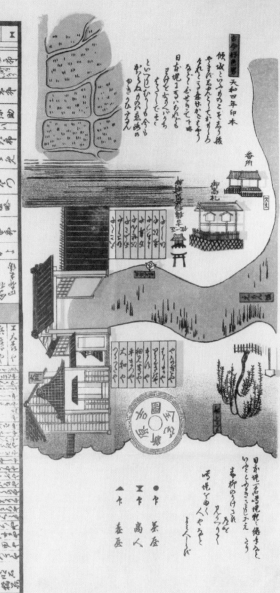

François Caron wrote:

'ONE MAN HATH BUT ONE WIFE, THOUGH AS
MANY CONCUBINES AS HE CAN KEEP; AND IF
THAT WIFE DO NOT PLEASE HIM, HE MAY PUT
HER AWAY, PROVIDED HE DISMISS HER IN A CIVIL
AND HONOURABLE WAY. ANY MAN MAY LIE WITH
A WHORE, OR COMMON WOMAN, ALTHOUGH HE
BE MARRIED, WITH IMPUNITIE; BUT THE WIFE
MAY NOT SO MUCH AS SPEAK IN PRIVATE WITH
ANOTHER MAN, WITHOUT HAZARDING HER LIFE.'[6]

PREVIOUS **A map of the Tokyo
Yoshiwara, 1846**
The map is taken from J. E.
De Becker's *The Nightless City:
or The History of the Yoshiwara
Yūkwaku* (1905). On the right is
the Ō Mon, the Great Gate to the
Yoshiwara. Once inside, there
was an abundance of brothels
for visitors to choose from.

ABOVE **Chōbunsai Eishi, *The
Yoshiwara Parade in Autumn*, 1793**
There were many such parades
and festivals held throughout
the year in the Yoshiwara.

Sex work has the potential to disrupt this order. Sex workers
were neither chaste, nor quiet, and they lived outside the
controlled domestic sphere. The selling of sex also facilitated
the mixing of different classes, and sexual desire was seen as
a direct challenge to Confucianist principles of self-control.
Recognizing this threat, the Japanese government moved to
control sex work by restricting it to enclosed *yūkaku*. *Yūkaku*
became worlds within worlds, where order and control could
be left at the gates for a short time and a hefty price.

The two most famous *yūkaku* in Edo Japan were Yoshiwara in
Edo (present-day Tokyo) and Yanagimachi in Kyoto. Writing
in 1661, Asai Ryōi called the *yūkaku* 'ukiyo' (浮世), or 'floating
worlds'. Whereas in China, the famous Cantonese brothels,
or 'flower boats', quite literally floated in the Delta River,
the 'floating' Ryōi describes here is metaphorical. *Ukiyo*
means transient pleasure, living in the moment and casting

off the anchors of everyday life. Ryōi described the fleeting hedonism the floating world offered thus:

> 'LIVING ONLY FOR THE MOMENT, GIVING ALL OUR TIME TO THE PLEASURES OF THE MOON, THE SNOW, CHERRY BLOSSOMS AND MAPLE LEAVES. SINGING SONGS, DRINKING SAKE, CARESSING EACH OTHER, JUST DRIFTING, DRIFTING. NEVER GIVING A CARE IF WE HAVE NO MONEY, NEVER SAD IN OUR HEARTS. ONLY LIKE A PLANT MOVING ON THE RIVER'S CURRENT; THAT IS WHAT IS CALLED *UKIYO* – THE FLOATING WORLD.'[7]

The floating worlds soon gave rise to a new genre of Japanese art, *Ukiyo-e*, meaning 'pictures of the floating world'. *Ukiyo-e* were woodblock prints that depicted life in the pleasure quarter: the courtesans, their clients and later the *geishas* (芸者) who flourished in the floating world. The word '*geisha*' translates to 'artist', and although great pains are taken to distance the modern *geisha* from sex work, there is no denying their shared history. Artist or not, the *geisha* was born in the pleasure quarters of Edo Japan.

The Kamakura-period tradition of the *shirabyōshi* had largely disappeared by the start of the Muromachi period in the 14th century, but women continued to take to the stage as dancers and singers, often securing patrons with whom they had sex. One of the most famous female performers of Edo Japan was Okuni. As a young girl, she joined the Izumo shrine as a *miko* (巫女, shrine maiden). *Mikos* earned money for their shrines

ABOVE **Hokusai,** *New Year's Day at the Ōgiya Brothel, Yoshiwara,* 1804 While the artist Hokusai is primarily known for his works depicting nature and landscapes, he also produced prints and paintings of more traditional *ukiyo-e* subjects, including courtesans and brothels.

ABOVE **Utagawa Kunisada II,**
Main Street of the Yoshiwara
on a Starlight Night, 1852–64
In this woodblock print two love
poems, one by Chokujuen Junma
and one by Kiō Enba, are hidden
in the night sky, lending a more
romantic air to the *yūkaku*.

ABOVE **Totoya Hokkei,** *Courtesan by a Lantern, c.* 1820
This illustration demonstrates the elaborate clothing worn by many courtesans, a level of luxury otherwise unattainable for the poor women sold into the profession.

through song, dance and sexual services. Okuni was sent by the shrine to Kyoto to solicit for further contributions. Here she performed dances that were both humorous and erotically charged. By 1603 Okuni had recruited other women to join her, particularly sex workers and other social misfits. The dance style she pioneered was loud, aggressive, colourful and highly sexual. It became known as *kabuki* (歌舞伎) and became wildly popular, soon being imitated throughout the pleasure quarters. Today it remains one of the most popular traditional styles of Japanese drama.

The *kabuki* actresses became superstars and men began to fight one another for their attention. *Kabuki* caused such

chaos that in 1628 the Japanese authorities banned women from performing it, effectively outlawing women appearing on the stage. Forbidden to perform, the dancers were forced to seek other work. Some went to work in the brothels, others taught dance and music and others set themselves up as private performers for wealthy patrons. It is here that the *geisha* emerged. It is true they did not work in the brothels, or on the street. They were highly educated and trained in the art of dance, music and entertainment, but, as the great courtesans before them, the *geishas* were still expected to be sexually available to their patrons.

The authorities' effort to establish order by forbidding women to perform the *kabuki* did not go according to plan. Beautiful young men soon filled the roles women had vacated, introducing acrobatics and feats of strength to the *kabuki*, and they too were selling sex. Male sex workers were known as *kagema* (陰間) and were often passed off as *kabuki* actors.

ABOVE LEFT **Miyagawa Isshō,** *Spring Pastimes,* 1750
Miyagawa Isshō painted in the *ukiyo-e* style and captured the *kabuki* actors, sex workers and sumo wrestlers of the floating world. He also painted several homoerotic images like this one.

ABOVE RIGHT **Miyagawa Isshō,** *Spring Pastimes,* 1750
Nanshoku (male colours) was a term used to refer to homosexuality throughout Japan. Here an older samurai monk embraces his young apprentice.

Homosexuality carried no stigma at all in Edo Japan. Indeed, for the samurai, sex between an older, experienced man and his younger apprentice was considered honourable. Soon, young men were also banned from performing and only older men were allowed to appear as *kabuki* actors.

There is no doubt that the male clientele who flocked to give their time 'to the pleasures of the moon' in the floating worlds were seduced by the glamour and heady sensuality they offered, but the reality for most of the people who worked there was very different. The courtesans, actors and *kagema* were certainly very beautiful, but few were free to live their own lives.

In keeping with Neo-Confucian principles, the sex workers were divided by class: *tayū* (太夫), who were considered to be the elite, then the *kōshi* (格子) and finally the *hashi* (端), who were considered to be 'ordinary', though still beautiful, and sat in latticed parlours soliciting trade from passers-by. The services they offered were available to anyone, and a poor man could buy the services of an elite *tayū*, as long as he had the money and the *tayū* accepted him. Each class had different prices, services and privileges. While the *tayū* could refuse clients, the *kōshi* and *hashi* could not. *Tayūs* made the most money but were also expected to maintain a very lavish lifestyle, wear the most expensive clothes and retain child servants called *kamuro* (禿) – all of which the brothel owner paid for, creating a heavy debt for the *tayū* that was unlikely to ever be paid off. Likewise, the *kōshi* and *hashi* would be indebted to their brothel owners for their clothing, food and accommodation. Many had been sold to the brothels by their family for a contract of ten years, during which time their

ABOVE **Sex workers on display in
the Yoshiwara district of Tokyo,
c. 1910**
These women were likely the *hashi*,
sex workers displayed for selection
in latticed parlours.

ABOVE **Sex workers of the Yoshiwara, early 20th century**
These postcards show a group of *oirans* from the Yoshiwara (top), and a young sex worker getting dressed in the morning (bottom).

debt increased to such an extent that they could not leave even when the contract had expired.

It was not uncommon for impoverished parents to sell their young children to the pleasure quarters. Pimps and procurers scoured the countryside for beautiful girls to work as *kamuros* and would buy them from their father. The practice was not thought of as abusive and immoral; daughters sold off to the *yūkaku* were considered very fortunate. The standard of education and living they would receive was far beyond anything a peasant family stricken with famine could hope to offer. If a *kamuro* showed promise, she would be trained as a *tayū*, where there was always the chance she could marry well, or at least secure a wealthy patron who would buy her out of her debt to the brothel. As appalling as this sounds to modern ears, the pleasure quarter offered a route out of terrible poverty, and many were glad to take it.

Children as young as 7 and 8 years old would be apprenticed to a brothel where they would learn the trade until they were old enough to legally work in the *yūkaku*. This was supposed to be at 18 years old, but records show girls as a young as 12 and 13 working in the brothels.[8] These fledgling courtesans were called *shinzō* (新造) and clients would pay handsomely to take their virginity in a ritual known as *mizuage* (水揚げ). This was considered their official debut into brothel life.

Regardless of class, these women were not allowed to leave the pleasure quarters and would know little of the world outside. Brothel owners controlled what they ate, where they went, what they wore, who they had sex with, and even when they went to the toilet. A derogatory term for brothel owners was *bohachi* (忘八) or 'forgetting eight', because it was said they had forgotten the eight principles of filial piety, respect for elders, loyalty, faithfulness, politeness, righteousness, modesty and sense of shame.[9]

The hope for the women working in the pleasure quarters was always to retire aged 27, after their contract had expired, with a number of marriage offers. But of course, the reality was often very different. Having few life skills to support them on the outside, without an offer of marriage, many continued to sell sex, or turned to brothel keeping. Disease, abuse and exhaustion all took their toll, and many died young, were wrapped in a straw mat, and left at the back of door of the Jōkan-ji temple.

ABOVE **Types of courtesans'
coiffures, c. 1899**
The illustrations are taken from
J. E. De Becker's *The Nightless City:
or The History of the Yoshiwara
Yūkwaku* (1905) and show the wide
variety of hairstyles modelled by
sex workers in the Yoshiwara.

ABOVE **Tombs at Jōkan-ji temple, Tokyo,** *c.* 1899
These are the tombs of a courtesan and
her client, who killed themselves together
in 1880. The photograph is taken from
J. E. De Becker, *The Nightless City: or The
History of the Yoshiwara Yūkwaku* (1905).

ABOVE **Tombs at Jōkan-ji temple, Tokyo,** *c.* 1899
Jōkan-ji was the final resting place for sex
workers too poor to afford a funeral. The
photograph is taken from J. E. De Becker,
*The Nightless City: or The History of the
Yoshiwara Yūkwaku* (1905).

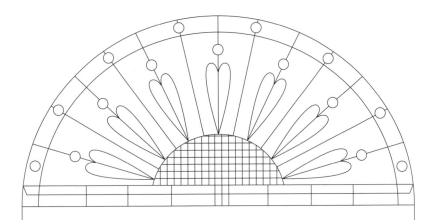

6

Men Selling Sex in
REGENCY BRITAIN

Molly Houses & MARY-ANNS

THE MEN CALLING ONE ANOTHER MY DEAR,
AND HUGGING, KISSING AND TICKLING EACH
OTHER, AS IF THEY WERE A MIXTURE OF WANTON
MALES AND FEMALES, AND ASSUMING
EFFEMINATE VOICES AND AIRS.

Jonathan Wild, *An Answer to a Late Insolent Libel*, 1718

OVID'S
METAMORPHOSES
done into
English

YET CRACKS
ARE SAINTS
COMPAR'D
WITH THEM,
WHO LEAVE
THE WHORES
TO PICK UP MEN.
ALL CRACKS
ARE FOUND SO
FULL OF AILS,
A NEW SOCIETY
PREVAILS, CALL'D
S[O]D[OM]ITES;
MEN WORSE
THAN GOATS,
WHO DRESS
THEMSELVES
IN PETTICOATS.

John Dunton, *The He-Strumpets: A Satyr on the Sodomite Club,* 1707–10

OPPOSITE *A Morning Frolic, or the Transmutation of the Sexes, c.* 1780 A woman wears a soldier's hat and adopts a masculine stance, while a man wears a lady's wig and sits primly with a fan. That gay men, or 'mollies', would often dress or act as women horrified reformers in the 18th century, who feared the corrupting and unnatural effect of this 'transmutation of the sexes'.

John Dunton's savage *The He-Strumpets: A Satyr on the Sodomite Club* (1707–10) mocks London's 'lewd cracks' (sex workers) whose 'Tails have burnt so many beaus / That now he-whores are come in use', and remarks that 'now men's tails have all the trade'.[1] Just months before Dunton penned his satire on the men selling sex in London, the city had been scandalized by the mass arrest of forty gay men, or 'mollies', who had been caught propositioning other men for sex in places where 'leud and scandalous persons' were known to meet to enjoy 'unlawful meetings and wicked conversation'; the 'Royal Exchange, Leaden-Hall-Market, Moorfields, [and] White-Chappel' were all identified.[2] Tragically, three of the men arrested took their own lives while awaiting trial; a man known only as 'Jones' hanged himself, as did Augustin Grant, a woollen-draper, while a clerk of the Church called 'Jermain' cut his own throat with a razor.[3] Far from eliciting sympathy, Dunton saw their suicide as further evidence of their guilt. He wrote:

> 'THEY J[O]NES NO SOONER DID ACCUSE, AND TWO I'TH' COMPTER FULL AS LOOSE, BUT THEY STRAIT FLY TO HEMPEN NOOSE. JERMAIN — A CLERK THAT LIV'D I'TH' EAST, BER—DEN A HE-WHORING BEAST, AND FORTY S[O]D[O]MITES AT LEAST, NO SOONER DID THEIR LEWDNESS FLAME, BUT CUT THEIR VERY THROATS FOR SHAME.'[4]

There is no surviving evidence to corroborate Dunton's accusation that these men were 'he-whores', depriving London's 'cracks' of a dishonest living, rather than simply gay men. For Dunton, and doubtless many others, there was little distinction to be made between men paying other men for sex and those looking for sex in the city's cruising hotspots: as far as he was concerned, they were all 'Men worse than goats'. In 18th-century London, men selling sex and men looking to have sex with other men occupied many of the same secretive spaces. Where else would a Regency hustler solicit for clients but in the areas gay men congregated? The first genuine evidence of men selling sex to other men is found in the court records of men charged with sodomy almost twenty years later.

On the morning of 9 May 1726, a crowd of several hundred gathered at Tyburn in London to watch the execution of ten prisoners. Public executions always drew a crowd, but that day's spectacle promised something really special. Not only were three of the condemned convicted highwaymen, but 36-year-old Catherine Hayes was to be burned to death for the murder of her husband. Until 1828, English common law regarded a wife murdering her husband as petty treason and the punishment was being burned at the stake.

At midday, the nine men were taken from their cells, had their irons removed and nooses placed around their necks, and were loaded onto carts to make the roughly 5-km (3-mile) journey from Newgate Prison to Tyburn. Catherine was dragged along behind a cart on a wooden panel. Despite a strong start, the executions did not run smoothly that day. On the way to the noose, two of the highwaymen, John Mapp and Henry Vigus, managed to free themselves and leaped from the cart in a final bid for freedom. They were quickly recaptured and forced to finish their journey. The grandstand that had been erected to seat the gawping crowds collapsed, killing at least two and injuring many others. But worst of all, the executioner failed to strangle poor Catherine to death before the flames got her, as was the custom on such occasions. *The Newgate Calendar* (1824) recorded what happened:

> 'BUT THIS WOMAN WAS LITERALLY BURNED ALIVE; FOR THE EXECUTIONER LETTING GO THE ROPE SOONER THAN USUAL, IN CONSEQUENCE OF THE FLAMES REACHING HIS HANDS, THE FIRE BURNED FIERCELY ROUND HER, AND THE SPECTATORS BEHELD HER PUSHING AWAY THE FAGGOTS, WHILE SHE RENT THE AIR WITH HER CRIES AND LAMENTATIONS. OTHER FAGGOTS WERE INSTANTLY THROWN ON HER; BUT SHE SURVIVED AMIDST THE FLAMES FOR A CONSIDERABLE TIME, AND HER BODY WAS NOT PERFECTLY REDUCED TO ASHES UNTIL THREE HOURS LATER.'[5]

Before her gruesome death, Catherine witnessed the hanging of her fellow prisoners, one of whom, Thomas Billings, was her son. However the first men to be loaded onto the carts, and the first to suffer the terrible drop, were three men convicted of the crime of sodomy: 43-year-old William Griffin, 43-year-old Gabriel Lawrence and 32-year-old Thomas Wright. As the fateful day approached, each man must have reflected on the events that had brought them there. And each one of them must have cursed the day that they hired the services of the 30-year-old hustler who turned informant to save his own neck, Thomas Newton.

OPPOSITE *Ganymede & Jack Catch,* **1771**
Samuel Drybutter, a well-known homosexual, is shown standing in fetters, conversing with Jack Catch (or Ketch, the public hangman) who holds a halter in his right hand and says, 'Dammee Sammy you're a sweet pretty creature and I long to have you at the end of my string,' to which Drybutter replies, 'You don't love me Jacky.' Drybutter was accused on several occasions of homosexual acts, though never convicted.

Drawn & Etchd by R Newton

PROGRESS of a WO

London Pub April 20

b Champaigne and not possessing the
the world in liquor, you give your
st of it in flinging a glass of wine

You are now turned off, and your only
consolation is that your Hair Dresser
promised to marry you.

He loves you to distraction but he thought
you'd have an annuity of 200 a year!
I have you now out? You dirty rascal I could
get the smartest Linen Drapers Man in London
with that money!

You now dance away at the Hop in
Queen Ann Street East, and captivate
all the men with your airs and graces!

You wind up the evening with a
Boxing match and a Warrant
and Two Black Eyes serve you in
the Morning.

You are now over head and ears in debt or
have some lawsuit and I see you shifting or
pawning your little wardrobe to Coventshford

t few years bury the Mistress of
ushman, a Sea Jam Attorney, and
en who went transported, I now
your last shift pawning your
mble for a groat to purchase
ast

Your Son is now setting very fast and I see
you the Servant of a woman who was formerly
your Servant, you live on Board Wages, which
seldom afford you more than a Bunch of
Raddishes and a Pint of Porter for your Dinner.

You take sick in the service of
this female monster and she
turns you out of doors fearing
your Funeral expences should
fall upon her.

50, Oxford Stt

N of PLEASURE.

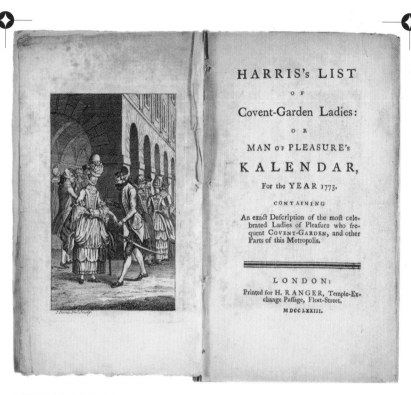

The Cov.t Garden Morning Frolick

Sodomy had been a capital offence in England since the passing of the Buggery Act in 1533, and remained as such until 1861. Despite the threat of the noose, if one knew where to look, gay brothels, or 'molly houses', could be found across 18th-century London. As early as 1649, the politician Clement Walker referred to 'new-erected sodoms and spintries at the Mulberry Garden at St James's'.[6] 'Spintry' is a Latin word for a male brothel, and the one at Mulberry Garden once stood where Buckingham Palace does today. In 1709, journalist Ned Ward went undercover and published an exposé of the goings-on at the capital's molly houses:

'THERE ARE A PARTICULAR GANG OF SODOMITICAL WRETCHES, IN THIS TOWN, WHO CALL THEMSELVES THE MOLLIES, AND ARE SO FAR DEGENERATED FROM ALL MASCULINE DEPORTMENT, OR MANLY EXERCISES, THAT THEY RATHER FANCY THEMSELVES WOMEN, IMITATING ALL THE LITTLE VANITIES THAT CUSTOM HAS RECONCIL'D TO THE FEMALE SEX, AFFECTING TO SPEAK, WALK, TATTLE, CURSY [I.E. CURTSEY], CRY, SCOLD AND TO MIMICK ALL MANNER OF EFFEMINACY, THAT EVER HAS FALLEN WITHIN THEIR SEVERAL OBSERVATIONS; NOT OMITTING THE INDECENCIES OF LEWD WOMEN, THAT THEY MAY TEMPT ONE ANOTHER BY SUCH IMMODEST FREEDOMS TO COMMIT THOSE ODIOUS BESTIALITIES, THAT OUGHT FOREVER TO BE WITHOUT A NAME.'[7]

Despite the obvious disdain shown for the mollies, in the first years of the 18th century there were few sodomy trials at the Old Bailey, and those that made it to court rarely returned a guilty verdict. But towards the end of the 17th century attitudes towards sexual morality had started to change, and these new ideas were to have a considerable impact on London's mollies. The Society for the Reformation of Manners was established in London in 1691. It was one of many such groups, led by prominent politicians and religious leaders, that sought to suppress vice by using the courts to punish immoral behaviour.

Although selling sex was not illegal in Georgian Britain, the jails and 'houses of correction' were full of female sex workers who had been detained on grounds of disorderly and lewd conduct. Among the general populace attitudes towards women selling sex were ambivalent at best.

PREVIOUS **Richard Newton, *Progress of a Woman of Pleasure*, 1796** In this illustration Newton traces the progress of a young woman who starts out as a servant but is soon seduced by the money and glamour of sex work, which ultimately leaves her destitute.

OPPOSITE TOP **Cover, *Harris's List of Covent Garden Ladies*, 1773** Half pornographic and half practical, Harris's annual list gave the names, addresses, tariffs and detailed descriptions of services offered by the sex workers in and around London's Covent Garden.

OPPOSITE BOTTOM **Louis Philippe Boitard, *The Covent Garden Morning Frolick*, 1747** In this satirical take on London life, night-time revellers – one wielding a large artichoke and another riding atop a sedan chair, in which sleeps a woman whose breasts are falling out of her bodice – are led home after a night of carousing, while a crowd of market people look on disapprovingly.

A Lugsail Privateer *towing* A Crippled Man of War *into* Port

London, Printed for R. Sayer & J. Bennett. Map, Chart & Printsellers, & Globe Manufacturers, N.º 53, Fleet Street, 10 April 1783.

ABOVE John Raphael Smith, *A Lugsail Privateer towing a Crippled Man of War into Port*, 1783
In this satirical print a harlot entices an old sailor with a wooden leg into the 'Rose Tavern'.

KIND AND TENDER USAGE.

WINES. &c.

A DECOY for the OLD as well as the YOUNG.

Printed for Carington Bowles, at his Map & Print Warehouse, No 69 in S.t Pauls Church Yard London.— Published as the Act directs.

ABOVE **John Raphael Smith,** *A Decoy for the Old as well as the Young,* 1773 In this illustration an elderly fop peers through a lorgnette at a harlot and a madam standing in the doorway to a brothel.

Harris's List of Covent Garden Ladies (1757–95) was
a popular annual almanac of London's sex workers. It gave
the addresses, services and prices of women selling sex
in and around Covent Garden in the West End, but it also
offered its readers titillation from the graphic descriptions
of its subjects. The list suggests an attitude of permissive
acceptance towards sex work, but this is far from the
whole picture. Court records, sermons, pamphlets and
newspaper articles from the time reveal a growing anxiety
around sex work. For many moralizers in Georgian London,
prostitution was a major problem. In 1758, Saunders
Welch, a Justice of the Peace for both the County of
Middlesex and the City and Liberty of Westminster,

NOW SⁱʳYOU'R A COMPLEAT MACARONI.   The ORIENTAL MACARONI.   The MACARONI MERCER.

ABOVE LEFT **J. Caldwell,** *Now
Sr. You're a Compleat Macaroni,*
1733–1807
The men in these caricatures are
'macaronis' – elite young Englishmen
who wore tight-fitting clothes, delicate
shoes, huge wigs and a lot of makeup.

ABOVE CENTRE **M. Darly,**
The Oriental Macaroni, 1773
In the late 18th century macaroni
fashion became associated with
an excessive lifestyle, effeminacy
and possible homosexuality.

ABOVE RIGHT **M. Darly,** *Macaroni
Mercer,* 1772
Between 1771 and 1773, the print
publishers Matthew and Mary
Darly produced nearly 150 satirical
macaroni prints with resounding
success.

published *A Proposal to Render Effectual a Plan, To remove
the Nuisance of Common Prostitutes from the Streets of this
Metropolis* and conservatively estimated that there were some
3,000 women who made their living selling sex in the capital.
When the Prussian historian Johann Wilhelm von Archenholz
visited London in 1789, he estimated there were 30,000 ladies
of pleasure living in the district of Marylebone alone. Given
that we do not even have reliable statistics on how many
people are selling sex in London today, there is simply no
way that accurate data could be gathered in the 18th century.
But, the vastly inflated numbers in circulation do tell us one
thing: sex work was thought to be a vast issue. The Society for
the Reformation of Manners campaigned relentlessly for the
abolition of sex work, as well as for suitable punishments for
anyone not toeing the line, and London's molly houses were
at the top of their hit list.

A molly house was not technically a brothel. Rather it was an establishment where gay men could meet to socialize and have sex. Sex was for sale in these establishments and many sex workers met their clients here, but facilitating the sale of sex was not the primary purpose of the molly house. These were social spaces where you could have sex, some of which was sold and some of which was not. The proprietors of these establishments made their money by renting out beds and selling food and drink to their clientele. In 1725, the Society for the Reformation of Manners began keeping a close watch on molly houses. Fired by moral outrage at what they regarded as 'unnatural practices', they recruited informants and gathered evidence. By 1726 they were ready to pounce.

ABOVE LEFT *The Macaroni Painter, or Billy Dimple sitting for his Picture,* 1772
Popular macaroni prints depicted macaronis enjoying various different pastimes, whilst highlighting their extravagant style and affected manner.

ABOVE CENTRE **Philip Dawe,** *The Macaroni, a Real Character at the Late Masquerade,* 1773
The macaroni was made distinctive in these prints through the exaggerated depiction of his towering wig.

ABOVE RIGHT *How d'ye Like Me,* 1772
This illustration shows an ageing macaroni, though the fashion was usually associated with young men.

In August 1726 Mr Mugg was arrested for keeping a house in Piccadilly for the 'entertainment of persons to commit that abominable crime'.[8] In December 1726, Robert Whale and York Horner were convicted of keeping a 'house in King Street, Westminster, with conveniences to commit the detestable sin of sodomy'.[9] Later that month Samuel Roper, otherwise known as 'Plump Nelly', died in jail while awaiting charges of keeping a disorderly house for 'sodomitical practices' in Giltspur Street, Smithfield.[10] Before he met his fate at the end of a rope, Thomas Wright ran a molly house in Christopher's Alley, and then another in Beech Lane, both in Moorfields. But the most famous molly house, and the establishment at the very epicentre of this wave of persecution, belonged to 'Mother' Margaret Clap in Field Lane, Holborn; it was tucked away between an arch on one side and the Bunch o' Grapes tavern on the other. It was an area of London that struck fear into the well-to-dos. A tangled maze of dark alleys, gin shops and dosshouses, the streets around Field Lane were known as a hotbed of vice. On a cold Sunday night in February 1726, Mother Clap's establishment was raided and forty men in various states of undress were hauled away to Newgate.

The Society for the Reformation of Manners had been investigating Mother Clap for months and when the time came, they had ample evidence against her and her patrons. Samuel Stevens, a reforming constable, had infiltrated Mother Clap's molly house by pretending to be the 'husband' of an informant in November 1725. He reported what he found to the courts in great detail.

> 'I FOUND BETWEEN FORTY AND FIFTY MEN MAKING LOVE TO ONE ANOTHER, AS THEY CALL'D IT. SOMETIMES THEY WOULD SIT ON ONE ANOTHER'S LAPS, KISSING IN A LEWD MANNER, AND USING THEIR HANDS INDECENTLY. THEN THEY WOULD GET UP, DANCE AND MAKE CURTSIES, AND MIMICK THE VOICES OF WOMEN. "O, FIE, SIR! – PRAY, SIR. – DEAR SIR. LORD, HOW CAN YOU SERVE ME SO? – I SWEAR I'LL CRY OUT. – YOU'RE A WICKED DEVIL. – AND YOU'RE A BOLD FACE. – EH YE LITTLE DEAR TOAD! COME, BUSS!" THEN THEY'D HUG, AND PLAY AND TOY, AND GO OUT BY COUPLES INTO ANOTHER ROOM ON THE SAME FLOOR, TO BE MARRY'D, AS THEY CALL'D IT.' [11]

It was in establishments like this that 'he-strumpets' like Thomas Newton found 'molly-culls' (male clients) and made their money. We do not know when Newton was press-ganged into working for the authorities, but it is almost certain that he did so to save his own life. Whatever the reason, his testimony, and that of his fellow hustler, 18-year-old Edward Courtney, were crucial in securing the 1726 convictions and provide the fullest account of male sex work in 18th-century London.

Newton had been a regular at Thomas Wright's molly house and testified that he had not only been sodomized by Wright but had also been pimped out to his many customers, stating that 'he has often fetched me to oblige company that way'.[12] At the trial, further evidence against Wright was offered by Joseph Sellers, who had also gone undercover to investigate Wright's molly house. 'On Wednesday the 17th of November last, I went to the prisoner's house in Beech Lane, and there

OPPOSITE *Mademoiselle de Beaumont or The Chevalier D'Eon*, 1777
The Chevalier d'Éon was a French diplomat, spy and soldier, and was one of the most celebrated characters in 18th-century Britain. They lived openly as a man and as a woman in both France and England at different stages of life.

MADEMOISELLE de BEAUMONT, or the
CHEVALIER D'EON.
Female Minister Plenipo. Capt. of Dragoons &c.&c.

I found a company of men fiddling, and dancing and singing bawdy songs, kissing and using their hands in a very unseemly manner.'[13] Wright offered only one character witness in his defence, who swore that he was an 'honest man'.[14] Honest or not, the jury found him guilty and sentenced him to death.

Newton also testified against Gabriel Lawrence, who he claimed that he had first met at Mother Clap's establishment, which he described as follows:

'IT BORE THE PUBLICK CHARACTER OF A PLACE OF ENTERTAINMENT FOR SODOMITES, AND FOR THE BETTER CONVENIENCY OF HER CUSTOMERS, SHE HAD PROVIDED BEDS IN EVERY ROOM IN HER

HOUSE. SHE USUALLY HAD THIRTY OR FORTY OF SUCH PERSONS THERE EVERY NIGHT, BUT MORE ESPECIALLY ON A SUNDAY.'[15]

ABOVE LEFT **M. Darly,** *A Macaroni Dressing Room,* **1772**
In this macaroni print, a man is shown not just in an elaborate wig and extravagant clothing, but wearing a woman's dress.

ABOVE RIGHT *Love-a-la-mode, or Two Dear Friends,* **1820**
A satirical print of Lady Louisa Strachan and Sarah Greville, Countess of Warwick, making love in a park, while their husbands look on with disapproval. The relationship between these two women was read by some at the time as more than a close friendship, and they were widely mocked in the press.

Newton claimed Lawrence had sodomized him and another sex worker called Partridge on 10 November 1725. Lawrence admitted he was a regular at Mother Clap's but denied knowing that it was a molly house. He produced several witnesses to attest to his character, but it did not go well and Gabriel Lawrence too was sentenced to hang.

The same sorry fate awaited William Griffin, a furniture upholsterer, whom Newton testified had been living at Mother Clap's for two years and had sodomized him on 20 May 1725. Griffin admitted living at Mother Clap's but denied knowing it was a molly house. He produced no witnesses and was found guilty of all charges against him.[16]

By the age of 18, Edward, or 'Ned', Courtney had already been sent to Bridewell Prison three times; he had assaulted a woman, stolen from his employer George Whittle and caused enough of a scene in Covent Garden to be arrested for disturbing the peace. He agreed to turn informer against George Kedger in April 1726 and testified that the accused had paid to have sex with him. Kedger denied this and claimed he had 'advised him [Ned] to leave off that wicked course of life; but he said, he wanted money, and money he would have, by hook or by crook; and, if I would not help him to some, he would swear my life away.'[17] Courtney very nearly did 'swear his life away', as Kedger was found guilty and sentenced to death, though this was later reprieved. Ned was not as convincing in the witness box as Thomas

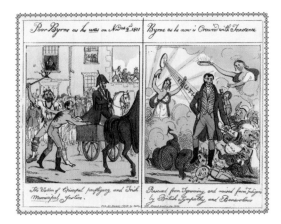

ABOVE LEFT *Poor Byrne as he was on Novmbr 2nd 1811 / Byrne as he now is Crown'd with Innocence*, 1822
In 1811 coachman James Byrne was publicly flogged after making allegations of homosexuality against Percy Jocelyn, the Bishop of Clogher. However, when they were proved to be true in 1822 his good reputation was restored.

ABOVE RIGHT **George Cruikshank,** *The Arse Bishop Josling a Soldier,* 1822
A print mocking the disgraced Percy Jocelyn, the Bishop of Clogher. The scene shows a police constable separating the clergyman and a soldier, while the bishops begs, 'Do let me go, I'll give you £500.'

Newton and when he claimed that his former employer George Whittle kept a molly house and had pimped him out for sixpence, the jury suspected that the accusation was motivated by spite and acquitted Whittle.

Finally, in July 1726, two months after the executions of three of her patrons, Margaret Clap, mother to the mollies of Holborn, was brought to trial. She was indicted for keeping a disorderly house for the purposes of sodomy. The evidence against her was overwhelming and the only defence she could mount was that she was 'a woman, and therefore it cannot be thought that I would ever be concerned in such practices'.[18] She was found guilty and was sentenced to a hefty fine and two years' imprisonment, but not before she had faced the public in the pillory at Smithfield market. On Tuesday 23 July 1726, Margaret Clap was placed in the pillory for her crimes. The newspapers at

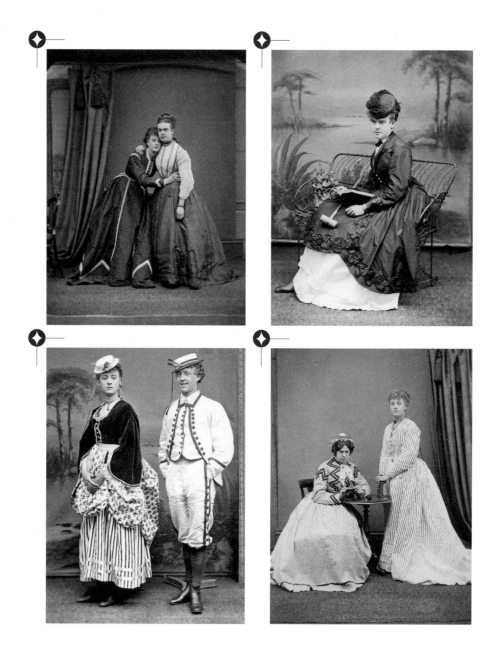

PREVIOUS *Drag* album, 1860–1950
The album contains thirty-five
photographs of cross-dressers and
trans women, including those from
music hall and theatre, mostly
from the 1860s and 1870s.

ABOVE **Frederick Park and Ernest
Boulton, AKA Fanny and Stella,** *c.* 1870
Park and Boulton were homosexuals
and cross-dressers, and were
arrested in 1870 for conspiracy
to commit sodomy.

the time reported that 'the populace treated her with so much severity that she fell once off of the pillory, and fainted upon it several times' and was eventually 'carried off in convulsion fits to Newgate'.[19] After this, Mother Clap vanishes from history. We do not even know if she survived her ordeal.

The Society for the Reformation of Manners had succeeded in destroying Mother Clap and her molly house. Their zeal for persecuting the abominable sin of sodomy ignited new waves of homophobia across the city. Few had any compassion for the men dragged before the court. Indeed, the anonymous author of a 'modest proposal', published in the *Weekly Journal: or, The British Gazetteer* in 1726, felt that these 'monstrous wretches' should face the 'common hangman' who would 'tie him hand and foot before the judge's face in open court', where 'a skillful surgeon be provided immediately to take out his testicles, and that then the hangman sear up his scrotum with a hot iron.'[20]

The public may have been whipped up into a frenzy of homophobia, but the trials of 1726 cost the Society for the Reformation of Manners dearly. They had secured multiple convictions, but their methods were highly questionable. That these convictions depended entirely on the testimonies of 'he-strumpets' in fear of their lives had not escaped public attention. In 1727, the Society had to defend itself against accusations of corruption, bribery and extortion.[21] Their zeal for moral reform may have remained undimmed, but the courts and the public were growing weary of their tactics. Just ten years later, there were only a handful of reform societies left in England, and in 1738 they disbanded entirely.[22]

Judicial persecution of gay men continued in waves throughout the 18th and into the 19th century. The last man to be sentenced to death for sodomy at the Old Bailey was John Spenser in 1860, though the sentence was never carried out. The impolitic cruelty meted out to men simply for having sex with one another did nothing to rid the world of either homosexuality or the sex trade.[23] Mother Clap and her boys may have lost the fight against pious reformers, but ultimately, the mollies won the war. Despite centuries of executions, maiming, imprisonments and state-sanctioned homophobia, gay subculture has always thrived in London. Long may it continue to do so.

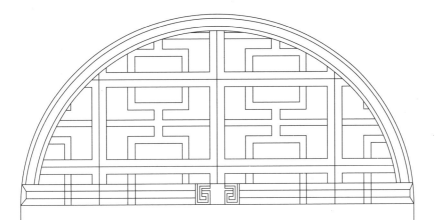

7

**Sex in the
QING DYNASTY**

~~~~~~~~~~

Master
OF THE
PLUM BLOSSOMS

~~~~~~~~~~

SOME YEARS AGO, NONE BUT WASHERWOMEN WERE
ALLOWED TO VISIT THE SHIPS, BUT NOW ALL SORTS ARE
PERMITTED, AND AN UNRESTRAINED INTERCOURSE
IS AS COMMON AT WHAMPOA AS AT LONDON OR
PORTSMOUTH. CERTAIN BOATS, HAVING LICENSES
FROM THE MANDARINS, VISIT THE SHIPS AS SOON
AS IT IS DARK, LITERALLY LOADED WITH WOMEN.

Peter Dobell, *Travels in Kamtchatka and Siberia*, 1830

THEY [THE WOMEN] COME VERY OFTEN ON BOARD THE SHIPS TO SEE THEIR OLD FRIENDS, AND TO TALK OVER OLD TIMES. BESIDES THESE, THERE ARE A FEW WOMEN, BOTH OLD AND YOUNG, WHO HAVE ALWAYS MAINTAINED, AND STILL PRESERVE, AN EXCELLENT CHARACTER.

Charles Downing, *The Fan-Qui in China, in 1836–37* (1838)

OPPOSITE **Erotic painting, late 18th century**
Concubinage was officially recognized in China until 1950, and concubines played an important role in the courts of the Qing emperors.

On the evening of 6 December 1806, several pirate ships, or 'junks', weighed anchor just off the coast of Ponta Cabrita in the Macau region of southern China. Shivering on deck stood John Turner, formerly the chief mate of the British Country Ship *Tay* and now a hostage to the infamous Captain Cheng I and the Red Flag Fleet that sailed under his command. Fearing a pirate attack, Captain William Greig had sent Turner to find help – only for him to sail straight into the pirates they had been trying to avoid. Ransoming hostages was a lucrative business for pirates and Turner spent the next five months at their mercy. His account of what happened provides a rare and valuable insight into organized Chinese piracy at the turn of the 19th century. The Red Flag Fleet was a vast criminal enterprise, more akin to a floating mafia than to the lovable pirate rogues of popular imagination. Captain Cheng I commanded over 25,000 men, aboard 600 hundred ships, ranging in size from 15 to 200 hundred tons. Turner saw for himself how the Fleet dealt with anyone who opposed them.

'IF A VESSEL WHICH THEY CAPTURE HAS MADE RESISTANCE, THEY IN GENERAL MURDER SOME OF THE CREW, AND CRUELLY TREAT THE REST. IF SHE HAS MADE NO RESISTANCE, BUT THEY SUSPECT THE CREW OF HAVING DESTROYED OR SECRETED ANYTHING, THOUGH NONE ARE MURDERED, THEY ARE VERY SEVERELY PUNISHED... THIS PUNISHMENT IS INFLICTED IN THE FOLLOWING CRUEL MANNER; THE UNHAPPY SUBJECT, HAVING BEEN FIRST STRIPPED OF ALL BUT HIS TROUSERS, HAS HIS HANDS TIED TOGETHER BEHIND HIS BACK; A ROPE PASSING FROM THE MAST HEAD, IS THEN MADE FAST TO HIS JOINED HANDS, BY WHICH HE IS HOISTED FROM THE DECK; AND, WHILE THUS SUSPENDED, REPEATED STRIPES ARE INFLICTED ON EVERY PART OF HIS BODY, WITH A ROD FORMED OF TWO OR THREE RATTANS TWISTED TOGETHER. BLOOD FREQUENTLY FOLLOWS THE STRIPES, AND IN SOME CASES THE MISERABLE SUFFERER IS LEFT SUSPENDED BY HIS HANDS FOR UPWARDS OF AN HOUR.'[1]

In November 1807, the year after Turner was freed, Captain Cheng I was killed in a hurricane and his wife, Shih Yang, known as Cheng I Sao (wife of Cheng), assumed command of the Red Flag Fleet. Not much is known about this formidable woman, and where fact fails, legend supplies. However a clutch of truths are known. Under Cheng I Sao's rule, the

Red Flag Fleet expanded significantly to include over 70,000 pirates and some 1,200 vessels along the coast of Guangdong Province. She maintained her authority through fear and intimidation, and by demanding strict adherence to her code of conduct.

Everything that the pirates looted was put into a common fund (*kung-hsiang*, 供剩) and distributed throughout the fleet. Anyone caught pilfering or withholding funds was decapitated. Those who disobeyed orders, stole from the villages that supplied the fleet or went ashore without

permission more than once could also expect to lose their heads. Raping female captives was made a capital offence, but any pirate found to be having a consensual sexual relationship with a woman they were not married to was also put to death. So too was the woman, who would have cannonballs attached to her legs before being thrown overboard.[2] Cheng I Sao did allow her crew to choose wives from their captives, who would then be forced into marriage and life aboard a pirate ship. Women thought to be ugly were rowed back to shore and the rest were either forced into marriage or slavery, or ransomed back to their families.

Civilians did not escape Cheng I Sao's brutality either, as she extorted money from towns and villages up and down the coast of the Shizi Channel. The pirates offered 'protection' for an exorbitant fee. Those who failed to pay the demands were met with brutal reprisals. In the coastal village of Sanshan,

Cheng I Sao's crew murdered 2,000 inhabitants who refused to pay the protection levy and enslaved the surviving women and children. In 1809, captive Richard Glasspoole witnessed this extortion racket first-hand when the pirates holding him hostage laid siege to a town on the Pearl River, demanding 10,000 Spanish silver dollars (also known as pieces of eight) be paid annually. After much negotiating and threats of mass murder, the pirates accepted 6,000 dollars just to leave.

Unable to defeat her, in 1810 the Qing Imperial government offered all pirates who surrendered an amnesty which

pardoned their crimes and allowed them to keep their money. The pirate queen retired a wealthy woman and died in 1844, surrounded by her family. Cheng I Sao's rise to power and vast pirate empire are made all the more impressive in light of her comparatively humble origins, selling sex in the floating brothels of Canton.[3]

There is no surviving record of Cheng I Sao's life in Canton, also known as Guangzhou, before she married Cheng I and took to the seas, but the floating brothels, or 'flower boats', had been a familiar sight along the Pearl River Delta for hundreds of years before the Qing dynasty (1644–1912). As early as the 7th-century Tang Dynasty, floating brothels were referred to as 'hua chuan' (畫船) or 'hua fang' (畫舫). Until the 20th century, Chinese culture was based on Confucianist philosophical and moral values, which taught that women were inferior to men. For Chinese families, sons

ABOVE **Large boats for the accommodation of sex workers, c. 1805**
In Canton, sex workers lived aboard 'flower boats' floating in the Pearl River. As one of the world's great ports, Canton provided them with plenty of customers.

ABOVE **Chen Mei,** *Amusements of*
the Concubines of the Emperor, 1738
Chen Mei served as a court painter
for both Emperor Yongzheng and
Emperor Qianlong, and depicted the
daily lives of the many concubines
living in the imperial palace.

were of paramount importance, while daughters were costly and could not continue the family name. Marriages were arranged and a wife was expected to serve her husband, bear sons and live a life of domesticity and submission. Sexual service was an extension of this deeply patriarchal society in which women existed to serve men. Concubinage was officially recognized in China until 1950, when it was made illegal by the Marriage Law.[4] Faced with the financial burden of raising daughters, many poor families sold their daughters to brothels, rather than attempting to broker a marriage and pay for a dowry. As brutal as this sounds, at least these girls escaped infanticide, which was widespread. Many families simply chose to murder their newborn daughters in a practice Qing texts refer to as 'ni nü' (to drown girls, 溺女).[5]

For a select few, sex work offered a life of power and privilege that was unobtainable to other women. The courtesans of ancient China were not only legendary for their sexual skills, but for their dancing, poetry and painting. In the 1st century BCE Zhao Feiyan was born into poverty but her skills as a dancer caught the eye of the Emperor Cheng, who made her his concubine. It is said that the first time Zhao came to the emperor's bedchamber, she was so beautiful that all he could do was stare at her for hours. Zhao became indispensable to the emperor and eventually he made her empress of China, the only courtesan ever to rule as queen.[6] Li Shishi was the favourite concubine of Emperor Huizong of the Song dynasty (960–1279). She was orphaned at a young age, taken in by a procuress named Li Yun and eventually put to work in Jinqian Xiang, the entertainment district of Kaifeng. Her beauty and skill at playing the lyre soon brought her to the attention of the emperor, who started to visit her in secret. It is said that he had a tunnel built between the palace and Li Shishi's home, much to the fury of his wife and other concubines. When one of them asked the emperor why he favoured Li Shishi over all others, he replied, 'None of you know about the art of love. With her, I never have to labour, and yet she offers me so much pleasure. In bed, she is always so lively and so full of fun. Compared with her, all of you are like beauties made of clay or wood.'[7]

The sexual artistry of these women was clearly considerable, and it was a skill that they were trained in before being set to work. One of the most thorough accounts of the techniques Chinese courtesans were apprenticed in comes from an

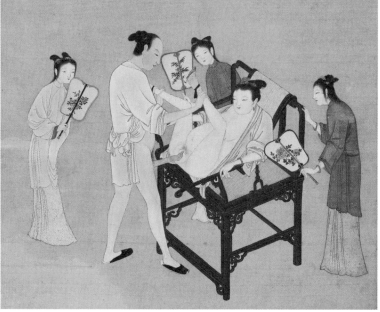

ABOVE **Erotic paintings, *c.* 16th century**
The elegant furniture and attendant
servants in these paintings indicate
that they are depicting the upper
classes. The audience for the works
was likely to be wealthy elites as well.

ABOVE **Erotic paintings, 19th century**
Chinese erotic art can be found
on inlaid boxes, porcelain figurines,
silk or rice paper paintings and
even the soles of ceramic shoes.

anonymous 19th-century text called *Memoirs of the Plum Blossom Cottage*, penned by an author calling himself 'Master of Plum Blossoms'.

> 'AS MOST MALES WANT TO DEEM THEMSELVES POTENT AND VIRILE, YOUR PRIMARY CONCERN IS NOT TO HURT THEIR EGO... LET THEM IMAGINE THEY HAVE THE INITIATIVE, THOUGH IT IS IN YOUR HANDS. WITH SOMEONE WHO DOES NOT HAVE THE STAMINA, YOU MUST FEIGN SATISFACTION EVEN THOUGH HE MAY DISCHARGE THE MOMENT HE ENTERS YOU. YOU CAN STILL LET HIS SHRUNKEN ORGAN REMAIN INSIDE, EMBRACING AND CARESSING HIM AS IF HE WERE THE MOST WONDERFUL MAN YOU HAD EVER HAD... FOR YOUR OWN GOOD, YOU HAVE TO MAKE HIM DISCHARGE AS QUICKLY AS YOU CAN. YOU MUST TAKE THE INITIATIVE WITHOUT HIS KNOWLEDGE. YOU CAN MOVE YOUR HIPS LIKE A MILLSTONE IN ACTION, HOLDING HIS WAIST TIGHTLY AND STROKING HIS SPINE NEAR THE WAIST GENTLY BUT PERSISTENTLY... BUT BE SURE TO LET HIM HAVE SOME FUN, OR HIS EGO WILL BE PRICKED AND YOU WILL LOSE A CUSTOMER.'[8]

Of course, the life of a wealthy courtesan was a world apart from those aboard the floating brothels of Canton, where life was tough, and punctuated with poverty, pimps and punters.

The flower boats in Canton accepted Chinese clients only, but those anchored at Whampoa, also known as Huangpu, serviced foreigners, who referred to them as 'lob-lob boats', thought to be a corruption of the English 'love-love boats'.[9] Indeed, much of what we know about this world comes from the memoirs of fascinated western travellers. In his *A Voyage to the East Indies in 1747 and 1748* (1762), Charles Frederick Noble recalled the poverty he saw amongst the floating Cantonese community: 'These boats come crowding about the European ships at Whampoa, especially at dinner time, begging victuals from the people aboard. In return for which they offer to wash their linen and to do other menial services.'[10] While Noble occasionally employed these 'miserable wretches' out of pity, he records there were many European sailors who took 'advantage of their necessity' and would bargain 'with a father and mother for an embrace of their daughter'.[11] Such arrangements had to be made discreetly as prostitution was under the control of local government bureaucrats called mandarins, who demanded regular fees for their trouble.

OPPOSITE **Porcelain fruit containing figurines engaged in sexual foreplay, early 20th century**
These porcelain fruits were known as 'trunk bottoms', as they were placed in the bottom of women's bridal chests by their mothers. When the daughter came to marry, her mother would reveal the porcelain figures inside the fruit, offering some helpful instruction as to what her daughter could expect on the wedding night. For the upper classes, erotica could be artistic and respectable, in the same way that their courtesans were admired and highly trained.

Anyone caught selling sex without offering up a cut to the state faced severe punishments, as Noble described.

> 'THESE MANDARINS ARE CONTINUALLY GOING UP AND DOWN THE RIVER, SEARCHING SUCH BOATS AS THEY HAVE ANY REASON TO SUSPECT; AND, IN CASE A EUROPEAN IS CAUGHT IN THEM, WITH YOUNG WOMEN, HE, TOGETHER WITH THE PEOPLE OF THE BOAT, MUST UNDERGO CHASTISEMENT OF THE BAMBOO, OR BRIBE THE MANDARIN WITH A DOLLAR OR TWO TO LET THEM PASS.'[12]

The English lawyer William Hickey travelled through Canton around 1770 and, being a self-proclaimed womanizer, made

sure to visit 'lob-lob creek'. In his memoirs, he recorded the legal system within which the floating brothels operated.

> 'THE FEMALES WHO PLY AT LOB-LOB CREEK ARE SUPPOSED TO DO SO BY STEALTH. I SAY *SUPPOSED*, BECAUSE THE FACT IS THEY PAY A PROPORTION OF THEIR EARNINGS TO THE MANDARIN UPON DUTY, WHO THEREUPON, LIKE AN UPRIGHT ADMINISTRATOR OF JUSTICE, SHUTS HIS EYES AND EARS TO THE BREACH OF THE LAW, WHOSE PUBLIC OFFICERS BEING INVARIABLY CORRUPT.'[13]

ABOVE LEFT **Tankas, 19th century**
The Tanka people were an ethnic subgroup in southern China who traditionally lived on junks in coastal regions. They were viewed as outcasts and sometimes referred to as 'sea gypsies' by both the Chinese and British. The Tanka also formed a class of sex workers in Canton, operating on the boats in Canton's Pearl River.

ABOVE RIGHT **William Alexander, a disorderly sex worker, late 18th century**
A Chinese sex worker who has been accused of disorderly conduct is depicted being brought before a judge.

The system was certainly corrupt, but as Noble observed, there was 'so good an understanding between the mandarins and the proprietors of these boats, that they deal pretty extensively and with great safety'.[14] Precisely whose 'safety' Noble is referring to is debatable, as many of the women had been sold into sexual slavery by their families and were poorly treated by their masters. Peter Dobell was an Irish-born Russian citizen who travelled to China in 1798 and made it his home for seven years. In his travel memoirs he described the lob-lob boats of Canton and the treatment of the women aboard.

'MOST OF THOSE BROUGHT AT NIGHT ARE POOR GIRLS, WHOM THE EXTREME DESTITUTION OF THEIR PARENTS HAS OBLIGED THEM TO SELL FOR A CERTAIN TERM OF YEARS; AND THEY ARE SLAVES UNTIL THAT TIME EXPIRES. WHATEVER THEY CAN EARN BELONGS TO THEIR MASTER; HE DISPOSES OF THEM AS HE PLEASES, OFTEN TIMES BEATS THEM AND CLOTHES AND FEEDS THEM BADLY.'[15]

Understanding the experience of these women is an exercise in cognitive dissonance; they were slaves, but within that status there were freedoms available that were denied to other women. Most received an education and were trained in the arts, diplomacy and social etiquette. They were often beautifully groomed and elaborately dressed. While Chinese wives were not permitted to accompany their husbands outside of the home, sex workers on the other hand were able to participate in public life, attending social functions and so forth. As young women, who were often little more than children, they were known as '*mui tsai*' (妹仔), meaning they were unpaid servants, or slaves. But they were also called '*p'êi-pá-t'chái*' (琵琶仔), which comes from *p'i-p'a* (琵琶), a short-necked four-string lute that they were taught to play.[16] Indeed, many travellers described with admiration how skilled lob-lob girls were in the arts of music, poetry and dance.

The surgeon Charles Downing was one of many who recalled *p'êi-pá-t'chái* fondly. He travelled to China in the 1830s, and wrote about how 'handsome' they were and their 'lively disposition'.[17] But does any of this mean they were happy, or in any way liberated? It is impossible to say. The complexity of sex work during the Qing dynasty frustrates neat binaries of enslaved and empowered. Men and women selling sex did so in a cruel and unfair world, with few options available to them. Confucianist teaching severely restricted the rights of women, so prostitution could offer limited agency within a very suppressive culture. Flower and lob-lob girls, courtesans, *p'êi-pá-t'chái* and the *mui tsai* operated outside of the domestic world. Historians have long questioned how

ABOVE LEFT **Rice merchants at a banquet with 'sing-song' girls in Beijing, *c.* 1900**
'Sing-song' girls (also known as flower girls) is an English term for the courtesans of 19th-century China.

ABOVE RIGHT **A staged studio image of opium smoking and 'sing-song' girls, *c.* 1900**
This staged image was likely taken for a western audience fascinated by the 'exotic' practices of the Far East, and shows opium smoking and young 'sing-song' girls with bound feet.

Cheng I Sao was able to amass her pirate empire. Why did men follow a woman in the first place? Cheng I Sao was everything a good woman was not. But as a flower girl from the brothels, she was not expected to be servile and she knew the world of men. Her training in business, politics and, of course, how to control and manipulate men all served her well when it came to running the Red Flag Fleet.

By the 19th century, attitudes to prostitution were changing. China came under increasing pressure from European powers to bring an end to their tradition of selling and buying sex. The region of Macau, for example, was a Portuguese colony from 1557 until 1999, and in 1851 laws that regulated sex work in Portugal were exported there. These regulations required sex workers to register with the Procuratory of Chinese Affairs, and brothels were limited and brought under state control. In 1905, the Chinese government

introduced their own version of the British Contagious
Diseases Acts (1864–69) that forced women to submit
to regular vaginal examinations. The flower boats were
eventually forced out of business and fell into decay.

The Chinese Communist Party assumed control of Beijing
in February 1949. On 1 October 1949 the People's Republic
of China was declared, and less than eight weeks later,
officials in Beijing set about closing down brothels and
arresting sex workers, pimps and procurers. Other cities
swiftly followed suit. In Shanghai alone, between 1950
and 1955, there were 5,333 arrests for prostitution.[18]
The communists loathed prostitution as they believed

Chinese food seller in front of brothel, Scott road, Shanghai.

Chinese Sing Song Girls.

it to be the result of capitalism and poverty. In a world
with no poverty, they reasoned, there would be no need for
anyone to sell sex. As a result, sex work and sex workers were
viewed as failures of the state. Thousands were rounded up
and retrained to be 'new persons' for the 'new society' in
specifically designated re-education centres. By the mid-
1950s, the Chinese government was boasting that it had
eradicated prostitution. This was not true, of course. The
arrests and forcible retraining alone tell another story.
The communists were successful in forcing sex work
underground, which only resulted in fewer rights for those
selling sex. Sex work is still illegal in mainland China and
yet it continues to thrive in criminalized conditions. The
flower boats are long gone, and mercifully so is the Red
Flag Fleet, but their cultural descendants are still in
need of the rights and respect that the flower girls on the
lob-lob boats so desperately needed two centuries ago.

ABOVE LEFT **A Chinese food seller
in front of a brothel, c. 1910s**
This photograph was captured on
Scott Road, Shanghai. The road was
at the centre of the city's infamous
red-light district, an area known
as the 'trenches'.

ABOVE RIGHT **A Chinese stamp,
c. 1900**
This stamp shows 'sing-song' girls
playing musical instruments. Like
many other courtesans throughout
history, the 'sing-song' girls were often
skilled in the arts of music and dance.

8

Prostitution in the
19th CENTURY

THE
GREAT
Social Evil

YOU MUST KNOW THERE ARE MANY GOOD MEN
AND WOMEN IN OUR COUNTRY WHO HAVE DEVOTED
THEIR LIVES TO THE WORK OF RECLAIMING
PROSTITUTES, AND OF OFFERING PROTECTION
AND AID TO WOMEN AND YOUNG GIRLS, WHO THROUGH
POVERTY, IGNORANCE OR EVIL COMPANIONSHIP
ARE IN DANGER OF FALLING INTO SIN.

Josephine Butler, *Letter to my Countrywomen,* 1871

BEWARE OF
PURITY WORKERS
[WHO ARE]...
READY TO
ACCEPT AND
ENDORSE
ANY AMOUNT
OF COERCIVE
AND DEGRADING
TREATMENT OF
THEIR FELLOW
CREATURES IN
THE FATUOUS
BELIEF THAT
YOU CAN OBLIGE
HUMAN BEINGS
TO BE MORAL
BY FORCE.

Josephine Butler, *Truth Before
Everything*, 1897

OPPOSITE **George Cruikshank,**
*The poor girl, homeless, friendless,
deserted, destitute and gin-mad,
commits self-murder,* 1848
The fallen woman, literally falling
to her death as she chooses suicide
rather than the life she leads, became
a popular image in Victorian art.

Shortly after noon on Tuesday 15 March 1881, 17-year-old
Elizabeth Burley flung herself from Dover's Granville Dock
into the freezing sea below. Carley and Griffiths, the two
police officers who had chased the terrified teenager through
the cobbled streets until they cornered her at the marina,
watched Elizabeth struggle in the surf as the wet fabric of
her dress and petticoats tangled around her kicking legs and
pulled her beneath the waves. Then they turned and walked
away. It was left to a railway porter and a local mariner, John
Barber, to drag Elizabeth from the sea and her almost certain
death. Barber was so enraged at the lack of care shown to the
young girl by her pursuers that he later told the press, 'If I had
had a pistol, I feel sure I would have shot him.'[1] A shivering
and traumatized Elizabeth was taken to the nearby Sailors'
Home to recover. The following day, the Borough Police
charged her with attempted suicide.[2]

Elizabeth's callous treatment by the authorities was cause
enough for scandal, but what made her story national news
was that she had fled the police because they believed her to be
a 'fallen woman' and, under a series of controversial acts that
came to be known as the Contagious Diseases Acts (1864–69),
such a woman could be detained and forcibly subjected to a
vaginal examination to check for signs of venereal disease.
If she were found to be infected, she would then be sequestered
at a lock hospital for up to three months. If she refused to
be examined, she could be jailed for up to one year, with the
possibility of hard labour.[3] It is little wonder that Elizabeth
fled the police.

During the reign of Queen Victoria, from 1837 to 1901, the
population of England and Wales more than doubled, rising
from 15,914,148 to 32,527,843 people.[4] In 1801, the only
British city that had a population of over 100,000 was London;
by the end of the century there were thirty more. London
itself grew at an exponential rate throughout the 19th
century. The 1801 census recorded one million people living
in London, by 1850 that had doubled and by 1911 London
was home to over seven million men, women and children.[5]
Where there is poverty there is prostitution, and the people
who flooded into the city from the countryside found poverty
waiting for them on a scale that London had never seen before.

The subject of prostitution was a source of great anxiety to the
Victorians. It is impossible to know exactly how many people
were selling sexual services in 19th-century Britain – we

ABOVE *The Ups and Downs of a Prostitute*, 1871
This pair of images was designed to illustrate the precarity of the lives of sex workers.

ABOVE *The Ups and Downs of a Prostitute*, 1871
Victorian moralizers were at pains
to warn women that sex work would
leave them outcast and impoverished.

still do not know precisely how many sex workers there are in the UK today. But a lack of empirical data did not deter many concerned Victorians from guessing, and the figures they came up with are testament to an obsession with what was termed the 'great social evil'.

In 2016, a Home Office Affairs Committee report on prostitution estimated that there were around 72,800 sex workers in the UK.[6] In 1851, Dr William Acton claimed there were 210,000 in London alone. Acton arrived at this astonishing figure by taking the number of illegitimate births recorded that year, 42,000, and then assuming each

of these mothers would inevitably work as a prostitute for around five years each: giving him the number 210,000.[7] Other Victorian moralists, including the Bishop of Exeter, put the number at 80,000.[8] There is no credible evidence to support this figure. Indeed, if it were true it would mean that one in every fifteen women in London was selling sex – regardless of their age or marital status.[9] But these gross over-estimations were accepted by many as fact. The 'great social evil' was truly thought to be a crisis of national proportions. But just what was to be done about it?

Historians have long noted that debates around sex work intensified in the middle of the 19th century, and that there was a notable softening of public attitudes towards women selling sex. Rather than viewing the sex worker as a lustful sinner, the media repackaged her as the pitiful victim of an uncaring world – she became the 'fallen', 'unfortunate woman'. Doctors, the police, social reformers and the

ABOVE **Prostitutes 'in and out of luck', 19th century**
The illustrations above, paired with those opposite, were designed to demonstrate the destructive power of a life of prostitution. On this page the women appear in luck, well dressed and in fashionable neighbourhoods, but on the opposite page they are shown fallen out of luck, in shabby clothes and poor surroundings.

Church all claimed ownership of the 'problem' and tried to remedy it. The debate was thrashed out in parliament as lawmakers sought to save these women from themselves. Hundreds of charitable organizations sprang up to rescue and reform 'fallen women', including the Cardiff Female Refuge Society, the London Society for the Rescue of Fallen Women, the Portsmouth Social Purity Organization, the Glasgow Midnight Rescue Brigade, the Staffordshire County Refuge for Discharged Prisoners and Fallen Women and the Liverpool House of the Ford. The cause was supported by many high-profile public figures, including Charles Dickens, William Gladstone and Christina Rossetti.

ABOVE **Prostitutes 'in and out of luck', 19th century**
The follow-up illustrations to those shown opposite demonstrate the eventual destitution of those who choose a life of prostitution. On the left of this page, a woman is seen buying a ticket to the music hall, whereas her previous self gave money to the poor. The next finds herself at a broker, and the last languishes in a seedy bar.

Of course, these efforts only work if there is a victim to save, and the reformers were very particular about the kind of woman they wanted to rescue. Many of these organizations only accepted women who were within a certain age range, childless, free from disease and generally appearing contrite and subdued. The Marylebone Female Protection Society, for example, would not accept 'openly depraved prostitutes', and only deemed first-time offenders as worthy of help. These groups also put pressure on parliament to come up with a remedy for the 'great social evil'. Although the government expressed concern, they favoured regulation over rescue, and viewed sex work not as an issue of public morality but of public health – not the health of the women selling sex, of course, but the health of the men who were paying for sex.

Between 1864 and 1869, the British government passed a series of laws that came to be known as the Contagious Diseases Acts. Initially, the Acts were brought in to try

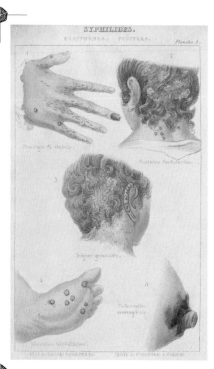

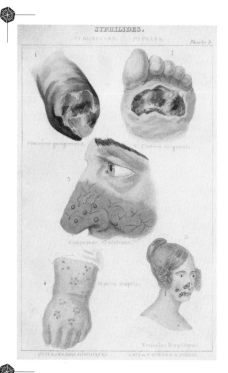

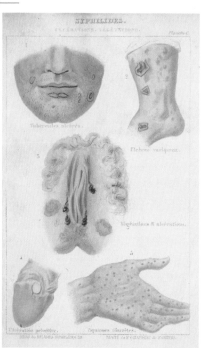

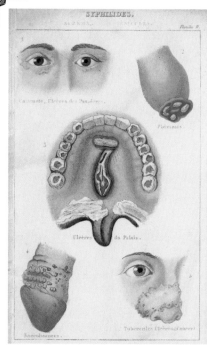

and control the epidemic-scale levels of venereal disease that were crippling the armed forces, but it was hoped that they would eventually be rolled out across the country to safeguard the health of the nation.

The War Office and the Admiralty discouraged serving men from marrying but did not expect them to embark on a life of celibacy either. By 1864, one in every three cases of sick leave in the army was due to a sexually transmitted infection; in the navy it was one in every eleven.[10] Infection rates in the port towns of Plymouth and Portsmouth were of particular concern. The Admiralty's chief inspector of hospitals, Dr William Sloggett, noted that, 'Whenever the crew of a seagoing ship is permitted to land on liberty at either of these ports, the indulgence is sure to be followed by a sudden rise in the sick list.'[11] The amount of manpower the War Office was losing each year meant that venereal disease was no longer a personal matter, but one of national security.

Initially, the military tried to control rates of venereal disease by mandating regular examinations of their men, but this proved to be very demoralizing and deeply unpopular. The authorities therefore looked at the regulatory systems adopted across the Channel in France for a new way of controlling the spread of venereal disease.

Detaining women suspected of prostitution to forcibly treat them for venereal disease had been legal in France since 1778, but in 1802 Paris initiated a new system of *hygiène publique* (public hygiene) that aimed to control the spread of venereal disease by directly targeting the women selling sex.[12] Laws were drawn up that dictated where brothels could operate and what hours they could keep. An approved madam would be put in charge of each establishment and was required to keep a clean shop, pay taxes, keep records on all women working there and admit an inspector whenever he should make an appearance. The *brigade des mœurs* (morality police) were formed to ensure the new rules were followed and that punishments were enforced. They also collated the data kept by the brothel owners and kept meticulous records of their own, updating their register daily.

Then, of course, there were the mandatory health checks that were at the forefront of what came to be known as the 'French system' of regulating prostitution. In Paris, these checks were carried out in a clinic on the rue Croix-des-Petits-Champs

OPPOSITE **Jean Giraudeau,**
The Syphilitic Diseases with Comparative Examination of their Various Healing Methods, 1841
Without antibiotics, the effects of advanced syphilis were devastating. Painful ulcers appeared on the face, and as the sores got deeper, the flesh simply rotted away. The ulcers also ate away at the bone, often causing the bridge of the nose to cave into the face, a condition known as 'saddle nose'. Towards the end, victims suffered blindness, paralysis, dementia and seizures as the nervous system was attacked.

or within the city's licensed brothels where they were performed by the *dispensaire de salubrité* (health dispensary). Any woman found with symptoms of a sexually transmitted infection was detained and treated. This approach did very little to help the women selling sex as no one was screening their clients, but within a few years, the same system had been adopted across France – and the British government had been watching closely.

Hoping to implement their own 'French system', in July 1864 the British parliament quietly passed the first Contagious Diseases Act but restricted it to a handful of port and army towns in England and Ireland.[13] The police were granted

  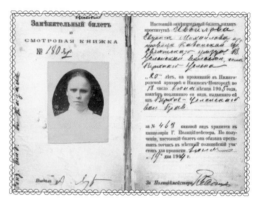

powers to detain any woman suspected of prostitution, who could then either submit to a medical examination by an army or naval surgeon followed by hospitalization (if required), or she would be imprisoned for up to three months. If she were found to be free from signs of infection, the woman was issued with a certificate of good health and sent on her way.

The Act was passed with very little parliamentary debate and even less preparation for its implementation. The result was a frantic scramble by the local authorities to appoint enough medics, magistrates, police officers, hospital staff and jailers to make the new system work. The Act also lacked a sound legal framework and raised more issues than it solved. It was unclear if prostitution had been legalized or was still a criminal offence. Were the certificates of health issued to the women after an examination a licence to continue selling sex, or just a health check? In short, it was a mess. But within five years, the Act had been reformed twice to include six new

ABOVE LEFT **J. P. Maygrier,** *New Childbirth Demonstrations,* **c. 1822–25**
This illustration shows a gynaecological examination, performed in a manner designed to protect the lady's modesty.

ABOVE CENTRE **Félicien Rops,** *Speculum,* **19th century**
This provocative sketch shows a surgeon or gynaecologist examining a woman with a vaginal speculum. The French system for regulating sex work included mandatory health checks for workers.

ABOVE RIGHT **A Russian sex worker's 'yellow ticket' and observation booklet, 1904**
This ticket listed a woman's name, age and address, and left room for a physician's stamp or mark regarding her state of health, and right to work.

towns and had extended the maximum amount of time
a suspected woman could be detained from three months
to one year, which brings us back to the teenage Elizabeth
Burley, who decided to take her chances with the English
Channel, rather than its police officers.

It transpired that Elizabeth had not been selling sex to the
soldiers stationed in Dover, but had been 'stepping out' with
one, unidentified, corporal in the army.[14] Elizabeth was an
orphan who had spent most of her short life in and out of
the workhouse. She had been working as a servant but lost the
position some three weeks before she was chased into the sea.
Without a permanent address, Elizabeth had been living in

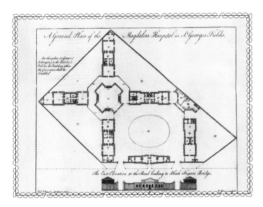

ABOVE LEFT **A ground plan of the
Magdalen Hospital in St George's
Fields, 1769**
Magdalen hospitals were established
to house and reform 'fallen women'.
However many effectively operated
as penitentiary workhouses.

ABOVE CENTRE **An advertisement
for the London Lock Hospital
and Asylum, 19th century**
Founded in 1747, the London Lock
Hospital was the first voluntary
hospital for the treatment of venereal
diseases. In 1787 it expanded to
include a rescue home for the
reformation of women who had
been treated there.

ABOVE RIGHT **J. Shury,** *The Lock
Hospital, Hyde Park Corner,
Westminster,* **19th century**
An illustration of the London Lock
Hospital in its original location
near Hyde Park Corner.

various lodging houses around Dover. Homeless, poor
and without any kind of familial support, Elizabeth soon
caught the attention of the police officers charged with
rounding up 'fallen women' under the Contagious Diseases
Act. By the time Elizabeth was brought before a magistrate
in March 1881, charged with attempted suicide and under
suspicion of being a prostitute, the Contagious Diseases
Acts were being widely challenged. For the activists who
campaigned tirelessly for their repeal, Elizabeth was about
to become the cause célèbre.

Despite parliament's efforts to quietly introduce the 1864
Act, the legislation had not gone unnoticed. Opposition
grew steadily at both the local and national level. By 1869,
two organizations had been founded with the single aim of
abolishing the Acts: The National Association for Repeal
of the Contagious Diseases Acts and the Ladies' National
Association for Repeal of the Acts. For most people, opposing

the Acts was not about protecting the rights of women selling sex so much as it was about condemning what was regarded as sexually immoral behaviour. The Acts had created a system of state-regulated prostitution and many felt this was simply encouraging vice. Others objected on the grounds that 'innocent women' could be falsely accused of prostitution and subjected to examination. In 1872, the Working Men's National League sent a delegate to speak to the Home Secretary about repealing the Acts on the grounds that working-class women were being forced to 'place their reputations and their persons at the mercy of an irresponsible secret police' which was 'a violation of the principles of our laws which

It appears from the Handbills issued by MR. CHILDERS this morning, that

HE IS AFRAID TO MEET US,

And answer our questions on the Contagious Diseases Acts.

THEREFORE

MRS. **BUTLER**

REQUESTS THE

WOMEN OF PONTEFRACT

TO MEET HER AT THE

LARGE ROOM, IN SOUTHGATE,

(USED BY MR. JOHNSON AS A SPINNING ROOM),

THIS EVENING AT SEVEN O'CLOCK.

MRS. BUTLER will shew that the Bill of which MR. CHILDERS says he is now a supporter, while pretending to Repeal the "Contagious Diseases Acts" is an extension of their principle to the whole country. MRS. BUTLER will shew that MR. CHILDERS belongs to a Government which has extended these Acts not only to this Country but to the Colonies and Dependencies of the British Empire.

JOSEPHINE E. BUTLER, Hon. Sec. of the Ladies' National Association.

PREVIOUS **Christian Krohg,** *Albertine in the Police Doctor's Waiting Room,* 1887
This painting shows a scene from Krohg's novel *Albertine* (1886), in which Albertine has to undergo the compulsory gynaecological exam that all Norwegian sex workers were subjected to.

ABOVE LEFT **The English social reformer Josephine Butler, 1876**
Butler campaigned against the Contagious Diseases Acts in the UK that forced sex workers to submit to a gynaecological examination or face arrest.

ABOVE RIGHT **Notice of a public meeting issued by Josephine Butler during the Pontefract by-election, 1872**
Butler campaigned against the re-election of Liberal MP Hugh Childers as part of her fight against the Contagious Diseases Acts.

require the accuser to prove his charge before the accused is called upon to prove her innocence'.[15]

One campaigner who did not marginalize the plight of sex workers was Josephine Butler. The daughter of anti-slavery campaigners John Grey and Hannah Annett, Butler had been schooled in Christian philanthropy and social activism since infancy. Following the tragic death of their 5-year-old daughter Eva in 1864, Josephine and her husband George Butler moved to Liverpool, where she started caring for women and girls imprisoned in workhouses and jails. She later wrote that she 'became possessed with an irresistible desire to go forth and find some pain keener than my own, to meet with people more unhappy than myself'.[16] Butler soon turned her home into a 'house of help' for poor women and 'unfortunates', and began campaigning for these women to have access to an education. When the government first brought in the Contagious Diseases Act, Butler was already staunchly opposed to the 'French system' of legalized prostitution and ideally placed to fight for the rights of Britain's sex workers.

She co-founded the Ladies' National Association for the Repeal of the Contagious Diseases Acts with Elizabeth Wolstenholme in 1869, and began a tireless campaign for the repeal of what she called the 'surgical rape' of vulnerable women. She wrote pamphlets and books, lobbied parliament, gathered petitions and hosted rallies and lectures across the country. She was often shouted down, attacked and subjected to malicious smear campaigns. But Butler did not shy away from pointing

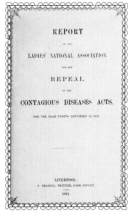
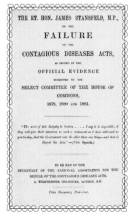

ABOVE LEFT **Charles Washington Shirley Deakin,** *The Contagious Diseases Acts,* 1871
Physician Charles Washington Shirley Deakin was in support of the Acts.

ABOVE LEFT CENTRE **Charles Washington Shirley Deakin,** Tables concerning prostitutes, 'houses of bad character' and syphilis, 1871
The tables are taken from Shirley Deakin's publication.

ABOVE RIGHT CENTRE *Report for the Ladies' National Association for the Repeal of the Contagious Diseases Acts,* 1871
Elizabeth Wolstenholme and Josephine Butler established the association in 1869.

ABOVE RIGHT **James Stansfeld,** *On the Failure of the Contagious Diseases Acts,* 1881
Stansfeld was a key supporter of Josephine Butler's work.

out the hypocrisy of targeting women who sold sex and not the men who paid for it, and she openly demanded sex workers have the same legal rights as everyone else. Butler's work was underpinned by her faith, and although she adopted the potentially problematic role of saviour, she did more than anyone else to highlight the injustices faced by Britain's 'unfortunates'. Perhaps nowhere is this more succinctly done than in her essay *The Constitution Violated* (1871), in which she quotes a young woman sentenced to a month's imprisonment for refusing to be examined: 'I did find it rather hard that the gentleman on the bench who gave the casting vote for my imprisonment had paid me five shillings the day before to go with him!'[17]

Alfred S. Dyer was a Quaker who published books on social reform, including those of Josephine Butler. He joined Butler in campaigning against the Contagious Diseases Acts and to have the age of consent raised from 12 to 18. When Butler

FAMOUS VICTORIAN COURTESANS, *c.* 1860–70

Clockwise from top left: Annie Bridgeman, Catherine 'Skittles' Walters, Nelly Hague
and Carry Blackwood. These women were referred to as 'pretty little horsebreakers'
as many courtesans rode horses near fashionable Hyde Park in London.

FAMOUS VICTORIAN COURTESANS, *c.* 1870

Clockwise from top left: Fanny Peel, Clara Rousby, Lizzy Dickson and Baby Thornhill.
Courtesans with wealthy patrons could expect to live a very different kind of life
from the impoverished women who worked on the streets or in brothels.

and Dyer heard of the plight of poor Elizabeth Burley, forced to defend herself against the might of the Dover constabulary, they were determined to help. Dyer and his wife, Helen, took Elizabeth into their home in Middlesex to recover. They also made sure the case made the national newspapers, which led to widespread public outcry. Several meetings were held in Dover and a petition was sent to the government, calling for the repeal of the Acts. The case of the 'Burley girl' caused such outrage that the Home Secretary, Sir William Harcourt, was forced to address the scandal in the House of Commons. Harcourt acknowledged that the police had shown a 'want of discretion' and had been reprimanded, but he was determined that Elizabeth Burley had led an 'immoral life'.[18] But Elizabeth was adamant she had done no such thing and, now backed by Dyer and Butler, she was able to publish an open letter to the Home Secretary in the *London Evening Standard*. She wrote, 'I suppose Sir Harcourt is a great man and I am only a poor girl; but my character is worth as much to me as the character of a lady.'[19] Her letter was swiftly followed by another from Alfred S. Dyer who wrote that he had conducted a thorough investigation of Elizabeth's character and found her to be 'perfectly virtuous'.[20] A poor, 'friendless' girl, unfairly accused of immorality and then hounded to the point of suicide was campaign gold for those against the Contagious Diseases Acts, and when the Home Secretary chose to attack her, rather than apologize, the PR war was won.

Elizabeth never did get her apology, but the scandal that was unleashed when she was chased off the docks at Dover did more to end the injustice of the Contagious Diseases Acts than years of campaigning ever did. Her case turned public opinion and directly led to the suspension of the Acts in 1883, and their eventual abolition in 1886.

The Acts were abolished but that did not mean sex workers ceased to be targeted by the police, far from it. However their abolishment did lead to the Criminal Law Amendment Act of 1885, which raised the age of consent from 13 to 16 and made it illegal to procure girls for the purposes of prostitution. Public attitudes had changed, and by the end of the century there was a willingness to view sex workers as victims of sin rather than the portents of it. The victim narrative went a long way in challenging stigma, but it created a binary between the penitent and unrepentant prostitute, neither of which captured the complexity of sex work. The shadow cast by Victorian attitudes to sex work has been long indeed.

OPPOSITE **Gustave Doré,** *Low-life Girls Dancing for Trade, Drury Lane, City of Westminster, London,* c. 1852–83
In 1885, the editor W. T. Stead published a series of controversial articles in the *Pall Mall Gazette* entitled 'The Maiden Tribute of Modern Babylon', in which he exposed the sexual exploitation of children in London. The articles caused national scandal and resulted in the age of consent in Britain being raised from 13 to 16.

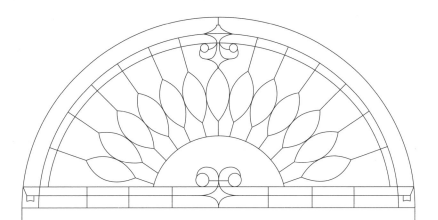

9

Sex for Sale in the
LAND OF THE FREE

~~~~~~~~~~~~~~~~

Soiled
Doves &
JAILBIRDS

~~~~~~~~~~~~~~~~

SHE HAS MADE A FEATURE OF BOARDING
NONE BUT THE FAIREST GIRLS – THOSE GIFTED
WITH NATURE'S BEST CHARMS, AND WOULD,
UNDER NO CIRCUMSTANCES, HAVE ANY
BUT THAT CLASS IN HER HOUSE.

Lulu White, *New Mahogany Hall*, 1898–99

WHAT IT COMES
DOWN TO IS THIS:
THE GROCER,
THE BUTCHER,
THE BAKER... THE
POLICEMAN, THE
DOCTOR, THE
CITY FATHER AND
THE POLITICIAN
– THESE ARE
THE PEOPLE
WHO MAKE
MONEY OUT OF
PROSTITUTION,
THESE ARE THE
REAL REAPERS
OF THE WAGES
OF SIN.

Polly Adler, *A House is Not
a Home*, 1953

OPPOSITE **E. J. Bellocq, Portrait of
a woman working in the Storyville
District of New Orleans, *c.* 1912**
Bellocq was an American
photographer who is known for
his portraits of sex workers in
New Orleans during the early
20th century. What makes his
work so extraordinary is his refusal
to sensationalize or sexualize his
subjects. Instead, he captures the
humdrum of everyday life in
the brothels.

Writing in 1844, Dr Francis Lieber recalled a conversation
he once had with a Dr Ferguson regarding the beauty of
American women.

'I REMARKED HOW CURIOUS A FACT IT WAS THAT ALL
AMERICAN WOMEN LOOK SO GENTEEL AND REFINED,
EVEN THE LOWEST [BORN] – SMALL HEAD, THIN
SILKY HAIR, DELICATE EYEBROWS YET THICK SET
ONES. [THE DOCTOR ANSWERED,] "OH, THAT IS EASY
TO BE ACCOUNTED FOR. THE SUPERABUNDANCE OF
PUBLIC WOMEN, WHO ARE ALWAYS RATHER GOOD
LOOKING, WERE SENT OVER IN FORMER TIMES.'[1]

The role 'public women' played in the founding of modern
America is one that has long been downplayed in favour of the
more wholesome narrative of pilgrim settlers, the founding
fathers and the Declaration of Independence. But the America
that we know today was built on the backs of thieves and
whores. In 1718, Britain passed the Transportation Act which
allowed courts to transport criminals to America for seven
years for the theft of items valued at under one shilling. It is
impossible to know the exact number of convicts Britain sent
to the American colonies in the 18th century, but conservative
estimates suggest it was over 50,000 people.[2] As historian
Roger Ekirch noted, 'Next to African slaves, they constituted
the largest body of immigrants ever to be compelled to go
to America.'[3]

Perhaps the most famous reference to the convict women
transported to America is in Daniel Defoe's *Moll Flanders*
(1722). Moll's mother, who is described as a 'thief and a
whore', is transported to America, after giving birth to
Moll in Newgate jail.[4] Moll embarks on a similar career,
and is eventually condemned to the same fate and likewise
transported to Virginia. Moll and her husband work out
their sentence and she then returns to England to 'spend the
remainder of [her] years in sincere penitence for the wicked
lives [she had] lived'.[5] Defoe affords his eponymous heroine
a happy ending, which was something few real-life Molls
could hope for.

Transportation was a punishment for larceny, not
prostitution. But, as Defoe's work attests, the stereotype
of the woman convict as 'a thief and a whore' was well
established – and this was not without reason. The grinding
poverty of 18th-century Britain was relentlessly cruel.

For many poor women, stealing and whoring were the last dependable means of feeding themselves. But we must not make the mistake of assuming all women who stole also sold sex, and vice versa. In the Old Bailey records the largest group of women convicted of theft and sentenced to transportation, 64% in fact, were domestic servants who stole from their employers.[6] 'Prostitute' was the second largest occupational category given for women transported to America between 1718 and 1775, just over 14%.[7] This 14% was made up of career sex workers and does not account for those who occasionally sold sex to supplement their income, a hustle known as 'dollymopping', or those who simply did not disclose how they made their money to the courts. Regardless of their profession, women found guilty of theft could expect to be transported to America. Those found guilty of stealing valuable goods could expect to be hanged.

The prisoners that survived the two-month journey in the hull of a ship would then be auctioned off to private employers to serve out their sentence as indentured servants, but female convicts never shook off the stigma of sex work. Although American colonists benefited greatly from convict labour, the public perception of transported women was overwhelmingly negative. Benjamin Franklin suggested the colonists send back ships of rattlesnakes to Britain as 'the most suitable returns for the human serpents sent us by our mother country'. He continued:

> 'WHAT IS A LITTLE HOUSEBREAKING, SHOPLIFTING, OR HIGHWAY ROBBING, WHAT IS A SON NOW AND THEN CORRUPTED AND HANGED, A DAUGHTER DEBAUCHED AND POXED, A WIFE STABBED, A HUSBAND'S THROAT CUT OR A CHILD'S BRAINS BEAT OUT WITH AN AXE, COMPARED WITH THIS "IMPROVEMENT AND WELL PEOPLING OF THE COLONIES!"'[8]

Once America broke from British rule in 1775, she refused to accept any more of these 'human serpents', but that did not stop immigrants from across Europe risking it all to make a new life in the land of the free. But the reality that greeted them was often far from the promised land they had hoped for. Wave after wave of immigration in the 19th century brought opportunity for some, but poverty, precarity and prostitution for many more.

OPPOSITE TOP **Thomas Rowlandson,** *Black, Brown and Fair,* 1807 This illustration shows a scene from Wapping dock, London, in which four sex workers lean out of the window of a building named 'Wapping Bagnio Hot Baths'. The racial diversity of the women and their customers is indicative of the broad mix of nationalities found at busy international ports in this period.

OPPOSITE BOTTOM **Thomas Rowlandson,** *The Last Jig, or Adieu to Old England,* 1818 A young woman is shown dancing a jig with sailors who will shortly set sail from England. Many people emigrated to America hopeful for the opportunities that they would find there.

As European settlers pushed further west, employment opportunities for women became increasingly scarce. In the cities, poor women might find work in the factories, the mills or domestic service, but they would also find terrible pay and dangerous working conditions. A woman selling sex could make four times what she could slaving away in a textile mill.[9] The heavy industries of the western frontier towns, such as mining and construction, largely excluded women altogether. Men seeking work in the West rarely took their families with them, preferring instead to send money home. As a result, few women made these emerging towns their home. But the shortage of women and an abundance of working men allowed the sex industry to flourish.

Women working in these early frontier communities came to be known as 'soiled doves' and they are as much a part of the American pioneers' story as the prospectors and the wagon trains. They came from North and South America, Britain, France, Germany, Spain, the Netherlands and China.[10] They sold sex in tents and, as towns became established, out of cottages, saloons and boarding houses. For the most part, the authorities turned a blind eye or accepted sex work as the inevitable result of men's lusts. Besides, as one of the first governors of Louisiana remarked when he was urged by a priest to banish all disreputable women from the colony, 'If I send away all the loose females, there will be no women left here at all.'[11] Some of the most notorious unofficial red-light districts in 19th-century America included New York's Tenderloin, San Francisco's Barbary Coast, Chicago's Levee and Fort Worth's Hell's Half Acre.

By the late 19th century, the authorities could no longer ignore the issue. Some cities looked to the regulatory models being used in Europe to try and 'control' what was now being called the 'great social evil'. Virginia City, Nevada, was one of the first cities to enact laws restricting sex work to one area in 1865. St Louis followed suit and legalized sex work in 1870 when they passed the Social Evil Ordinance, requiring all sex workers to register with the authorities and submit to regular vaginal examinations by an appointed doctor. Omaha, Nebraska, and Waco, Texas, also introduced similar legislation, but by the 1870s new waves of anti-vice sentiment were gaining traction in middle-class America, and any form of toleration was severely condemned.

OPPOSITE TOP **George Cantwell, Klondike City, c. 1893–1903**
The red-light district known as Klondike City was just across the Klondike River from Dawson, Yukon, Canada. The settlement was also known as 'Louse town', 'White Chapel', in reference to London's disreputable East End, or 'Oshiwora', inspired by the Yoshiwara district in Tokyo.

OPPOSITE BOTTOM **Sex workers in the red-light district of Dawson, Canada, c. 1899–1904**
The women are standing in Dawson's red-light district, known as Paradise Alley. The original caption on the image reads 'a group of hard workers, Dawson, YT'.

In Louse Towne

A Group of Hard Workers, Dawson, Y.T.

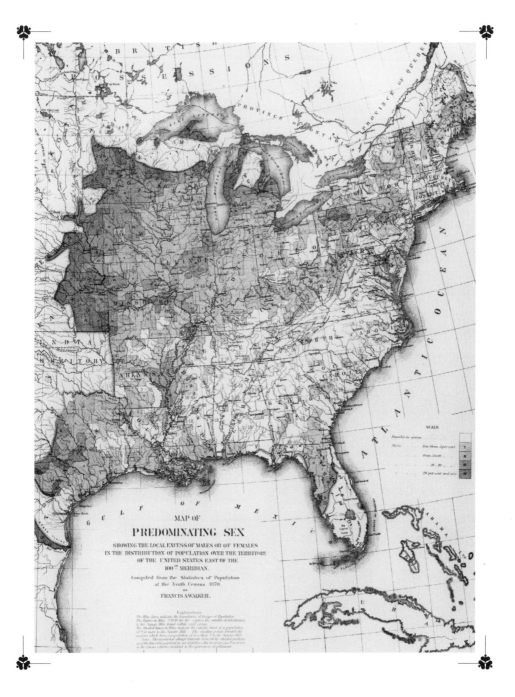

MAP OF

PREDOMINATING SEX

SHOWING THE LOCAL EXCESS OF MALES OR OF FEMALES
IN THE DISTRIBUTION OF POPULATION OVER THE TERRITORY
OF THE UNITED STATES EAST OF THE
100TH MERIDIAN.

Compiled from the Statistics of Population
at the Ninth Census 1870,
BY
FRANCIS A. WALKER.

OPPOSITE TOP **Belle Brezing at 59 Megowan Street, 19th century**
Belle was a famous madam in Lexington, Kentucky, at the end of the 19th century.

OPPOSITE BOTTOM **59 Megowan Street, c. 1895**
Belle Brezing's lover, Billy Mabon, inside her bordello. The couple stayed together until his death in 1907.

ABOVE **Francis A. Walker, *Map of Predominating Sex*, 1870**
Compiled from population statistics in the 1870 census, this map shows the concentration of men across America. In white areas women are 'in excess', and in purple areas men predominate, shown in four gradations of severity.

In 1873 Anthony Comstock founded the New York Society for the Suppression of Vice, one of many anti-vice organizations that policed public morals and specifically targeted sex work. In March 1875, under considerable pressure from Comstock, Congress passed what became known as the 'Comstock Law', which made it illegal to use the postal service to deliver 'obscene, lewd or lascivious' material, including information about birth control. The same month Congress also passed the Page Act which prohibited 'undesirable' East Asian women from emigrating to the United States. The Act was named after the Republican Representative Horace F. Page, who sought to 'end the danger of cheap Chinese labour and immoral Chinese women'.[12]

St Louis abandoned their system of regulation after four years following widespread condemnation from anti-vice groups. New York, Chicago, San Francisco and Philadelphia all tried to pass similar regulation bills, but were all defeated on the grounds that such tolerance only encouraged vice.[13] But one city successfully passed an ordinance to regulate sex work that remained in force for twenty years: New Orleans, the 'Big Easy'.

On 29 January 1897 an ordinance to restrict all sex workers in the city of New Orleans to a contained area, just north of the French Quarter, was passed into law. As the ordinance was prepared and sponsored by alderman Sidney Story the area came to be known as 'Storyville', and it operated until 1917 when the USA entered the First World War and the federal government made it illegal to sell sex anywhere within a 8-km (5-mile) radius of any military base.[14] Rather than viewing the new law of 1897 as punitive, the sex workers of New Orleans celebrated its passing by staging a parade down Canal Street and marching to their new district while dancing, singing and wearing elaborate, provocative costumes. Crowding the dance halls, saloons, bars, hotels and, of course, brothels into a few blocks cemented New Orleans's reputation as a place where a man could spend a month's pay in a single night.

OPPOSITE Udo Keppler, *The Tenement – A Menace To All*, 1901 This satirical cartoon shows the spirits of alcoholism, opium, prostitution, gambling and death lurking above a tenement house. Tenements were multi-storey apartment buildings built in the late 19th century to house the working class across America.

Sex could be purchased for less than a dollar in one of the single-room, no-frills establishments known as 'cribs'. Or in one of the upmarket, luxury brothels, the services on offer could cost up to ten dollars. One of the most famous, and the most expensive, brothels in Storyville was Mahogany Hall, belonging to the legendary Lulu White.

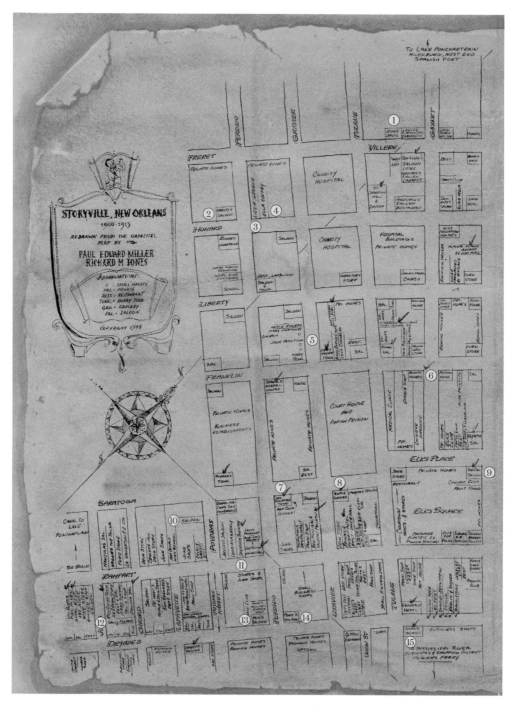

1 *Rose Davis* (below)
2 *Marley's Saloon* (right)
3 *Lizzie Greene* (above)
4 *Ella Coffey* (left)
5 *Janie Pattepson* (left)

6 *Bonnie Hoore's* (left)
7 *Joe Sogretto's Tonk* (below)
8 *Temple Theatre* (below)
9 *The Owl Saloon* (left)
10 *Mae Doland High School* (below)

11 *Iroquois Theatre* (above)
12 *Sally Pierre* (right)
13 *Tammany Club* (above)
14 *Pratt's Saloon* (left)
15 *Tulane Theatre* (above)

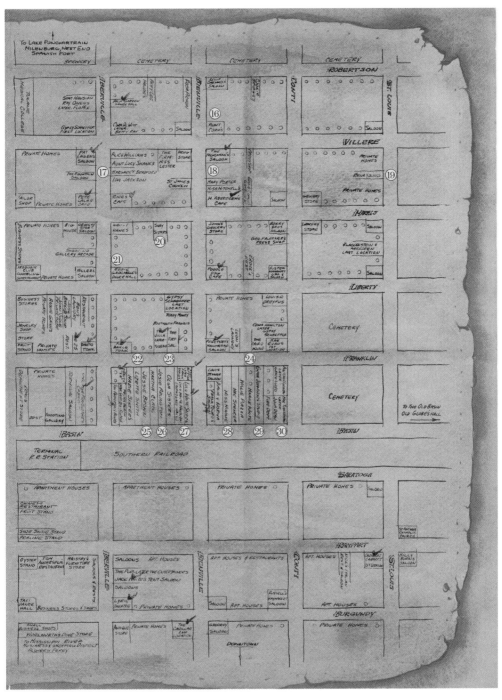

16 *Aunt Cora's* (below)
17 *Margaret Bradford* (right)
18 *Mary Porter* (below)
19 *Rena Young* (left)
20 *Shay Sisters* (above)
21 *Eddie Grochelle's Dance Hall* (below)
22 *Lizette Smith* (below)
23 *Olga Sisters* (below)
24 *Minnie White* (below)
25 *Jessie Brown* (above)
26 *Josie Arlington* (above)
27 *Lulu White's Saloon* (above)
28 *Miss Minnie* (above)
29 *Emma Johnson's Studio* (above)
30 *Mae Tuckerman* (above)

Little is known about Lulu's early life, and she was so adept at promoting an image she knew would sell that teasing out the truth from the titillation is very difficult. She was likely born in Selma, Alabama, although she claimed to be an immigrant from the West Indies and marketed herself as an 'octoroon', meaning she was one-eighth black. She settled in New Orleans in around 1880 and was soon well known to the police for 'pandering' and 'disorderly conduct'. Lulu ran a brothel at 166 Customhouse Street, but spying a lucrative business opportunity, she relocated to Storyville and invested an alleged $40,000 in building her 'Octoroon Parlour', Mahogany Hall, at 235 N. Basin Street. Lulu had booklets printed to advertise her establishment. The 1898-99 edition contained this description of Mahogany Hall:

'THE HOUSE IS BUILT OF MARBLE AND IS FOUR STOREY; CONTAINING FIVE PARLOURS, ALL HANDSOMELY FURNISHED, AND FIFTEEN BEDROOMS. EACH ROOM HAS A BATH WITH HOT WATER AND EXTENSION CLOSETS. THE ELEVATOR, WHICH WAS BUILT FOR TWO, IS OF THE LATEST STYLE. THE ENTIRE HOUSE IS STEAM HEATED AND IS THE HANDSOMEST HOUSE OF ITS KIND. IT IS THE ONLY ONE WHERE YOU CAN GET THREE SHOTS FOR YOUR MONEY – THE SHOT UPSTAIRS, THE SHOT DOWNSTAIRS AND THE SHOT IN THE BEDROOM.'[15]

Lulu presided over forty women in her employ, and cut a distinctive figure, draped in ropes of diamonds and wearing a ring on every finger. Mahogany Hall was one of the last Storyville brothels to be closed in 1917, and the building itself was finally demolished in 1949 to make way for a car park. In fact, very little remains of Storyville at all. However, thanks to the work of the photographer E. J. Bellocq we may glimpse inside that world.

Bellocq was born in New Orleans into an aristocratic white Creole family. He earned his living as a commercial photographer, but whenever he could he went to Storyville to photograph the women working there. What makes his work remarkable is that he had no interest in sexualizing his subjects. His photographs are a behind-the-scenes account of brothel life, and it is believed that many of his subjects were shot inside Mahogany Hall.[16] His documentary work

PREVIOUS **Paul Edward Miller, Richard M. Jones,** *Storyville, New Orleans,* **1900–15**
This map shows New Orleans's infamous red-light district, Storyville, with the buildings labelled to show the multitude of entertainments and attractions on offer. The district was overflowing with brothels, saloons, boarding houses, theatres, tonks and dance halls.

OPPOSITE **Lulu White,** *New Mahogany Hall,* **c. 1898–99**
Mahogany Hall was run by one of the most famous madams of Storyville, Lulu White. Lulu earned fame and fortune as the 'handsomest octoroon' in the south (an octoroon was someone who is an eighth black). Staying 'on brand', Lulu marketed Mahogany Hall as an 'octoroon palace', and the 'most elaborately furnished house in the city of New Orleans'.

NEW MAHOGANY HALL.

NEW
Miss Lulu Hall.
Desires to ...

A picture which appears on the
cover of this souvenir was erected
specially for Miss Lulu White at a
cost of $40,000. The house is built of
marble and is four story; containing
five parlors, all handsomely furnished,
and fifteen bedrooms. Each room has
a bath with hot and cold water and
extension closets.

The elevator, which was built for
two, is of the latest style. The entire
house is steam heated and is the
handsomest house of its kind. It is
the only one whose you can get those
shots for your money.

The shot upstairs,
The shot downstairs,
And the shot in the room.

INTRODUCTORY.

In presenting this souvenir to my
multitude of friends, it is my earnest
desire to, in the first place, would any
and all equalize, and, secondly, to im-
press them with the fact that the name
of my customers must certainly be attributed to their loyalty and generous
support of my customers in making
their visits to my establishment a
moment of pleasure.

While, desiring it necessary to
give the history of my boarders from
their birth, which would no doubt
prove reading of the highest grade.
I trust that what I have mentioned will
not be misconstrued, and will be read
in the same light as it was written, and
in mentioning the fact that all are born
and bred Louisiana girls, I trust that
my exertions to that direction will be
as appreciated as yours has been to me.

Yours very sincerely,
LULU WHITE.

MISS LULA WHITE.

This famous West
Indian octoroon first
saw the light of day
thirty-one years ago.
America is this coun-
try at a pretty tender
and having been
horoscope gifted
with a good education
it did not take long for
her to find out what
the other sex were in
search of.

As everyone knows, Miss
Lulu, so she is more
familiarly called. It would not be quite to say
that besides possessing an elegant form she has
beautiful black hair and blue eyes, which have
rouge gained her the title of the "Queen of
the Demi-monde."

Her establishment, which is situated in the centre part of the city, is unquestionably the most
elaborately furnished house in the city of New
Orleans, and without a doubt one of the most elegant places in this or any other country.

She has made a fortune of boarding and being
the Queen of gaye—those gifted with natures least
charmer, and would cater to circumstances have
put her that she is best loved.

As an entertainer Miss Lulu stands foremost,
having made a life-long study of music and literature. She is well read and can thus converse
anyone, and can make a visit to her place a moment
round of pleasure.

And when asking that she would be pleased to
see all her old friends and make new ones. What
more could be added?

Clara Miller.

Denise
everybody's friend, can sit up all
night if necessary, and headcap to
put a friend on to a good thing.
Why? Because it is her disposition,
and who don't want to meet such a
young lady? Not one with real
blood in his veins. She has been in
the principal cities of Europe and
the Continent, and can certainly interest you as she has a host of others. When we add that the famous
octoroon was born near Baton
Rouge we trust you will call on her.

Emma Sears.

This clever girl has been justly
termed the colored Carmencita, and
the name has certainly not been misplaced. As a tambourine dancer she
has no superior and very few equals.
Tall, graceful, winning. What
more can be said! Let me add; Gentlemen, a visit to New Orleans is
incomplete if you fail to visit Lulu
White's and ask to see Miss Sears
dance, sing or play some of her own
compositions on a Steinway Grand.

Victoria Hall.

A member of Miss White's Club,
as accomplished as she is beautiful,
a form equal to Venus, a voice not
unlike Patti. How could a more accurate description be printed, and
what more could be said.

Sadie Levy.

Miss White's Octoroon Club would
certainly be incomplete without
Sadie. Accomplished, beautiful,
and charming. We are not given
to flattery, so invite you to call and
cognize yourself that, while there
are others there is only one Sadie
Levy. Born and bred right here
in this city and a girl which any
city should feel proud of.

"Prettie Sadie Reed."

Such is the sobriquet Miss Sadie
has gained, and properly—as pretty
a form and as accomplished as could
be asked for. We cannot possibly
do the lady justice by the writing
of her accomplishments, so gently
request you to personally attend to
her by a call at the famous Octoroon
Club, presided over by Miss Lulu
White.

Middie Cook.

Miss White's house would be incomplete without Middy Cook. She
is everything that one desires—
charming, pretty, sweet. There
are lots of pebbles on the beach,
but there is only one Middy Cook.
She is a native of Alabama, and a
girl to be proud of. Call and see
her.

"Chippie" McKee.

The name often tells the tale.
Miss Chippie is a young lady whom
any man would call to see the second
time. Why? Because she can make
your visit one never to be forgotten.
You may have heard Paderewski
play the piano, but hear Miss Chippie. While we do not claim that
she is a superior player, we do say,
with emphasis, that she can interest
you equally as well—demure, petite.
"Nuff sed."

Annie Stone.

Who has not heard of this beauty
of Louisiana! Not any who has
lived in New Orleans. Miss Stone
is one of the best entertainers in
New Orleans; and if she can not
show you a royal time no one can.
Make up a club, and go in a crowd
to see Miss White and don't forget
to ask for Miss Stone. You will
have a great time.

Petite Irene Mantley.

There are others, lots of others,
but there is only one Irene Mantley,
who has accomplished that which
others have failed to do—to win
your esteem at once. Can sing you
a song, can play a violin or man-
dolin solo, and if you are in search
of a good time, desire to come in
contact with a good fellow, look no
further, but invite yourself to Miss
White's Octoroon Club and ask for
Miss Mantley.

Margaret Ellis.

This clever girl has been called
the colored Carmencita and this
term has not been misplaced. As
a dancer she has no equal in New
Orleans. Let us say that a visit to
New Orleans is incomplete without
seeing Miss Ellis dance, sing and
play some of her own compositions.

Your old friend Georgie Wilson,

a striking contrast to the many so-
called beauties. Fair, blue eyes, a
typical blonde, a royal entertainer
and a "good fellow" generally.

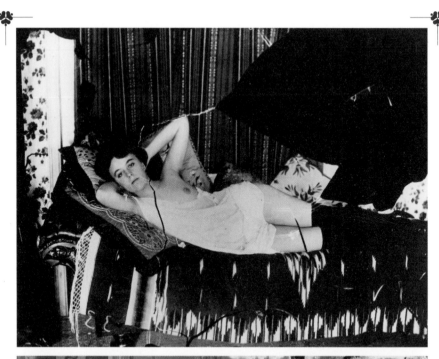

ABOVE & OPPOSITE **E. J. Bellocq,**
sex workers in Storyville, *c.* **1912**
Bellocq's work is all the more
remarkable for the frank and relaxed
demeanour of his subjects. Many of
them are wearing masks, and others
have their faces scratched out, likely
in order to protect their anonymity.

was only discovered in 1958 when American photographer Lee Friedlander acquired a battered chest containing the unpublished negatives and restored them. In several images, Bellocq has deliberately scratched out the faces of his subjects. Quite why he did this is unknown, but it is thought that it was to protect the identity of the women in the pictures.

Storyville had its own press which produced guides to the area known as the 'Blue Books'. 'Blue' referred to the content, rather than the colour, of the book. They were handed out at the railway station and in bars, hotels and barber shops.

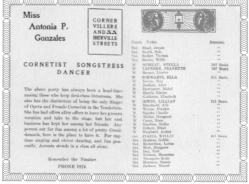

The earliest surviving copies date to 1900, though they were likely being produced earlier than this. Each book's preface introduces the reader to the area and explains why the 'Blue Books' are necessary.

ABOVE LEFT **A Mardi Gras pageant in New Orleans, performed by the Krewe of Rex, _c._ 1907**
The annual Mardi Gras celebrations were a major tourist attraction for the city, and therefore an important opportunity for the madams of Storyville. Blue Books would have been distributed among the crowds, often featuring advertisements for special Mardi Gras balls.

ABOVE RIGHT **Advertisement for the madam Antonia P. Gonzales, _Blue Book_, 1905**
As well as a sex worker, Gonzales was a musician and is known to have played with the ragtime and jazz musicians Tony Jackson and Jelly Roll Morton.

'BECAUSE IT IS THE ONLY DISTRICT OF ITS KIND IN THE STATES SET ASIDE FOR THE FAST WOMEN BY LAW. BECAUSE IT PUTS THE STRANGER ON A PROPER AND SAFE PATH AS TO WHERE HE MAY GO AND BE FREE FROM "HOLD-UPS" AND OTHER GAMES USUALLY PRACTICED UPON THE STRANGER. IT REGULATES THE WOMEN SO THAT THEY MAY LIVE IN ONE DISTRICT TO THEMSELVES INSTEAD OF BEING SCATTERED OVER THE CITY AND FILLING OUR THOROUGHFARES WITH STREET WALKERS. IT ALSO GIVES THE NAMES OF WOMEN ENTERTAINERS EMPLOYED IN THE DANCE HALLS AND CABARETS IN THE DISTRICT.'[17]

The 'Blue Books' contained details of the most prominent working girls, but more commonly advertised the madams at whose establishments they worked. One example is Miss Antonia P. Gonzales of Iberville Street.

'THE ABOVE PARTY HAS ALWAYS BEEN A HEADLINER AMONG THOSE WHO KEEP FIRST-CLASS OCTOROONS. SHE ALSO HAS THE DISTINCTION OF BEING THE ONLY SINGER OF OPERA AND FEMALE CORNETIST IN THE TENDERLOIN. SHE HAS HAD OFFERS AFTER OFFERS TO LEAVE HER PRESENT VOCATION AND TAKE TO THE STAGE, BUT HER VAST BUSINESS HAS

KEPT HER AMONG HER FRIENDS. ANY PERSON OUT FOR FUN AMONG A LOT OF PRETTY CREOLE DAMSELS, HERE IS THE PLACE TO HAVE IT. FOR RAGTIME SINGING AND CLEVER DANCING, AND FUN GENERALLY, ANTONIA STANDS IN A CLASS ALL ALONE.'[18]

ABOVE LEFT **A group of jazz musicians playing saxophones, *c.* 1900**
Storyville was filled with cabarets, dance halls, saloons and honky tonks, supplying plenty of work for musicians and providing the cultural milieu in which the emerging jazz genre was developed and brought to a wider audience.

ABOVE RIGHT **Williams-Piron Band, *c.* 1916**
Many jazz greats cut their musical teeth in the Storyville district. Standing, from left: Jimmie Noone, William 'Bebe' Ridgley, Oscar 'Papa' Celestin and John Lindsay. Seated, from left: Ernest Trepagnier, Armand J. Piron, Thomas Benton and Johnny St Cyr. Front: Clarence Williams.

Another Storyville sex worker who sang the blues was Mamie Desdoumes, immortalized in the song 'Mamie Desdoumes Blues' (1938) by Jelly Roll Morton.

CAN'T GIVE ME A DOLLAR, GIVE ME A LOUSY DIME CAN'T GIVE ME A DOLLAR, GIVE ME A LOUSY DIME JUST TO FEED THAT HUNGRY MAN OF MINE.[19]

There are no pictures of Mamie, nor is there any surviving official documentation pertaining to her life, but other Storyville musicians remembered her fondly too.

ABOVE **Cover, *Tenderloin Blue Book*, 1901**
A directory of sex workers in New Orleans's Tenderloin district, more commonly known as Storyville.

Like the Stars above,

MISS

Olive Russell,

Of CUSTOMHOUSE ST.,

has appeared before the better class of
sporting gentlemen of this community
and never has her reputation been other
than a highly cultivated lady. As an
entertainer and conversationalist she has
no equal; so when out for a good time
don't over-look her house, her ladies are
of a like character.

They are Misses Adele Richards, Ollie
Young, Camile Lewis, Minnie Mc-
Dohald and others.

MISS

Josie Arlington,
225 N. BASIN ST.

No pen can describe the beauty and
magnifiance that reign supreme within
the walls of Miss Arlington's Mansion.
The draperies, carved furniture and oil
painting or of foreign make and a visit
will teach more than man can tell.

Her women are also beautiful and are
as follows: Ollie Nicholls, Minnie White,
Marie Barrett, Bench Mathews, Thelma
Clayton, Myrtle Rhea, Frankie Sawyer,
Madeline Vales, Freda Dunlap, May
Spencer, Louise Ward, Florence Russell,
Mate Gordon, Marie Cole, Amber Shipp-
herd, Unice Derring and Madme Annie
Casey, Manager. PHONE 1888.

A MERE DREAM
is the new

Arlington Annex,
COR. N. BASIN AND CUSTOMHOUSE STS.

In having this place constructed the
owner, Tom Anderson, has spared no
money, so you can imagine its beauty.
Connausser's say it is the finest place
where sports congregate in the South.
The best service can be had here at
all times. Eatables and drinkables are
of the very best the land affords.
Private dining rooms up and down
stairs.

Tom Anderson, Proprietor.

FRENCH 69.

SALVINO JENNETTO, 321 Basin
PAULA LAROSIE,
LILLY SUMMONS, 307 Basin
MARGARITE DELBER, 1542 Customhouse
DRAGETH LANDRY, " "
JENNIE WEST, 1407 Customhouse
ISABELLA LAURENT, 1415 Customhouse
LENA FREDMAN, 1319 Customhouse
EMMA CRASSON, 1518 Bienville
ALICE CODE, " "
BLANCH DUBOIS, 1416 Bienville
BLANCH WHITE, 1204 Customhouse
1204-1206-1208-1210-1214-1216 Customhouse street
are among the bunch.

P. S.—There are also 7 or 8 roping in french re-
sorts on Customhouse between Basin and Franklin, opposite the negro dance halls.

The "Grotto" white dance hall in 320 Marais
st. Every old thing goes here—don't miss it.

OCTOROONS.

WILLIE V. PIAZZA, 319 Basin
BERTHA WASHINGTON, Basin
MARGARET LEVY,
PAULINE JONES, 325 Basin
CORA DeBLANC, "
BERTHA GOLDEN, 329 Basin
EDITH HOWARD, " "
PRESCILLA CONSCINTRIO, 329 Basin
GERTRUDE HAWKINS, " "
HILDA CLARKE, " "
ALISTINE CARDOTY, " "

ABOVE **Interior,** *Tenderloin Blue Book,*
1901
Josie Arlington's brothel was one of
the most expensive establishments,
only employing experienced women.

FUN! FUN!! FUN!!

DON'T MISS THE
French Balls
GIVEN BY THE
C. C. C. Club and
Two Well-Known Gentlemen

ODD FELLOWS' HALL
FEBRUARY 29TH AND
MARDI GRAS NIGHT

¶ The Balls have
been the Real
Thing for years,
so if you are out
for a good time
don't miss'em.
Tickets for sale
at TOM ANDER-
SON'S TWO
SALOONS, and
LAMOTHE'S
RESTAURANT,
716 Gaavier St.

"Honi Soit Qui Mal y Pense"

"Honi Soit Qui Maly Pense"

The trumpet player Bunk Johnson recalled:

> 'I KNEW MAMIE DESDOUMES REAL WELL. PLAYED
> MANY A CONCERT WITH HER SINGING THOSE
> SAME BLUES. SHE WAS PRETTY GOOD LOOKING –
> QUITE FAIR AND WITH A NICE HEAD OF HAIR. SHE
> WAS A HUSTLIN' WOMAN. A BLUES-SINGING POOR
> GAL. USED TO PLAY PRETTY PASSABLE PIANO
> AROUND THEM DANCE HALLS ON PERDIDO STREET.
> WHEN HATTIE ROGERS OR LULU WHITE WOULD
> PUT IT OUT THAT MAMIE WAS GOING TO BE
> SINGING AT THEIR PLACE, THE WHITE MEN
> WOULD TURN OUT IN BUNCHES AND THEM
> WHORES WOULD CLEAN UP.'[20]

Legend has it that many of the great blues and jazz
musicians, such as Jelly Roll Morton and pianist Tony
Jackson, got their break performing in the brothels of
Storyville, when they were not welcome in more respectable
establishments. Although this is not quite true, music lay
at the heart of Storyville and as many people flocked there
for the jazz as for the sex. Jazz great Louis Armstrong
himself wrote:

> 'I ALSO LOOKED FORWARD TO EVERY NIGHT IN
> THE RED-LIGHT DISTRICT, WHEN I WAS DELIVERING
> STONE COAL TO THE GIRLS WORKING IN THOSE
> CRIBS. I COULD HEAR THESE WONDERFUL JAZZ
> MUSICIANS PLAYING MUSIC THE WAY IT SHOULD
> BE PLAYED.'[21]

It was said that when Storyville closed, the musicians left
New Orleans and it was this that brought blues and jazz to the
rest of the world. The truth is that jazz musicians performed
in New Orleans long before and after Storyville, but the myth
alone is testament to the close association between sex and
music in the brothels of the 'Big Easy'.

When Storyville was closed down in 1917 the brothels,
bars and 'Blue Book' press all went with it and the sex
workers relocated to the French Quarter where they had to
work illegally. All that remained of America's most famous
official red-light district was an old chest full of unprinted
photographs, some empty buildings and the few 'Blue Books'
that survived, each one inscribed with the motto *honi soit
qui mal y pense* (shame on him who thinks evil of it).

OPPOSITE **Interiors of 'Blue Books',**
c. 1906–08
The top left page shows a promotion
for one of the 'French' Mardi Gras
balls that were thrown each year to
bring in the customers. The other
pages show the motto *honi soit qui
mal y pense* (shame on him who
thinks evil of it), and an advertisement
for Lamothe's Restaurant.

10

Sex and the
BELLE ÉPOQUE

~~~~~~~~~

MAISONS
DE
Tolérance

~~~~~~~~~

EVERYONE WHO VISITED THE SPHINX REMEMBERS
THE QUIET ATMOSPHERE OF A DELICATE, AMIABLE
AND EXQUISITE PARTICIPATION REIGNED IN A
DIFFUSED PINK LIGHT WITH A HUGE HALL ON
THE GROUND FLOOR WHERE CUSTOMERS WERE
MET BY GIRLS DRESSED IN LIGHT DRESSES.

Jean-Paul Crespelle, *Daily Life in Montparnasse*, 1976

ALBERT: I'VE SPENT ENOUGH ON YOU TO BUILD A BATTLESHIP! LILLIE: AND YOU'VE SPENT ENOUGH IN ME TO FLOAT ONE.

Reported conversation between Albert, Prince of Wales, and Lillie Langtry, actress, 1870s

When Albert, the Prince of Wales and future King Edward VII, was in Paris and in the mood to indulge his gargantuan sexual appetite, there was only one establishment that was truly fit for a king: Le Chabanais, a brothel so luxurious that its very name was a byword for the debauchery and decadence that defined France's Belle Époque era. The so-called 'beautiful time' between the end of the Franco-Prussian War in 1871 and the start of the First World War in 1914 was a period of peace, prosperity, artistic creativity and sex, lots and lots of sex. After the French government introduced a system of state-regulated prostitution in 1802, brothels, or *maisons de tolérance*, became a common sight in Paris, but no one had seen anything like Le Chabanais before. Situated close to the Louvre, Le Chabanais first opened its doors in 1878. Little is known about the Irish-born proprietor, 'Madame Kelly', but one thing is certain: she knew her market and spared no expense.

The reception area was furnished with gilt, inlaid panels and 18th-century paintings. Patrons could choose from individually themed grottoes, such as the Moorish Room, the Spanish Room, the Hindu Room, the Pompeian Saloon or the Japanese Room, which was so lavish it won a design prize at the 1900 World Fair. The rich and famous were drawn there like moths to the flame. Celebrated patrons included Guy de Maupassant, Henri de Toulouse-Lautrec, Cary Grant, Humphrey Bogart and Mae West. The Prince of Wales had his own suite with the royal coat of arms above the bed and furnished with an ornate copper bath, decorated with a bare-breasted woman, where the prince and his lovers would bathe in champagne.

In 1890, Edward commissioned the famous cabinet maker Louis Soubrier to build a *siège d'amour*, or 'seat of love', to be installed in his suite. The chair was designed to allow the prince to enjoy two partners at once, as well as supporting the bulk of his weight. The prince's passion for women was matched only by his passion for food and his love chair took the pressure off any woman struggling underneath the royal belly. As well as patronizing the many women of Le Chabanais and paying court to his wife, Edward found time to have none-too-discreet affairs with Sarah Bernhardt, Lady Randolph Churchill, Mary 'Patsy' Cornwallis-West, the Countess of Warwick Daisy Greville, Alice Keppel, Agnes Keyser, Lillie Langtry, Lady Susan Vane-Tempest, Carolina Otero, Hortense Schneider and many, many more. It is not hard to see how he earned the nickname 'Dirty Bertie'.

OPPOSITE **French postcard of a young woman in a brothel, early 20th century**
The French government introduced a system of regulated prostitution in 1802. By law sex workers were required to register with the state and to submit to a regular vaginal examination to check for symptoms of venereal disease. It was a brutal and deeply unjust system that did little to protect women selling sex. Nevertheless, it was a system that was adopted throughout much of the Western world.

ABOVE **Parisian brothels, 20th century**
Paris of the Belle Époque was a city for
the sexual connoisseur. Bottom right
is the copper bath used by the Prince
of Wales to bathe in champagne.

ABOVE *Siège d'amour, c.* 1900
The 'seat of love', was commissioned
by the Prince of Wales, 'Dirty Bertie',
for his suite at Le Chabanais in 1890.

Those who lacked the funds to enjoy the opulence of
Le Chabanais, or one of the other exclusive *maisons de
tolérance*, such as the Sphinx or the One-Two-Two, were
still remarkably well catered for elsewhere. Paris was a city
for the sexual connoisseur. Devotees of the lash could find
specialist torture rooms awaiting them in La Fleur Blanche
on the rue des Moulins, or the Chez Christiane at 9 rue de
Navarin. The Hotel Marigny was a gay brothel that opened
on the rue de l'Arcade in 1917 and was a favourite haunt of

the novelist Marcel Proust. French novelist and playwright
Alphonse Boudard wrote about a brothel called the Abbey in
rue Saint-Sulpice that catered specifically for clergymen.[1]
The Aux Belles Poules could be found at 32-34 rue Blondel
and specialized in putting on erotic shows and *tableaux
vivants* (living pictures). In *La Belle Lurette* (1935)
Henri Calet describes how the ladies of Aux Belles Poules
impressed customers by asking them to place their money
on the edge of the table, which they then 'sucked' up into
their 'slits'. A talented performer could win up to forty
sous in a single game.[2]

But not all the *maisons de tolérance* were so concerned
with such theatrics. Legalized, state-regulated prostitution
strictly controlled where and when women could work.
For many, this meant that if they wanted to work legally,
they would have to work in one of France's budget
brothels, commonly known as *maisons d'abattage*,
or the 'slaughterhouses'.

A special 1939 edition of *Le Crapouillot* counted twelve *maisons d'abattage* in Paris, including Le Moulin Galant on rue de Fourcy, which employed sixty women who worked around the clock, and charged a flat rate of five francs and fifty sous – the fifty sous were for the use of a towel.[3] The Lanterne Verte was located on the corner of rue de Chartres and rue de la Goutte d'Or until 1921. The writer Sylvain Bonmariage described a visit there in *Gagneuses! Chronique de l'amour vénal* [Winners! Chronicles of Venal Love] (1951).

ABOVE LEFT **Albert Brichaut, *Maison de Tolérance, 226 Boulevard de la Villette, c. 1901***
In Paris there was a *maison de tolérance* to suit every budget and sexual preference.

ABOVE CENTRE ***Maison de Tolérance, 12 rue Chabanais, 'Le Chabanais', c. 1900***
Brothels such as Le Chabanais, the Sphinx, the One-Two-Two and the La Fleur Blanche only catered to the aristocracy.

ABOVE RIGHT ***Maison de Tolérance, 8 rue Colbert, 'Le Colbert', c. 1900***
From the exterior Paris's brothels were unassuming as regulations stipulated that they had to be discreet; any signage was forbidden.

'THE LANTERNE VERTE WAS A BROTHEL; IT WAS DECLARED AS SUCH, AND IN ITS LARGE HALL, FURNISHED AS A CAFÉ, NAKED GIRLS SERVED THE OFFER OF THE HOUSE. A SCHOPPEN WHITE WINE COST A FRANC AND [ANYONE] WHO WANTED TO FUCK WITH THE GIRLS OR WANK ONE... PAID [THE WAITRESS] FORTY SOUS. EVERYTHING HAPPENED ON A BENCH OR CHAIR OF THE ESTABLISHMENT: THERE WERE NO ROOMS. CUSTOMERS ENTERING WERE USUALLY SURPRISED AT TWO OR THREE PAIRS WHO WERE JUST IN FULL SWING. THIS LANTERNE VERTE WAS A PROSPEROUS BUSINESS; EACH WAITRESS SERVED THIRTY CUSTOMERS ON AVERAGE BETWEEN TWELVE O'CLOCK AND FIVE O'CLOCK IN THE MORNING, WHICH BROUGHT HER SIXTY FRANCS.'[4]

These 'slaughterhouses' were a world away from the glitz and glamour of Le Chabanais. The women who worked in them were invariably poor and frequently subjected to abuse,

ABOVE **Albert Brichaut,**
Maisons de Tolérance, c. 1900
Women at 2 rue de Londres, the
workplace of Amelia Elie, one of
Paris's most famous sex workers.

ABOVE **Albert Brichaut,**
Maisons de Tolérance, c. 1900
Women posing in the *maisons de
tolérance* located at 2 rue de Londres
(top) and 14 rue Monthyon (bottom).

SEX WORKERS IN THE *MAISONS DE TOLÉRANCE*, c. 1900
Women from 2 rue de Londres, clockwise from above, top left: 'Mother' Lacaisse
(the madam), Mlle Louisa and Mlle Georgette. Women from Le Chabanais, above,
bottom left: Mlle Andréa, and opposite: Mlle Margot.

not only from clients but from the police who enforced
the regulations they had to abide by.

It was Napoleon who had introduced the system of state-
regulated prostitution in 1802. Initially, all sex workers
were mandated to undergo regular examinations to check
for signs of venereal disease, but within a few years new laws
had been brought in to carefully control the entire industry.
By 1804, all brothels and sex workers were under the control
of a branch of the police known as the *brigade des mœurs*
(morality police). Every woman had to be officially registered
with the Préfecture de Police and was required to submit
to bi-monthly vaginal examinations at a dispensary if
they worked independently, or by sanitary inspectors
if they worked in a brothel. Should any woman be found to
have symptoms of disease, she would be taken to the Saint-
Lazare hospital for treatment. All sex workers were to be
issued with a registration card that had to be presented
to a police officer upon request.

Laws dictated what sex workers could wear, when and
where they could work and even where they lived. Brothels
were prohibited from operating near churches, schools,
public buildings, hotels or major factories. They had to
keep their windows closed, keep the volume down and,
above all, they had to be discreet. Signs were prohibited;
instead brothels had to identify themselves by the street
number on the building, which had to be 2-foot (61-cm)
high. No minors were to be admitted, and the police were
never to be refused. In order to prevent pimping, all brothels
were run by a madam, who had to keep detailed records on
both the women in her employ and their customers.[5] And it
was not just the authorities who wanted to know who was
selling sex and where they could be found.

The Pretty Women of Paris was published anonymously
in 1883 and is a comprehensive directory of the *poules de luxe*
(high-class prostitutes) of Paris. Its lengthy descriptions of
the women selling sex set it apart from other directories that
were on offer. It is an extraordinarily important document
that shines a light on lives lived in the shadows. The text
details the courtesans at the very top of their game, as well
as those living in destitution. Women such as Camille Faure,
who lived at 32 rue de Berlin, and is described as 'a time-
defying bag of bones' who has 'been on the town ever since we
remember'. Or Mathilde Lasseny of 20 rue Bremontier, who

OPPOSITE **Alexandre Jean Baptiste
Parent-Duchatelet,** *Distribution
of Prostitutes in each of the
Forty-eight Quarters of Paris,* **1836**
Dr Parent-Duchatelet was a hygienist
dedicated to public health, who
published works on a range of
subjects, including cholera, sewers
and tobacco. His publication on sex
work was particularly influential.
This map shows the distribution of
sex workers within Paris, as measured
by the metres of each area inhabited
by prostitutes. The figures for each
quarter are given beneath.

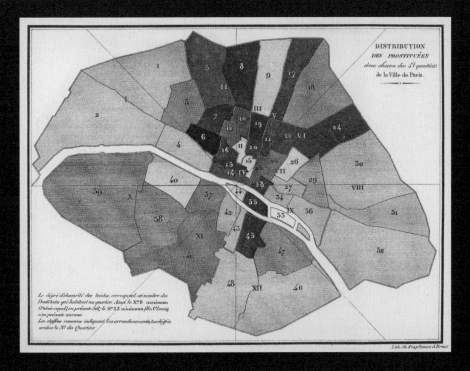

1   *Quartier du Roule*: 145,384
2   *Quartier des Champs-Elysées*: 490,000
3   *Quartier de la place Vendôme*: 16,153
4   *Quartier des Tuileries*: 96,600
5   *Quartier de la Chaussée-d'Antin*: 113,880
6   *Quartier du Palais-Royal*: 886
7   *Quartier Feydeau*: 1,843
8   *Quartier du Faubourg Montmartre*: 5,416
9   *Quartier du Faubourg Poissonnière*: 114,285
10   *Quartier Montmartre*: 1,910
11   *Quartier Saint-Eustache*: 32,500
12   *Quartier du Mail*: 2,238
13   *Saint-Honoré*: 494
14   *Quartier du Louvre*: 13,592
15   *Quartier des Marchés*: 5,333
16   *Quartier de la banque de France*: 774

17   *Quartier du Faubourg Saint-Denis*: 9,558
18   *Quartier de la Porte Saint-Martin*: 43,750
19   *Quartier Bonne-Nouvelle*: 1,136
20   *Quartier Montorgueil*: 1,630
21   *Quartier du Temple*: 11,235
22   *Quartier Saint-Martin-des-Champs*: 13,469
23   *Quartier des Lombards*: 3,181
24   *Quartier de la Porte Saint-Denis*: 2,676
25   *Quartier Saint-Avoie*: 3,921
26   *Quartier du Mont-de-Piété*: 125,000
27   *Quartier du marché Saint-Jean*: 10,000
28   *Quartier des Arcis*: 457
29   *Quartier du Marais*: 16,600
30   *Quartier Popincourt*: 315,000
31   *Quartier du Faubourg Saint-Antoine*: 54,736
32   *Quartier des Quinze-Vingts*: 306,666
33   *Quartier Ile-Saint-Louis*: 0

34   *Quartier de l'Hôtel-de-Ville*: 4,166
35   *Quartier de la Cité*: 731
36   *Quartier de l'Arsenal*: 20,625
37   *Quartier de la Monnaie*: 7,755
38   *Quartier de Saint-Thomas-d'Aquin*: 42,000
39   *Quartier des Invalides*: 82,777
40   *Quartier du Faubourg Saint-Germain*: 30,909
41   *Quartier du Luxembourg*: 31,458
42   *Quartier de l'Ecole-de-Médec*: 11,200
43   *Quartier de la Sorbonne*: 11,666
44   *Quartier du Palais-de-Justice*: 90,000
45   *Quartier Saint-Jacques*: 26,35
46   *Quartier Saint-Marcel*: 110,555
47   *Quartier du Jardin-des-Plantes*: 21,081
48   *Quartier de l'Observatoire*: 60,588

RÉPUBLIQUE FRANÇAISE

N. 11.

LIBERTÉ — ÉGALITÉ — FRATERNITÉ
SOLIDARITÉ

DÉLÉGATION COMMUNALE
Du 2me Arrondissement

Considérant que la Société est responsable et solidaire des désordres engendrés par la prostitution ;

Qu'en effet, le manque d'instruction et de travail, cause générale de la perte de tant de femmes, est sans nul doute imputable à un mécanisme social essentiellement vicieux ;

Que, par suite, la Société nouvelle, issue de la Révolution communale, doit poursuivre la guérison de toutes les plaies du passé monarchique ;

Que l'organisation intelligente du travail des femmes est le seul remède à la prostitution ;

Que cette organisation est en voie de formation ;

Que néanmoins, et quel que soit le sentiment de légitime pitié que peut inspirer la situation des victimes inconscientes de la prostitution, il importe de préserver pour le présent la pureté de la jeune génération et lui épargner le spectacle du vice s'étalant sur la voie publique ;

La Délégation communale du 2e Arrondissement arrête :

ARTICLE 1er. La circulation sur la voie publique des femmes livrées à la prostitution est absolument interdite dans toute l'étendue du 2e Arrondissement.

ART. 2. Toute femme contrevenant à cette disposition sera mise immédiatement en état d'arrestation.

ART. 3. La Garde Nationale est chargée de l'exécution stricte du présent Arrêté.

LA DÉLÉGATION COMMUNALE DU 2ME ARRONDISSEMENT :
EUGÈNE POTTIER, A. SERRAILLIER,
JACQUES DURAND, J. JOHANNARD.

Paris. — Imprimerie LEFEBVRE, passage du Caire, 87-89.

ABOVE **Announcement forbidding prostitution on public highways,** *c.* 1871
Prostitution in Paris was confined to carefully controlled areas.

ABOVE Poster announcing a public
meeting regarding the regulation
of prostitution, 1927
The creators oppose regulation, calling
it the 'official enslavement of women'.

was once a celebrated concert hall star, but was now 'a gutter wench of Belleville'. The work is also testament to the sheer diversity of women selling sex in the city. There are descriptions of women from Italy, Holland, Algeria, Spain, England, Scotland and Germany, as well as numerous Jewish women – such as Blanche Méry, residing at 44 rue Lafayette, who is described as a 'dark, podgy, Jewish maiden'. There were also several black sex workers trading in Paris, such as 'Gallayx', a 'little, black tickler', and 'Luciani' who was 'as black as a mulberry and twice as rich and juicy'. The majority of women listed are in their twenties, but there are plenty of women in their forties, fifties and even a few in their sixties. There are so many older women that the author gleefully informs the reader that 'the aged whores of Paris form what is called "the old guard", because they never die and always surrender.'[6]

The French system of regulation was clearly successful in gathering data, but it was a failure, nonetheless. The restrictions were so severe, and the compulsory gynaecological examinations so unpopular, that many women simply did not register. Unregistered sex workers, or *insoumises*, sold sex on the street, in bars, in hotels or in unregistered brothels, known as a *maisons de rendez-vous*. The police regularly raided addresses they suspected of operating illegally and had powers to arrest women suspected of being an *insoumise*. If caught, women would be automatically registered and forcibly examined for signs of disease. Once registered, it was very difficult to become unregistered.

Another loophole in the system was the emergence of so-called *brasseries à femmes* in the 19th century. France's regulatory system was comprehensive, but it fell at the same hurdle that has tripped every effort to police prostitution in history: it is very difficult to define what counts as prostitution. Legislating for the women working in the 'slaughterhouses' was relatively straightforward because the transaction was straightforward, but what about kept women, professional mistresses or the countless women who were happy to occasionally top up their income by indulging the lusts of wealthy men?

OPPOSITE **Women inside a French brothel, *c.* 1900**
The women have been captured in a relaxed setting, seated around a table drinking with a pet cat (top), and doing their hair and makeup (bottom).

The *brasseries à femmes* were bars and cafés that were staffed with attractive serving girls whose job it was to flirt with the customers and make them spend more money. The women were usually paid a pittance by the club, if they were

ABOVE **Erotic postcards of French
sex workers, *c.* 1910**
The prevalence of postcards like these
meant that erotic photographs were
dubbed 'postcards from Paris'.

ABOVE **French sex worker,**
c. 1890–1900
Japanese rooms with printed screens
and drapes like these were very
popular in Parisian brothels.

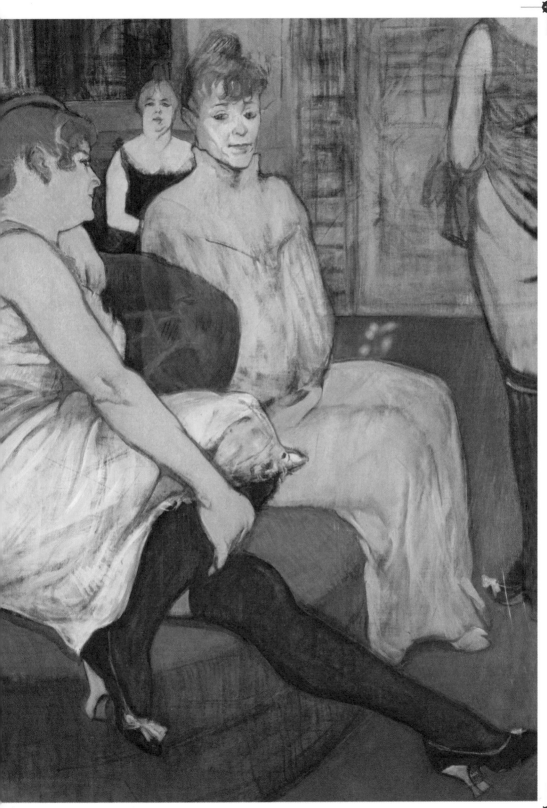

paid anything at all, and so relied on the tips and gifts of their customers. Some clubs charged women to work there, much like lap dancing clubs today. The clubs made their money through the sales the serving girls helped to generate. The serving girls did not have to have sex with their customers, but their incomes were dependent on maintaining the possibility that they might. One police report on the bar La Cigarette in December 1879 recorded that the serving girls made their money by 'sitting with the clientele, being informal with them, encouraging them to buy and having dirty and gross conversations with them.'[7] Technically, what transpired between the serving girls and their customers was nothing to do with the police. Needless to say, this greatly frustrated them, as they categorized these establishments as sites of prostitution but could do nothing to regulate them.

Then of course, there was the Moulin Rouge. The most famous dance and cabaret hall of all time first opened its doors on 6 October 1889. It was the brainchild of Joseph Oller and Charles Zidler, two formidable businessmen who knew how to throw a party. The Moulin Rouge was situated in the Jardin de Paris in the district of Montmartre. The location was an inspired choice as Montmartre was already home to many artists and writers. Oller and Zidler intended to create a truly extravagant venue that allowed the very rich to rub shoulders with the bohemian underclass.

The exterior of the venue was famously shaped like a red windmill. Inside, there was a dance floor, surrounded by tables, mirrors and elegant artwork. It was the first Parisian venue to be lit by electricity. Outside, there was an ornate garden with more seating, and a sculpture of a giant elephant. The champagne flowed freely and the money poured in. People flocked from all over the world to see the extravagant décor, but the star attraction was always the dancers who can-canned their way to international stardom.

Like the women working in *brasseries à femmes,* cabaret dancers could not be easily classified as prostitutes by the authorities, but it was no secret that many dancers offered extras to paying clients. Others became the mistress of very wealthy customers and for those working in the Moulin Rouge, there was no shortage of patrons. The more famous the dancer, the higher she could set her sights, and right at the top of the pile was Dirty Bertie.

PREVIOUS **Henri de Toulouse-Lautrec,** *Au Salon de la rue des Moulins* [At the Salon on rue des Moulins], 1894 Toulouse-Lautrec's painting captures a group of sex workers during one of the moments of boredom between clients. The woman lifting her dress on the right indicates that the women are attending their mandated medical examination.

SEX WORKERS IN PARISIAN HIGH SOCIETY, c. 1890
In this lively series of illustrations scantily clad women are shown
drinking and partying with upper-class gentlemen, sometimes
to the disapproval of those around them.

**Jules Chéret, poster for the
Moulin Rouge, 1890**
Chéret's brightly coloured poster advertises
an ochestra of fifty musicians, celebrity
choreographers and the Can–Can.

ABOVE **The Moulin Rouge, 1926**
The Moulin Rouge cabaret is famed as
the birthplace of the modern Can-Can
dance, created as a seductive dance
by the women who worked there.

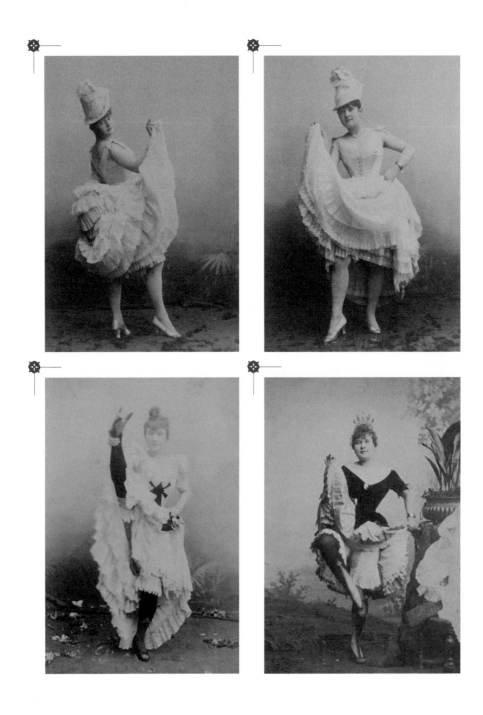

ABOVE **Louise Weber, *c.* 1895**
Louise was nicknamed *La Goulue*,
meaning 'the glutton', a sobriquet
earned through her habit of stealing
customers' drinks.

ABOVE **Louise Weber, *c.* 1881–91**
La Goulue performing the splits (top)
and with fellow Moulin Rouge dancers
(bottom) *Grille d'Égout* (centre right)
and Valentin le Désossé (right).

Perhaps the most famous dancer of the Moulin Rouge was Louise Weber, who was nicknamed *La Goulue*, meaning 'the glutton', because she stole customers' drinks in between dances. The daughter of a laundress, *La Goulue* came to be celebrated as 'the Queen of Montmartre'. Her risqué dancing and forthright manner earned her legions of fans. She was immortalized in the artwork of Toulouse-Lautrec and was a firm favourite of the Prince of Wales.

The first time they met, the Prince was watching her perform and she called out, 'Hey, Wales! Are you buying the champagne?' The audience was shocked, but the Prince could not get enough of her. Sadly, *La Goulue*'s decline was as dramatic as her rise. Buoyed by her success, she left the Moulin Rouge to strike out on her own. She invested all her money in her own show, but it was not a success. She disappeared from public view and spent what was left on drink. She spent her last years destitute, selling cigarettes and matches on the streets outside the Moulin Rouge.

La Goulue was one of several dancers painted by the post-impressionist, bohemian bon vivant Henri de Toulouse-Lautrec. Despite being born into the aristocracy, Lautrec lived his life amongst the Parisian underclasses. He rented rooms in brothels for months at a time so that he could draw and paint the sex workers as they went about their everyday lives. He was a client, but also a friend and

ABOVE LEFT **Henri de Toulouse-Lautrec,** *Moulin Rouge: La Goulue,* **1891**
Lautrec painted the Moulin Rouge dancer *La Goulue* several times.

ABOVE CENTRE **Henri de Toulouse-Lautrec,** *At the Moulin Rouge: La Goulue and Her Sister,* **1892**
Lautrec was a regular patron at the Moulin Rouge and the many brothels of Paris.

ABOVE RIGHT *Edward VII Promoting the Entente Cordiale with a Table of Can-Can Dancers,* **1899**
The promiscuous Prince of Wales was a known patron of the Moulin Rouge.

patron to many a poor woman whose likeness he captured in paint. He once said that 'the professional model is always like a stuffed owl... These girls are alive.' He was also a regular at the Moulin Rouge where he painted the dancers obsessively. His work immortalized not only *La Goulue*, but also the dancer Jane Avril, who was nicknamed *La Mélinite* after a firework; the gymnast known as Cha-U-Kao, a phonetic spelling of the dance style *chahut chaos*,

who performed on stage dressed as a clown; and the singer Yvette Guilbert.

Many of the great courtesans of the Belle Époque made their name in the dance halls. Women like Liane de Pougy, Emilienne d'Alenqon, Cléo de Mérode and Mata Hari set the stage alight and were as famous for their lovers as they were for their dancing. Carolina Otero, also known as *La Belle Otero,* is often called 'the last great courtesan'. Carolina was Spanish but made her name in the Folies Bèrgere dancehall in Paris. Her performances were notoriously erotic. Sem, the cartoonist, saw her perform and declared, 'I feel that my thighs are blushing.'[8] By the age of 25, *La Belle Otero* had the whole world at her feet. Some of her many lovers included King Edward VII (Dirty Bertie), Czar Nicholas II of Russia, Kaiser Wilhelm II, King Alexander II of Serbia, King Alfonso XIII of Spain, Prince Albert I of Monaco and statesmen such as France's Aristide Briand. Otero remained in demand until her

ABOVE LEFT **Del Baye, 1910**
Del Baye was a dancer at the Moulin Rouge.

ABOVE CENTRE *La Belle Otero, c.* 1909
Carolina Otero, better known by her stage name *La Belle Otero,* was a famed dancer and courtesan, known for her erotic performances on stage.

ABOVE RIGHT **Liane de Pougy,** *c.* 1910
Anne Marie Chassaigne, known as Liane De Pougy, was another famous Parisian dancer and courtesan.

fifties when she retired to Monte Carlo. Unfortunately, she did not adjust her spending habits and lost her fortune in the gambling houses. She died in a one-room flat in the Hotel Novelty in Nice, on 11 April 1965, without a penny to her name.

The police could not touch women like *La Belle Otero* or *La Goulue*. They were protected not only by their wealthy lovers but by their own celebrity. Courtesans, dancers and kept women traded in the grey area of sex work and so escaped the horrors of enforced vaginal examination and police harassment that their poorer sisters faced. Opposition to the regulatory system had been growing since Josephine Butler led a successful campaign in Britain against forced examinations in the 1860s. Not only was the system cruel and abusive, it also did not work. Without anyone testing their clients, regular screening offered no protection to sex workers. Despite the best efforts of the police there were always far more unregistered sex workers than registered ones. France's regulated system of prostitution was finally abolished under the Marthe Richard Law of 13 April 1946, named after Marthe Richard, a former sex worker and politician who campaigned for the closure of the brothels. Public opinion of sex workers and brothels had changed dramatically during the Second World War. During their occupation of Paris, the Nazis commandeered many of the city's brothels, including famed institutions such as Le Chabanais, the Sphinx, the One-Two-Two and La Fleur Blanche. When the war ended, retribution against anyone thought to have collaborated with the Nazis was swift: just one year after the war had ended, the French government gave the brothels six months to close.

In 1951, an auction was held by France's premier art connoisseur, Maurice Rheims, to sell the famous décor of Le Chabanais. Eager collectors snapped up the tapestries, the paintings by Toulouse-Lautrec, the Venetian glass and the gilded clocks. But the sale's most intriguing objects were a large copper bathtub, decorated with a naked woman, and an elaborate chair. Dirty Bertie's bathtub was bought by the artist Salvador Dalí for over 100,000 francs and then installed at his suite at the Hotel Meurice in Paris. The infamous love chair was purchased for 32,000 francs by Alain Vian, the brother of Boris Vian, a popular jazz musician. Since then it has changed hands several times. Its current location is unknown.

OPPOSITE **Brassaï**, *At Suzy's*, c. 1932–33
Brassaï was the pseudonym of Gyula Halász, the Hungarian–French photographer, artist and writer. Although he also photographed the world of high society, Brassaï's most enduring work was shot in his neighbourhood of Montparnasse, Paris, where he documented brothels, sex workers and other characters of the city nightlife.

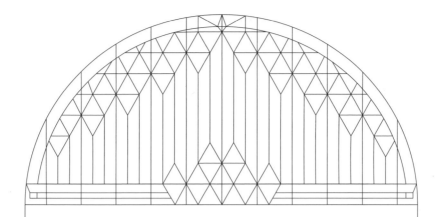

11

Sex in
WARTIME

~~~~~~~~~~~~~~

THE

Prophylactic

DICTATORSHP

~~~~~~~~~~~~~~

UNIFORMED GERMANS…GAZE FIXEDLY AT WOMEN
AND GIRLS BETWEEN THE AGES OF 15 AND 25.
ONE OF THE SOLDIERS PULLS OUT A POCKET
FLASHLIGHT AND SHINES IT ON ONE OF THE WOMEN,
STRAIGHT INTO HER EYES. THE TWO WOMEN TURN
THEIR PALE FACES TO US, EXPRESSING WEARINESS
AND RESIGNATION… THEY OPEN HER COAT AND
START GROPING HER WITH THEIR LUSTFUL PAWS.
THIS ONE IS IDEAL 'FOR BED', HE SAYS.

Franz Mawick, 1942

THE WAR WAS
THE BIGGEST
GODSEND
ON EARTH TO
THE MESSINAS...
LONDON BECAME
FILLED WITH
BRITISH AND
AMERICAN
TROOPS AND
WITH WAR
WORKERS
AWAY FROM
HOME. TIME
WAS SHORT,
MONEY WAS
LOOSE, MORALS
WERE OUT:
AND THIS, OF
COURSE, IS
WHERE I CAME IN.

Marthe Watts, *The Men in My Life*,
1960

OPPOSITE **Military police taking sex
workers in Naples to a hospital
to be treated for venereal disease,**
c. **1939–45**
During both the First and Second
World Wars, many warring nations
saw more troops admitted to hospital
with syphilis or gonorrhoea than for
any other ailment, excepting influenza.
Controlling venereal disease became
a matter of national security, and it
was sex workers who paid the price.

In August 1914, as the first British troops prepared to leave
for the trenches of France, Lord Kitchener, the formidable
Secretary of State for War, saw to it that every serving man
was issued with a copy of his advice on 'the true character
of the British soldier'. Printed on a single sheet of paper,
Kitchener's words were to be kept inside every soldier's
pay book. As well as cautioning his men to be 'invariably
courteous, considerate and kind' and to 'always look upon
looting as a disgraceful act', Kitchener addressed their sexual
conduct. 'In this new experience you may find temptations
both in wine and women. You must entirely resist both
temptations, and, while treating all women with perfect
courtesy, you should avoid any intimacy.'[1] Every serving
British soldier carried this advice with him throughout the
war. Ironically, inside the very pay book that logged the wages
being spent in the many brothels servicing the Western Front.

Kitchener may have hoped soldiers would abstain from 'wine
and women', but the reality was very different. Not only did
the troops freely ignore his advice, many did so with the full
understanding of their superior officers. As Irish brigadier
Frank Percy Crozier wrote:

> 'IT IS NOT REASONABLE TO EXPECT THE YOUNGSTERS
> TO KEEP THE TRENCHES FOR ENGLAND INTACT, AND
> THEIR CHASTITY INVIOLABLE AT ONE AND THE SAME
> TIME. HE WHO HOPES TO WAGE WAR WITHOUT WINE
> AND WOMEN IS LIVING IN A FOOL'S PARADISE, FOR
> THERE ARE NO HALF-MEASURES IN WAR, TRY HOW
> ONE WILL.'[2]

Or, as American general George Patton bluntly put it,
'If they don't fuck, they don't fight.'[3] But, as governments
around the world soon found out, soldiers that fuck
often do not fight at all.

By the time the war ended, venereal disease (VD) had
accounted for 416,891 hospital admissions among British
and Dominion troops. In 1918 alone 60,099 men were
admitted to hospitals in France and Flanders for venereal
disease treatment.[4] Similar casualties were seen amongst
the Canadian, Australian, New Zealand and German forces.
VD decimated armies and many warring nations saw more
troops admitted to hospital with syphilis or gonorrhoea than
for any other ailment, except for influenza. Patients were
treated for up to four weeks with various mercury compounds,

antiseptics and colloidal silver for gonorrhoea. The manpower being lost to wounds 'not sustained in the line of duty' was substantial. Responses to the crisis varied dramatically from country to country, ranging from enforcing abstinence in serving men (known as 'moral prophylaxis'), through to providing them with approved brothels and condoms ('physical prophylaxis'). But when it came to apportioning blame for the army's sexual health, all sides were united; it was wine and women.

Like most nations, during the first few months of the First World War, the Germans had initially hoped that

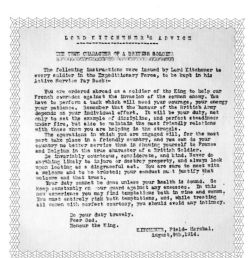

ABOVE LEFT **Lord Kitchener, *The True Character of a British Soldier*, 1914** These instructions were issued by Lord Kitchener to every soldier in the Expeditionary Force, to be kept in his Active Service Pay Book.

ABOVE RIGHT **A mobile brothel for troops close to the Front, c. 1916** Despite Kitchener's orders that British troops keep away from 'wine and women', there were hundreds of brothels serving troops at the Front.

simply telling their troops to not pay for sex and appealing to their Christian duty would be enough to curtail rising levels of venereal disease. Ever the pragmatists, when it became clear that advocating for abstinence alone was not keeping their men out of the brothels, the German military opted for physical over moral prophylaxis. They not only educated their recruits about venereal disease and instructed them on how to use a condom, but they quickly assumed control of sex work in occupied countries.[5] Prostitution was already under state regulation in France and Belgium, the so-called 'French system' of registration and compulsory health checks. The Germans quickly adopted the same system but implemented it with their famous Teutonic discipline and on a scale that had not been seen before.

On 11 February 1915, the German authorities occupying Belgium mandated the registration and twice-weekly inspection of all women suspected of prostitution in the areas immediately behind the frontline. Two days later, they established a *Sittenpolizei* (morality police), run by the German police and enforced in conjunction with local authorities. By the end of the year, Germany had installed a morality police force in all of its occupied towns. The system they introduced to regulate sex work and control venereal disease in the troops was so strict that French historian Jean-Yves Le Naour referred to it as the 'prophylactic dictatorship'.

ABOVE **A German brothel, c. 1916**
During the First World War, the Germans assumed control of all brothels in occupied cities across Europe. The sex workers who operated there were closely monitored, and subjected to mandatory health checks. The jovial air in this painting is likely unrepresentative of the experience of many of the women working in the brothels.

The German military assumed control over all new and existing brothels, which were then segregated by class into establishments for the officers and those for the grunts. (A similar system was unofficially adopted by the allied troops in France: 'blue lamp' brothels for the officers and 'red lamps' for everyone else.) Not only did sex workers have to submit to bi-weekly vaginal examinations by a German doctor, or face jail, but they had to keep and update the paperwork that proved they were healthy and allowed to work.[6] Should any woman be found to be infected, she was forcibly hospitalized in one of the new venereal disease centres that the Germans established in major occupied towns across Europe. The VD centres in Bruges and Antwerp treated over 1,000 women in 1917 and again in 1918.[7] Many of these treatment centres were little more than prisons, designed to humiliate as much as heal.

The German system of military brothels, condoms and forced examinations was certainly no friend to the women selling sex, but at the very least it viewed venereal disease as an issue of health, rather than one of moral failing – which is certainly more than can be said for the American approach. As far as General John J. Pershing was concerned, the American military was engaged in two wars: one against the central powers of Germany and the other against vice. It soon became obvious that if nothing was done to address the 'social hygiene' of their troops, America could lose both wars. When the Prime Minister of France, Georges Clemenceau, learned how many American men were being laid up with VD he wrote

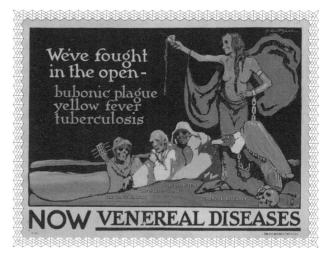

ABOVE LEFT **American poster warning troops about venereal disease, 1919**
During and following the First World War the Americans implemented an aggressive purity campaign to shame their men away from brothels.

ABOVE RIGHT **American poster warning troops about venereal disease, 1918**
Many of the images in the American anti-VD campaign demonize 'fast' women as vectors of disease. Here, a semi-naked woman, surrounded by skulls, is likened to death.

to Pershing offering to establish brothels for the exclusive use of American soldiers along the Western Front. This made perfect sense to Clemenceau as this was the system the French had used to control VD since the 19th century. The letter was then passed along to the American Secretary of War, Newton D. Baker, by Raymond Fosdick, the special assistant for troop morale. After reading and rereading the letter, a shocked Baker exclaimed, 'For God's sake, Raymond, don't show this to the president or he'll stop the war.'[8] Instead, the Americans chose moral prophylaxis and aggressively enforced abstinence amongst their serving men by embarking on a campaign to stigmatize and suppress sex work.

Pershing refused to issue condoms to American troops, believing they would simply encourage vice. Instead, in July 1917, he issued orders that prophylactic stations be established at every army camp and that men must undergo regular genital inspection for signs of disease. Every camp commander was made accountable for the sexual health of his men and required to keep detailed records on testing and treatment. All military camps had a single guarded entrance, and any man found to be showing symptoms, or who had recently had sex, was subject to postcoital chemical prophylaxis. This involved stripping naked in front of a medical orderly, who would scrub the penis, insert antiseptic into the urethra until the bladder was full, and then apply calomel ointment. The process was intentionally humiliating and painful so as to discourage repeat offenders. Pay was

suspended for the duration of treatment and any soldiers failing to report VD symptoms could be subject to a court martial. In Britain, any man found to have venereal disease had his pay stopped and a letter sent to his family, informing them of his conduct – a practice that was stopped after a major committed suicide when his wife was told the reason for his hospitalization. After that, next of kin were simply told that their loved one had been admitted for reasons 'not yet diagnosed'.[9] This regime was accompanied by an extensive propaganda programme that warned of the dangers of 'loose' and 'immoral' women.

ABOVE **The interior of an American army camp in France, 1918**
The sign warns of the range of punishments for soldiers who contract venereal disease.

Lectures, posters and leaflets blaming and stigmatizing French sex workers as vectors of disease and potential spies were widely distributed throughout the forces. Films, such as *Fit to Fight* (1918), showed the terrible consequences

of 'fast women' and organizations like the YMCA offered recreational activities to distract the troops from less wholesome pursuits. In France, the *maisons de tolérance* were completely off limits to US troops, while back in America, local authorities in garrison towns were granted powers to arrest and detain 'all persons not of good fame' to be held 'for such period as the health officer may deem best'.[10] Hundreds of women were rounded up and held in venereal disease centres across America until the end of the war.

The American government also put considerable pressure on its allies to end the system of regulated sex work in France. Prime Minister Clemenceau steadfastly refused to make any such changes, which created a tense situation for the British who did not want their men to visit brothels but worried that they would offend the French if they closed them down. Under mounting pressure from anti-vice organizations on the home front, the British finally ordered their troops to stay out of French brothels in 1918. Not that this provided much of a deterrent. Men continued to queue down the street to empty their wallets in the *maisons de tolérance* until the war was over and they were finally allowed to go home. George Coppard, a British soldier who served with the Machine Gun Corps, recalled such a scene in his memoir of the war.

'THERE WERE WELL OVER A HUNDRED AND FIFTY MEN WAITING FOR OPENING TIME, SINGING *MADEMOISELLE FROM ARMENTIÈRES* AND OTHER LUSTY SONGS. RIGHT ON THE DOT OF 6 PM A RED LAMP OVER THE DOORWAY OF THE BROTHEL WAS SWITCHED ON. A ROAR WENT UP FROM THE TROOPS, ACCOMPANIED BY A FORWARD LUNGE TOWARDS THE ENTRANCE.'[11]

The fear of being seen to encourage 'vice' by moralists at home prevented the British from offering basic prophylactics to their troops until the final months of the war, when tubes containing potassium permanganate were made available, though not easily so. Other nations, such as New Zealand, outwardly condemned vice but secretly started issuing troops with prophylactic kits in a desperate effort to curtail epidemic levels of venereal disease.

The amount of man hours lost to venereal disease during the First World War was substantial. So, when the Second World War broke out, no one was taking any chances with

PREVIOUS **Eugène Atget,** *La Villette, Public Girl Doing the Watch,* **1921 (left) and** *Versailles, Woman, Soldier, Brothel,* **1921 (right)**
During both world wars, the French attempted to control VD in their troops by strictly regulating sex workers through registration and compulsory health checks.

OPPOSITE **Sex workers in Marseilles, 1918–19**
These postcards show sex workers sitting outside their brothels, and some of the soldiers visiting them.

3 - VIEUX-MARSEILLE - Rue Lanternerie
Pensionnaires au repos - L.V.

MARSEILLE. - Rue Lantermery, près le vieux Port -

339 MARSEILLE. — Un Coin du Vieux Marseille. — La Rue Bouterie. — LL.

SELECTA

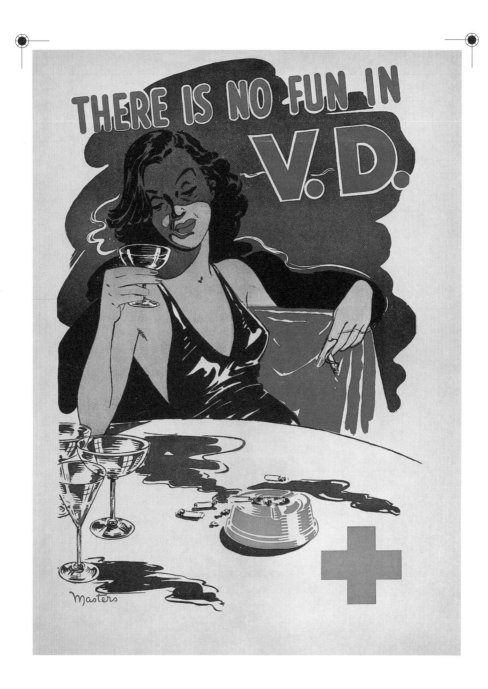

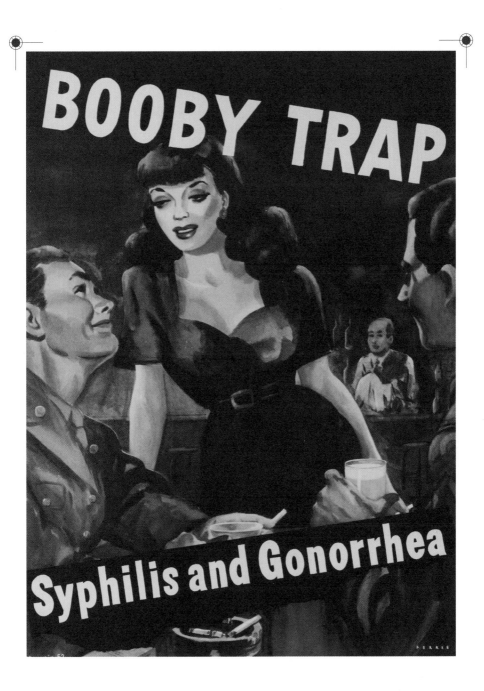

ABOVE **American anti-VD poster, 1940s**
During the Second World War, America attempted to educate its troops about venereal disease. However the campaign still blamed 'fast women' for VD in the army.

the sexual health of their troops. Even the American war office realized that attempting to enforce abstinence simply did not work, and instead issued all serving men with condoms and launched a safe sex campaign, largely stigmatizing 'fast women' and 'goodtime girls'. American servicemen were issued with six condoms a month and a 'pro-kit' (prophylactic kit), containing ointment, a cloth impregnated with soap and a cleansing tissue to use immediately after sex.[12] Condom production grew, and companies branded their products with exotic-sounding names, such as Ramses, Sheikh and Saxon.

Allied troops received education on safe sex and a prophylactic kit, but they were still discouraged from visiting brothels.

ABOVE LEFT **An officer guarding Chinese women forced in sexual slavery, c. 1948**
These women, known as 'comfort women', were forced into sexual slavery by the Japanese Imperial Army in occupied territories before and during the Second World War.

ABOVE RIGHT **Chinese and Malayan girls forcibly taken from Penang by the Japanese to work as 'comfort women' for the troops, c. 1939-45**
In 2015, a memorial hall dedicated to Chinese 'comfort women' was opened in Nanjing.

The British made efforts to close brothels in India, Nairobi and Sri Lanka, but to little effect. Once again, the Germans assumed control over prostitution in every occupied country and introduced a rigorous system of registration and mandatory inspection. Transactional sex was only permitted inside an authorized brothel, the most exclusive of which were reserved for German officers. The ready and enthusiastic provision of sexual services for German troops seemed at odds with Nazi propaganda that promoted marriage and sexual fidelity. But this was dismissed by Heinrich Himmler as 'falsely understood prudery, which is typically a very strong remnant of a specifically Christian way of thinking'.[13] For Himmler, state-approved brothels not only controlled VD, but also prevented Germans from having sex with local, racially inferior women. On 19 April 1939, following the invasion of Czechoslovakia, Himmler made sexual intercourse with any women of the 'Eastern deployment' illegal.[14] Thus, providing his men with brothels in Poland, and later Russia, prevented social contact with their racial inferiors. These brothels were still staffed by local women, but this glaring contradiction did not seem to worry Himmler; neither did forcing women to work against their will.

The Nazis may have viewed prostitution as an essential military provision, but they also categorized sex workers as 'anti-socials', and many were rounded up and sent to concentration camps like Ravensbrück women's camp, 90 km (56 miles) to the north of Berlin. These women would then be forced to work in one of the camp brothels that were established

to 'reward' non-Jewish prisoners for good behaviour. There were brothels in Mauthausen, Auschwitz, Buchenwald, Neuengamme, Dachau, Dora-Mittelbau and Sachsenhausen.[15]

ABOVE LEFT **The 'brothel' at Mauthausen concentration camp, c. 1942–44**
These brothels were designed to 'reward' good behaviour in non-Jewish prisoners. Very little is known about the women who were forced to work here.

ABOVE RIGHT **Heinrich Himmler visits the Gusen camp 'brothel' within Mauthausen concentration camp, c. 1941**
Mauthausen was the first camp to introduce a brothel in 1942, however many other concentration camps implemented them in the following years.

Those who escaped this fate could find themselves trafficked across Europe to work in German brothels on the Eastern Front. Once a woman was officially registered as a sex worker with the German authorities, she had very few rights and could be forced to work anywhere under Nazi control. Registered sex workers from France, the Netherlands, Bohemia and Moldovia were shipped to military brothels in the East. Even more women were forced into sexual slavery in September 1940, when Reich Governor Arthur Greiser passed a decree that made forced prostitution a punishment for any Polish woman who had violated the law against having sex with an Aryan German man.[16]

ABOVE *Freudenhäuser* (Houses of Joy)
established in Brest, France, c. 1940
The notice (bottom) – from a brothel
established in a former synagogue –
states that the use of condoms
is compulsory.

ABOVE *Freudenhäuser* (Houses of Joy)
established in Brest, France, *c*. 1940
The Germans attempted to control
VD in their troops by brutally
controlling sex work and the
health of sex workers.

ABOVE **Interior of a brothel**
in Naples, *c.* 1945
One American surgeon reported
that 'prostitutes from Naples
descended upon our encampment
by the hundreds, outflanking guards'.

ABOVE **Interior of a brothel in Naples, c. 1945**
In 1958 the passing of the Merlin Law made brothels illegal in Italy, forcing women onto the streets, and into private homes.

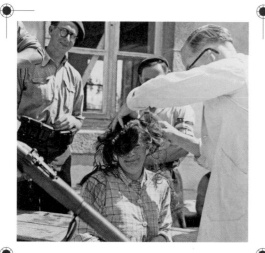

The Nazis' treatment of sex workers was unbelievably cruel, but their torment did not end with the war. The women who had been forced to work in the brothels could not shake off the stigma of prostitution and many were shunned by society after the war ended. Such was the shame of the survivors that it was not until the 1990s that researchers started to be able to bring the story of sexual slavery and the military brothels to light. In France, public opinion of sex workers and brothels had changed dramatically during the Second World War. When the Nazis occupied Paris, they commandeered many brothels for the exclusive use of German officers, including Le Chabanais, the Sphinx, the One-Two-Two and La Fleur Blanche. Under German patronage, these establishments flourished. But once the war was over, the French unleashed a savage wave of revenge against anyone suspected of collaborating with the Nazis. Some 6,000 people are known to have been murdered during what became known as the *épuration sauvage*, or the 'wild purge'.

Any woman who had a relationship with a German was accused of 'horizontal collaboration'. Even women who had just been seen talking to a Nazi were accused, but sex workers became obvious targets for the vigilante groups. The women who had worked in the brothels during the war had their heads shaved and were stripped naked, covered in tar and paraded through the streets. Many had swastikas painted on their bodies or daubed on their foreheads in red lipstick. They became known as *les femmes tondues,* or 'the shorn women'. It was just a year after the end of the war that the French government gave the brothels six months to close. Little to no provisions were made to support the women exiting sex work, so most were forced to continue operating under criminalization with even fewer rights than they had before. There is little surviving data on what happened to these women. They simply disappear from the records.

OPPOSITE **The *femmes tondues*, or 'shorn women',** *c.* 1945
Following the surrender of Germany in 1945, a wave of revenge was unleashed across France against anyone who was thought to have collaborated with the Nazis. Sex workers who had worked in the military brothels became obvious targets. Many had their heads shaved, were painted with swastikas and paraded through the streets.

Wartime policies on prostitution may have varied considerably, but they all blamed and heavily stigmatized women who sold sex. Anti-vice tactics cast 'loose women' as vectors of disease that must be avoided, while the 'prophylactic dictatorship' viewed them as vectors of disease that must be controlled. Either way, all fighting nations agreed 'wine and women' were to blame – and it was the women who paid the price.

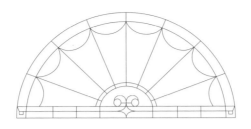

Conclusion

The

FIGHT

BACK

WE WILL NOT, WE WILL NEVER, BECOME
THE CIVIL SERVANTS OF SEX.
Ulla, sex worker activist, 1975

On the morning of Monday 2 June 1975, over one hundred sex workers marched into Saint-Nizier church in Lyon. Led by a woman known only as Ulla, they refused to leave until their complaints were heard by the highest authorities in France and the police changed the punitive tactics being deployed against them. By Friday, their numbers had grown to over two hundred as sex workers from across France came to stand with their sisters in Lyon. Churches were occupied in Marseilles, Paris, Grenoble and Saint-Étienne, while in Nice, sex workers went on strike, and a delegation of sex workers in Paris presented a petition to the newspaper *France-Soir*, calling for an end to police brutality against them. And the police had indeed been brutal.

Three years earlier, an anonymous whistle-blower had exposed several high-ranking police officers in the Lyon vice squad, who had been extorting money from sex workers and brothel owners in exchange for 'police protection'.[1] The ensuing scandal had rocked Lyon to its core and

the accused officers were quickly charged and jailed. In an effort to reassure the public that the police were not profiteering from prostitution, the authorities of Lyon resolved to purge the city of vice. In 1972, some 6,290 fines for soliciting were issued in Lyon, forty-three pimps were jailed, and forty-one hotels in the red-light district known to rent rooms to sex workers were closed down.[2] These establishments were illegal under French law, but until the scandal, the police had been prepared to tolerate them as long as everyone involved was discreet. But the revelation of police corruption changed all that.

Without a room to work from, many of the city's sex workers were forced to solicit on the streets, where they could be fined or charged with 'incitement to debauchery'. Those fined for prostitution had little option but to continue selling sex in order to pay the fine, which only increased the risk of incurring yet more fines. Enraged at this treatment, on 24 August 1972, approximately forty sex workers met at the

Place des Jacobins near the main red-light district to plan a protest march the following day. They were swiftly dispersed by the police. The brave few who turned up for the protest the next day were met by yet more police who said they would take the women to a meeting with a city prefect, but took them to the central police station instead, where they were detained for several hours.

As the authorities clamped down on sex work, violence against sex workers increased. In 1974, between March and August alone, three sex workers were brutally murdered in Lyon. The killer was never caught, and the newly formed Collective for the Defence of the Prostitutes of Lyon accused the police of not investigating the crimes properly. The first statement drawn up by the collective in 1974 was unequivocal: 'Six or seven prostitutes have been murdered since 1971...

They were ghastly murders and included torture. They still have not found the killers.'[3]

The final straw came when the city of Lyon reactivated article R37 of the French penal code, meaning anyone who had paid several fines for the same offence could be sent to jail. Forced onto the streets and already incurring multiple fines, the sex workers of Lyon knew all too well what this legislation meant for them. Little wonder that their first action in occupying the Saint-Nizier church was to hang a large banner from the steeple that read, 'Our children do not want their mothers to go to jail.'[4]

The women remained inside the church for ten days, receiving gifts of food and drink from local merchants, and telegrams of support from various unions, feminist groups and gay rights activists. The parish priest, the Reverend Antonin Bdal, refused to remove them and the world's media

ABOVE **The sex worker occupation of Saint-Nizier church, Lyon, 1975**
Over one hundred women occupied the church for ten days. To commemorate the event, 2 June is now marked around the world by sex workers as 'International Whores' Day'.

OPPOSITE LEFT **Stonewall Inn, Greenwich Village, New York**
The Stonewall Riots in 1969 were a pivotal moment in the fight for LGBTQ rights.

OPPOSITE RIGHT **Marsha P. Johnson and Sylvia Rivera,** *c.* **1969**
Johnson and Rivera were both sex workers, and important activists for LGBTQ rights.

descended, all clamouring to talk to the striking sex workers of Lyon. Eventually, without sending any representatives to meet with the women, the government ordered the police to forcibly clear the church.

Although the sex workers' demands were not met, the occupation of Saint-Nizier was an international event and a milestone in the early fight for sex worker rights: 2 June is now marked around the world by sex workers as 'International Whores' Day'. It was the first time collective action by sex workers had been played out on the world stage and received widespread support. But it was not the first time sex workers had joined together to demand their rights, protest police brutality and effect political change.

In August 1966, a riot broke out at Compton's Cafeteria in the Tenderloin district of San Francisco. In an effort to deter drag queens and transgender sex workers from gathering there, Compton's management frequently called the police on their patrons, who arrested them for prostitution and the crime of 'female impersonation'. Once in custody, these women faced severe abuse from the police, including

sexual and physical assaults, being put in male jail cells and even having their heads shaved.[5] When Compton's Cafeteria brought in a service fee targeted at transgender patrons, many of whom were sex workers, the transgender community began picketing outside. When the police were called and tried to arrest the protestors, the demonstration turned violent.

The restaurant's windows were smashed, tables and chairs were upturned and dishes were thrown as drag queens and sex workers spilled out into the street. When police reinforcements turned up, the windows of their cars were smashed. A newsstand was burned down, and dozens of rioters were arrested and dragged, kicking and screaming, into paddy wagons.

Three years later, sex workers played an integral role in the famous 1969 Stonewall riots in New York City. The Stonewall Inn was a popular late-night hangout for the LGBTQ community and subject to frequent police raids. But when the police descended yet again in the early hours of 28 June 1969, the Stonewall patrons fought back. Marsha P. Johnson and Sylvia Rivera, both sex workers and trans women of colour, have

both been credited with throwing the 'first brick' at Stonewall that night. Although Johnson and Rivera have denied this, what happened at Stonewall led to six days of protesting and clashes with the police as the gay, lesbian, transgender and queer communities refused to be brutalized by the police any longer. The Stonewall riots are now considered to be one of the most important events in the global fight for LGBTQ rights. In 2019, it was announced that Marsha P. Johnson and Sylvia Rivera would be commemorated with a monument in New York's Greenwich Village.

The rumblings of collective action among sex workers had been felt long before even Stonewall and the occupation of Saint-Nizier.[6] In January 1917, less than half a mile from where the Compton's Cafeteria Riots would erupt fifty years later, some three hundred sex workers marched through San Francisco to the Central Methodist church to confront the Reverend Paul Smith about his campaign to rid the city of prostitution. Led by a prominent madam named Reggie Gamble, the women were described in the press as 'of the underworld, 300 strong, bedecked, their eyebrows pencilled and their lips rouged'.[7] Gamble had told Smith 'a few' women wanted to talk to him, but he was completely unprepared for the crowd that

approached him. Before the women started to speak, Smith desperately tried to calm their anger by claiming to be on their side. 'This crusade, I want it understood, is not directed against you women,' he claimed. 'It is directed against the system of which you are some of the victims... This is a man-problem.'[8] But the assembled women were not convinced.

Gamble stood up and launched an impassioned speech about the 'hundreds and thousands of women in San Francisco who make their living in the underworld' because there were precious few other options available to them. She accused Smith of Christian hypocrisy and of not 'want[ing] women such as us around your church' and told him flatly to campaign against poverty, not prostitution. She demanded to know if Smith or his band of abolitionists would be prepared to take these women into their homes once they had succeeded in denying them a livelihood. One woman stood up and confronted Smith, saying, 'Let us understand each other. Are you trying to reform us or are you trying to reform social conditions? You leave us alone. It is too late to do anything with us. Give your attentions to the boys and girls in the schools and to the social conditions responsible for the spread of prostitution.'[9]

Outfaced and outnumbered, Smith resorted to asking the women how much money they needed to stop selling sex. When he suggested $10 a week, the women told him they would need $20 or $25. Smith told them that was unrealistic and then asked them if they would be willing to swap sex work for housework. To this, one woman shouted back, 'What woman wants to work in a kitchen?' The crowd laughed and Smith abruptly called an end to the meeting. Nothing said to Smith that day changed his mind, indeed he led an anti-vice rally that very afternoon, but this action is one of the first times the voices and demands of sex workers were recorded in the American press.

The right 'to be seen' is a demand that has echoed throughout history and still shapes the fight for sex worker rights today. What are largely missing throughout the history of sex work are the voices of sex workers themselves. They have always been there but have rarely been listened to or recorded. They have rarely been seen. They have been talked over, talked down or talked for. The history of sex work is a history of control,

exploitation and powerful people closing their eyes to the rights of those they legislate for. Narratives of sexual shame have long focused public attention upon specific scripts, such as the sex worker as a victim, in need of management, or as a subject of titillation, rather than as a human being who needs to earn a living.

The late 20th century saw the emergence of the sex worker rights movement, and activists who have fought hard to wrestle the narrative away from moralizers and would-be rescuers to instead focus on the issues of human rights and labour laws. COYOTE was founded in May 1973 by former sex worker Margo St James and was the first American organization dedicated to sex worker rights. The following month, sex workers in Sweden formed the Posing Girls and Trade Models' Union. Three months after that, sex workers in Rome came together and founded Partito per la Protezione delle Prostitute, or PPP, to fight against criminalization. Inspired by the political action in Lyon, the English Collective of Prostitutes was formed in London in 1975,

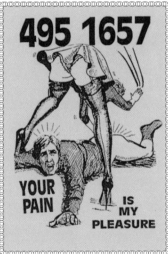

OPPOSITE **Tart cards in a phonebox in Tokyo, 2002**
Before the internet, tart cards – cards advertising the services of sex workers – were a common sight in city phoneboxes around the world. They generally avoid direct reference to prostitution, instead using euphemistic references to sex.

ABOVE **British tart cards, *c.* 1990**
Tart cards originated in areas such as Soho, London, in the 1960s as handwritten postcards. By the 1980s and 1990s they had evolved to be printed cards, often cheaply reproduced on brightly coloured paper.

and by the 1980s, sex worker rights groups had been established in countries across Europe, North and South America, Asia, Africa and Australia. In 1985, representatives from sex worker rights groups in North America and Europe formed the International Committee for Prostitutes' Rights (ICPR). That same year, the ICPR held the first World Whores' Congress in Amsterdam where they drafted the World Charter for Prostitutes' Rights. The Charter called for full decriminalization of sex work and established a distinction between forced and voluntary prostitution. It called for freedom of movement, an end to discrimination, to compulsory health checks and to zoning policies as well as 'human rights and civil liberties, including the freedom of speech, travel, immigration, work, marriage and motherhood and the right to unemployment insurance, health insurance and housing'. The Charter simply demanded the right for sex workers to 'provide their services under the conditions that are absolutely determined by themselves and no one else'.[10] Although the Charter was ridiculed in the press at the time, it became the cornerstone for sex worker rights around the world.

As this book has shown, no attempt to abolish or control either the selling or buying of sex in our collective history has worked. Not one, and there have been many. All that happens when either the provider or the client is criminalized is that sex work is forced underground, creating opportunities for exploitation and abuse without recourse to legal protection. This is why the overwhelming majority of sex worker rights groups today are calling for full decriminalization, which means the removal of laws and criminal penalties specifically pertaining to the selling and buying of sex, rather than 'legalization'.[11] Legalization means sex work is legal but only under specific, government-mandated conditions. Many of these conditions have been covered in this book: zoning, licences, specified clothing, forced health checks, etc.

Another system of legalization favoured by many radical feminist groups is the so-called 'Nordic Model', which has been adopted in Sweden, Norway, Iceland, France and Northern Ireland, which criminalizes the purchase of sexual services, but not the selling. The idea is to 'end demand' and eventually end all sex work. But the Nordic Model does not work because by criminalizing the client, you force the sex worker underground and, ultimately, this puts the police in charge of regulating the industry. Research from the countries that have adopted the Nordic Model shows again and again that 'end demand' legislation only places sex workers at significantly greater risk of harm, not only from clients but from increased levels of police harassment and difficulty accessing support services.

The decriminalization of sex work is not a political panacea to rid the world of stigma and discrimination against sex workers, but it is the first step towards achieving that. In 1995, sex work was decriminalized in the Australian state of New South Wales and it remains so. In 2003, New Zealand also decriminalized sex work and according to research carried out by the University of Otago in 2006, more than 60% of New Zealand sex workers reported feeling empowered to refuse to see certain clients, and 95% said they felt they had rights after decriminalization.[12] In 2014, a New Zealand sex worker took a brothel operator to a human rights tribunal, after being sexually harassed – and won her case.

Selling sex is a product of capitalism and commerce. It is not a moral failing, but the inevitable result of market forces that primarily disadvantage women. We are all selling something but throughout history sex workers have been punished, shunned, marginalized and ignored because they sold sex, rather than their labour in factories or on farms. It has taken thousands of years, but sex workers have finally managed to create space to speak for themselves. The modern-day sex worker rights movement asks for the same rights that the women who marched to the San Francisco Central Methodist church demanded over a hundred years ago: the right to dictate their own working conditions, without the threat of arrest or rescue. To work without harassment or abuse and, of course, the right to be seen.

ABOVE **A sex workers' rights protest
in Las Vegas, 2019**
The protest was sparked by two Acts
passed in 2018 that resulted in many
sex workers being banned from
advertising online.

INTRODUCTION: TALES FROM GROPECUNT LANE

1 Hallie Rubenhold, *The Five: The Untold Lives of the Women Killed by Jack the Ripper* (London: Doubleday, 2019)

2 Jeffrey Richards, *Sex, Dissidence and Damnation: Minority Groups in the Middle Ages* (London: Routledge, 1991)

3 John Lowman, 'Violence and the Outlaw Status of (Street) Prostitution in Canada', *Violence Against Women*, 6.9 (2000), pp. 987–1011

4 Ibid.

5 Rudyard Kipling, 'On the City Wall', in *Soldiers Three, and Other Stories* (London: Macmillan, 1914), p. 137

CHAPTER ONE: IN SERVICE OF THE GODS; SEX IN THE ANCIENT WORLD

1 George Smith, *The Chaldean Account of Genesis* (London: Sampson Low, Marston, Searle and Rivington, 1876), p. 202

2 A. R. George, trans., *The Epic of Gilgamesh* (London: Penguin, 2002), p. 7–8

3 Ibid, p. 8

4 Martha T. Roth, 'Marriage, Divorce and the Prostitute in Ancient Mesopotamia', in Christopher A. Faraone and Laura K. McClure, *Prostitutes and Courtesans in the Ancient World* (Madison: University of Wisconsin Press, 2006), p. 33

5 Patrick Olivelle, *King, Governance and Law in Ancient India: Kautilya's Arthaśāstra* (New York; Oxford: Oxford University Press, 2012), pp. 158–60

6 A. R. George, trans., *The Epic of Gilgamesh* (London: Penguin, 2002), p. 8

7 Ignace J. Gelb, *The Assyrian Dictionary of the Oriental Institute of the University of Chicago*, Vol. 6 (Chicago: Oriental Institute, Chicago, 1968), pp. 101–02; Julia Assante, 'The Kar.Kid/Arimtu, Prostitute or Single Woman? A Critical Review of the Evidence', *Ugarit-Forschungen*, 30 (1998), pp. 5–96, p. 60

8 Morris Silver, 'Temple/Sacred Prostitution in Ancient Mesopotamia Revisited. Religion in the Economy', *Ugarit-Forschungen*, 30 (2006), pp. 632–63, p. 640

9 Herodotus, *Delphi Complete Works of Herodotus* (Delphi Classics, 2013), Kindle location 1718

10 Strabo, *Delphi Complete Works of Strabo* (Delphi Classics, 2016) Kindle location 20295

11 Herbert A. Strong and John Garstang, *The Syrian Goddess: Being a Translation of Lucian's De Dea Syria, with a Life of Lucian* (London: Dodo, 2010), pp. 40–42

12 Justin, 'Epitome of the Philippic History of Pompeius Trogus', in John Selby Watson, ed., *Justin. Cornelius Nepos, and Eutropius, literally translated, with notes and a general index*, Books 11–20 (1886), pp. 90–171

13 Maria Costanza Torri, 'Abuse of Lower Castes in South India: The Institution of Devadasi', *Journal of International Women's Studies*, 11.2 (2009), pp. 31–48, p. 35

14 K. Jamanadas, *Devadasis* (Delhi: Kalpaz Publications, 2007), p. 300

CHAPTER TWO: TOADS AND SHE-WOLVES; SELLING SEX IN THE CLASSICAL WORLD

1 Plutarch, 'De Pythiae Oraculis, section 14', in Frank Cole Babbitt, trans., *Moralia* (Cambridge: Harvard University Press; London: William Heinemann Ltd, 1936)

2 Pseudo-Lucian, 'Affairs of the Heart, chapter 15', in M. D. Macleod, trans., *Lucian* (Cambridge: Harvard University Press, 1967)

3 Machon, *The Fragments*, XVIII, 11, ed. A. S. F. Gow (Cambridge: Cambridge University Press, 2004), pp. 450–55

4 Athenaeus, 'Deipnosophists, Book 13 (C)', in C. D. Yonge, trans., *The Deipnosophists, or, Banquet of the Learned of Athenaeus* (London: Henry G. Bohn, 1854), pp. 589–99

5 Pseudo-Plutarch, 'Lives of the Ten Orators', in William W. Goodwin, ed., *Plutarch's Morals* (Boston: Little, Brown, and Co., 1878), pp. 844–52

6 Konstantinos A. Kapparis, *Apollodorus 'Against Neaira' [D.59]* (Berlin: Walter de Gruyter, 1999), p. 161

7 Demosthenes, 'Against Neaera, Sections 18–48', in Norman W. DeWitt, trans., *Demosthenes* (Cambridge: Harvard University Press; London: William Heinemann Ltd, 1949)

8 Maurus Servius Honoratus, *Commentary on the Aeneid of Vergil*, Georgius Thilo, ed. (Leipzig: B. G. Teubner, 1881), line 273

9 Robin S. Karson and Kevin Consey, *Pompeii, As Source and Inspiration: Reflections in Eighteenth- and Nineteenth-Century Art* (Michigan: University of Michigan Museum of Art, 1977), p. 10

10 Mary Beard, *Pompeii: The Life of a Roman Town* (London: Profile, 2008), p. 232

11 Andrew Wallace-Hadrill, 'Public Honour and Private Shame: The Urban Texture of Pompeii', in Tim J. Cornell and Kathryn Lomas, *Urban Society in Roman Italy* (London; New York: Routledge, 1995), pp. 51–54

12 Sarah Levin-Richardson, *The Brothel of Pompeii: Sex, Class and Gender at the Margins of Roman Society* (Cambridge: Cambridge University Press, 2019), p. 40

13 Ibid.

CHAPTER THREE: THE GEESE THAT LAID THE GOLDEN EGG; SEX WORK IN MEDIEVAL LONDON

1 'Memorials: 1385', in Henry Thomas Riley, ed., *Memorials of London and London Life in the 13th, 14th and 15th Centuries* (London: Longman, 1868), pp. 483–86

2   Ephraim J. Burford, *The Orrible Synne: A Look at London Lechery from Roman to Cromwellian Times* (London: Calder & Boyars, 1973), pp. 151–52

3   'Liber Albus, Vol. 1', in Henry Thomas Riley, ed., *Munimenta Gildhallae Londoniensis: Liber Albus, Liber Custumarum, et Liber Horn*, Rolls Series, Vol. 12, Pt. 1 (London: Longman, 1859), p. 283

4   John Carpenter, *Liber Albus: The White Book of the City of London,* Henry Thomas Riley, trans. (London: Richard Griffin, 1861), p. 247

5   Henry Thomas Riley, ed., *Memorials of London and London Life in the 13th, 14th and 15th Centuries* (London: Longman, 1868), pp. 226–29

6   Karen Jones, *Gender and Petty Crime in Late Medieval England: The Local Courts in Kent, 1460–1560* (Woodbridge: Boydell Press, 2006), p. 162

7   John Carpenter, *Liber Albus: The White Book of the City of London,* Henry Thomas Riley, trans. (London: Richard Griffin, 1861), p. 395.

8   'Memorials: 1385', in Henry Thomas Riley, ed., *Memorials of London and London Life in the 13th, 14th and 15th Centuries* (London: Longman, 1868), pp. 483–86

9   Ibid.

10 John Stow, *A Survey of London, Written in the Year 1598*, William John Thoms, ed. (London: Whittaker and Co., 1842), p. 151

11 Ruth Mazo Karras, 'The Regulation of Brothels in Later Medieval England', *Signs*, 14.2 (1989), pp. 399–433, p. 427

12 Ibid., pp. 427–33

13 'Henry VIII: April 1546, 11–20', in James Gairdner and R. H. Brodie, eds., *Letters and Papers, Foreign and Domestic, Henry VIII, Volume 21 Part 1, January–August 1546* (London: His Majesty's Stationery Office, 1908), pp. 287–305

14 Hugh Latimer, *The Works of Hugh Latimer, Sometime Bishop of Worcester, Martyr, 1555*, George Elwes Corrie, ed. (Cambridge: Cambridge University Press, 1844–45), p. 133

CHAPTER FOUR: THE HONEST COURTESANS; SELLING SEX IN RENAISSANCE EUROPE

1   St Augustine, *De ordine*, 2.12 (386 CE), as cited in Alain Corbin, 'Commercial Sexuality in Nineteenth-Century France: A System of Images and Regulations', *Representations*, 14 (1986), pp. 209–19, pp. 213–14

2   St Thomas Aquinas, 'Unbelief in General', in Fathers of the English Dominican Province, trans., *The Summa Theologiae of St Thomas Aquinas* (London: Burns, Oates & Washbourne Ltd., 1920–25), article 11

3   Giordano de Pisa, *Quaresimale Fiorentino, 1305–1306*, Carlo Delcorno, ed. (Florence: G. C. Sansoni, 1974), p. 210

4   Richard C. Trexler, 'La Prostitution Florentine Au Xve Siècle: Patronages et Clientèles', *Annales. Histoire, Sciences Sociales*, 36.6 (1981), pp. 983–1015; Michael Rocke, *Forbidden Friendships: Homosexuality and Male Culture in Renaissance Florence* (New York; Oxford: Oxford University Press, 1996), p. 31

5   'Il Ponte Delle Tette, Ovvero Storia Delle Carampane', *Veneto World*, 2020, <https://www.venetoworld.com/il-territorio/curiosita-dal-veneto/il-ponte-delle-tette-ovvero-storia-delle-carampane.html> (accessed 24 January 2020)

6   Janet Sethre, *The Souls of Venice* (Jefferson; London: McFarland, 2003), p. 155

7   Diane Owen Huges, 'Earrings for Circumcision: Distinction and Purification in the Italian Renaissance City', in Richard C. Trexler, ed., *Persons In Groups. Social Behavior As Identity Formation in Medieval and Renaissance Europe* (Binghamton: Medieval & Renaissance Texts & Studies, 1985), pp. 155–94, p. 162

8   Carol Lansing, 'Gender and Civic Authority: Sexual Control in a Medieval Italian Town', *Journal of Social History*, 31.1 (1997), pp. 33–59, p. 39

9   Paolo Mantegazza, James Bruce and Robert Meadows, *Anthropological Studies of Sexual Relations of Mankind* (New York: Falstaff Press, 1937), p. 271

10 John K. Brackett, 'The Florentine Onesta and the Control of Prostitution, 1403–1680', *The Sixteenth Century Journal*, 24.2 (1993), pp. 273–300, p. 277

11 William W. Sanger, *The History of Prostitution: Its Extent, Causes and Effects Throughout the World* (New York: Harper & Brothers, 1858), p. 117

12 John K. Brackett, 'The Florentine Onesta and the Control of Prostitution, 1403–1680', *The Sixteenth Century Journal*, 24.2 (1993), pp. 273–300, p. 281

13 Paula C. Clarke, 'The Business of Prostitution in Early Renaissance Venice', *Renaissance Quarterly*, 68.2 (2015), pp. 419–64, p. 426

14 Janet Sethre, *The Souls of Venice* (Jefferson; London: McFarland, 2003), p. 155.

15 Diane Yvonne Ghirardo, 'The Topography of Prostitution in Renaissance Ferrara', *Journal of the Society of Architectural Historians*, 60.4 (2001), pp. 402–3

16 John K. Brackett, 'The Florentine Onesta and the Control of Prostitution, 1403–1680', *The Sixteenth Century Journal*, 24.2 (1993), pp. 273–300, p. 285

17 Ibid., p. 275

18 Ibid., p. 286

19 Richard C. Trexler, 'La Prostitution Florentine Au Xve Siècle: Patronages et Clientèles', *Annales. Histoire, Sciences Sociales*, 36.6 (1981), pp. 983–1015, pp. 985–88

20 Brian S. Pullan, *Tolerance, Regulation and Rescue: Dishonoured Women and Abandoned Children in Italy, 1300–1800* (Manchester: Manchester University Press, 2016), p. 36

21 Nick Squires, 'Italian Regions Battle Over Who Invented Tiramisu', *Telegraph*, 2016 <https://www.telegraph.co.uk/news/2016/05/17/italian-regions-battle-over-who-invented-tiramisu-in-long-runnin/> (accessed 5 February 2020)

22 'Pasta Puttanesca: What's With the Name?', *Italy Magazine*, 2020 <https://www.italymagazine.com/dual-language/pasta-puttanesca-whats-name> (accessed 5 February 2020)

23 Veronica Franco, *Poems and Selected Letters,* Ann Rosalind Jones and Margaret F. Rosenthal, eds. (Chicago: University of Chicago Press, 2007), p. 69

24 Ibid., p. 39

25 Kathryn Norberg, 'The Body of the Prostitute: Medieval to Modern', in Sarah Toulalan and Kate Fisher, eds., *The Routledge History of Sex and the Body: 1500 to the Present* (Abingdon; New York: Routledge, 2013), pp. 393–408

26 John Addington Symonds, *Renaissance in Italy,* Vol. 1 (London: Smith, Elder, 1909–11)

27 Madam Cresswell and Damaris Page, *The Poor-Whores Petition. To the most Splendid, Illustrious, Serene and Eminent Lady of Pleasure, the Countess of Castlemayne, &c. The Humble Petition of the undone company of poore distressed whores, bawds, pimps, and panders, &c.* (London: 1668)

CHAPTER FIVE: THE PLEASURES OF THE MOON; THE FLOATING WORLD OF EDO JAPAN

1 Jane Marie Law, *Puppets of Nostalgia: The Life, Death, and Rebirth of the Japanese Awaji Ningyō Tradition* (Princeton: Princeton University Press, 2016), p. 130

2 Cecilia Segawa Seigle, *Yoshiwara, The Glittering World of the Japanese Courtesan* (Honolulu: University of Hawaii Press, 1993), p. 6

3 Ibid., p. 9

4 Ibid., p. 11

5 Dominique Buisson, *Japan Unveiled: Understanding Japanese Body Culture* (London: Hachette Illustrated, 2003), p. 57

6 François Caron and Joost Schouten, *A True Description of the Mighty Kingdoms of Japan and Siam* (London: Robert Boulter, 1671), p. 74

7 Money L. Hickman, 'Views of the Floating World', *MFA Bulletin*, 76 (1978), pp. 4–33, p. 6

8 Cecilia Segawa Seigle, *Yoshiwara, The Glittering World of the Japanese Courtesan* (Honolulu: University of Hawaii Press, 1993), p. 82

9 Ibid., p. 34

CHAPTER SIX: MOLLY HOUSES AND MARY-ANNS; MEN SELLING SEX IN REGENCY BRITAIN

1 John Dunton, 'The He-Strumpets: A Satyr on the Sodomite Club, the Fourth Edition, Alter'd and much Enlarg'd', in *Athenianism*, Vol. 2 (London: Tho. Darrack, 1710), pp. 93–99

2 Rictor Norton, ed., 'Trial of Sodomites, 1707', *Homosexuality in Eighteenth-Century England: A Sourcebook*, 2003, updated 2008, <http://www.rictornorton.co.uk/eighteen/tryal07.htm> (accessed 10 February 2020)

3 Rictor Norton, ed., 'Newspaper Reports for 1707', *Homosexuality in Eighteenth-Century England: A Sourcebook*, 2000, updated 2008 <http://www.rictornorton.co.uk/eighteen/1707news.htm> (accessed 10 February 2020)

4 John Dunton, 'The He-Strumpets: A Satyr on the Sodomite Club, the Fourth Edition, Alter'd and much Enlarg'd', in *Athenianism*, Vol. 2 (London: Tho. Darrack, 1710), pp. 93–99

5 Andrew Knapp and William Baldwin, *The Newgate Calendar: Comprising Interesting Memoirs of the Most Notorious Characters Who Have Been Convicted of Outrages on the Laws of England* (London: J. Robins and Co., 1824–28), p. 268

6 Clement Walker, *Relations and Observations Historical and Politick upon the Parliament Begun Anno Dom. 1640* (London: 1648), p. 221

7 Edward Ward, 'Of the Mollies Club', in *Satyrical Reflections on Clubs,* Vol. 5 (London: J. Phillips, 1710)

8 *Caledonian Mercury*, 15 August 1726

9 *The British Journal*, 3 December 1726

10 *The London Journal*, 17 December 1726

11 Rictor Norton, ed., 'The Trial of Margaret Clap, 1726', *Homosexuality in Eighteenth-Century England: A Sourcebook*, 2002, updated 2008, <http://www.rictornorton.co.uk/eighteen/clap.htm> (accessed 10 February 2020)

12 *The London Journal*, 17 December 1726

13 Rictor Norton, ed., 'The Trial of Thomas Wright, 1726', *Homosexuality in Eighteenth-Century England: A Sourcebook*, 1999, updated 2008 <http://www.rictornorton.co.uk/eighteen/1726wrig.htm> (accessed 10 February 2020)

14 Ibid.

15 Ibid.

16 Ibid.

17 Ibid.

18 *The London Journal*, 30 July 1726

19 Rictor Norton, ed., 'Newspaper Reports, 1726', *Homosexuality in Eighteenth-Century England: A Sourcebook*, 2000, updated 2002 and 2018, <http://www.rictornorton.co.uk/eighteen/1726news.htm> (accessed 10 February 2020)

20 'Letter to the Editor', *The Weekly Journal: or, The British Gazetteer*, 14 May 1726

21 George Smyth, *A Sermon To the Societies for Reformation of Manners, Preach'd at Salter'-Hall, On Monday, June 26, 1727* (London: Eman. Matthews, 1727), pp. 19–20, pp. 31–33.

22 Rictor Norton, 'Mother Clap's Molly House', *The Gay Subculture in Georgian England*, 2005, <http://rictornorton.co.uk/eighteen/mother.htm> (accessed 10 February 2020)

23 'Communities – Homosexuality – Central Criminal Court', *Oldbaileyonline.org*, 2020 <https://www.oldbaileyonline.org/static/Gay.jsp> (accessed 5 February 2020)

CHAPTER SEVEN: MASTER OF THE PLUM BLOSSOMS; SEX IN THE QING DYNASTY

1 *Sufferings of John Turner, Chief Mate of the Country Ship, Tay, Bound for China, Under the Command of William Greig...* (London: T. Tegg, 1809), p. 13

2 Dian Murray, 'One Woman's Rise to Power: Cheng I's Wife and the Pirates', *Historical Reflections / Réflexions Historiques*, 8.3 (1981), pp. 147–61, p. 151

3 Ibid.

4 Rachel T. Hare-Mustin, 'China's Marriage Law: A Model for Family Responsibilities and Relationships', *Family Process*, 21.4 (1982), pp. 477–81

5 David Emil Mungello, *Drowning Girls in China: Female Infanticide in China Since 1650* (Lanham: Rowman & Littlefield, 2008), p. 9

6 Fang Fu Ruan, *Sex in China: Studies in Sexology in Chinese Culture* (New York: Springer, 1991), p. 70

7 Ibid., p. 71

8 Quoted in Fang Fu Ruan, *Sex in China: Studies in Sexology in Chinese Culture* (New York: Springer, 1991), p. 73

9 Paul A. Van Dyke, 'Floating Brothels and the Canton Flower Boats: 1750–1930', *Revista De Cultura*, 37 (2011), pp. 112–42, p. 112

10 Charles Frederick Noble, *A Voyage to the East Indies In 1747 And 1748, Containing an Account of the Islands of St. Helena and Java, of the City of Batavia, of the Government and Political Conduct of the Dutch, of the Empire of China, With a Particular Description of Canton, and of the Religious Ceremonies, Manners and Customs of the Inhabitants* (London: Becket, Dehondt, & Durham, 1762), pp. 278–79

11 Ibid., p. 281

12 Ibid.

13 William Hickey, *Memoirs of William Hickey*, Alfred Spencer, ed. (London: Hurst & Blackett, 1948), p. 198

14 Charles Frederick Noble, *A Voyage to the East Indies In 1747 And 1748, Containing an Account of the Islands of St. Helena and Java, of the City of Batavia, of the Government and Political Conduct of the Dutch, of the Empire of China, With a Particular Description of Canton, and of the Religious Ceremonies, Manners and Customs of the Inhabitants* (London: Becket, Dehondt, & Durham, 1762), p. 281

15 Peter Dobell, *Travels in Kamtchatka and Siberia; with a Narrative of a Residence in China*, Vol. 2 (London: Henry Colburn and Richard Bentley, 1830), pp. 140–41

16 Isabel Nunes, 'The Singing and Dancing Girls of Macau. Aspects Prostitution in Macau', *Instituto Cultural do Governo da Região Administrativa Especial de Macau*, 1994 <http://www.icm.gov.mo/rc/viewer/20018/994> (accessed 30 July 2020)

17 Charles Downing, *The Fan-Qui in China, in 1836–37*, Vol. 1 (London: Henry Colburn, 1838), pp. 245–46

18 Fang Fu Ruan, *Sex in China: Studies in Sexology in Chinese Culture* (New York: Springer, 1991), p. 75

CHAPTER EIGHT: THE GREAT SOCIAL EVIL; PROSTITUTION IN THE 19TH CENTURY

1 Bridget O'Donnell, *Inspector Minahan Makes a Stand: The Missing Girls of England* (Leicester: Thorpe, 2015), p. 104

2 Ibid.

3 Ibid.

4 *United Kingdom General Registrar Office, Census 1961, England and Wales, Preliminary Report* (London: Her Majesty's Stationery Office, 1961), p. 75, table 6

5 'London, 1800–1913', *Oldbaileyonline.org*, 2020 <https://www.oldbaileyonline.org/static/London-life19th.jsp> (accessed 7 March 2020)

6 'House of Commons Home Affairs Committee: Prostitution. Third Report Of Session 2016–17', *Publications Parliament UK*, 2016 <https://publications.parliament.uk/pa/cm201617/cmselect/cmhaff/26/26.pdf> (accessed 7 March 2020)

7 William Acton, *Prostitution, Considered in its Moral, Social, & Sanitary Aspects, in London and Other Large Cities: With Proposals for the Mitigation and Prevention of its Attendant Evils* (London: John Churchill, 1857), p. 7

8 Michael Ryan, *Prostitution in London: With a Comparative View of that of Paris and New York, as Illustrative of the Capitals and Large Towns of All Countries* (London: H. Bailliere, 1839), p. 90

9 Edward Cheshire, 'The Results of the Census of Great Britain In 1851, With a Description of the Machinery and Processes Employed to Obtain the Returns; Also an Appendix of Tables of Reference', *Journal of the Statistical Society of London*, 17.1 (1854), p. 55

10 Judith R. Walkowitz, *Prostitution and Victorian Society: Women, Class and the State* (Cambridge; New York: Cambridge University Press, 1980), p. 49

11 William Sloggett, 'History and Operations of the Contagious Diseases Acts in the Home Ports', *Admiralty Papers*, PRO 1/6418 (1873)

12 Alexandre Jean Baptiste Parent-Duchatelet, *De la prostitution dans la ville de Paris considérée sous le rapport de l'hygiène publique, de la morale et de l'administration*, Vol. 2, Chapter XVI (Paris: J. B. Baillière 1836)

13 Portsmouth, Plymouth, Woolwich, Chatham, Sheerness, Aldershot, Colchester, Shorncliffe, The Curragh, Cork, and Queenstown

14   Claire Kennan, 'Mistaken Identity: Elizabeth Burley and the Contagious Diseases Acts', *The National Archives Blog*, 2019 <https://blog.nationalarchives.gov.uk/mistaken-identity-elizabeth-burley-and-the-contagious-diseases-acts/> (accessed 2 March 2020)

15   Quoted in *The Times*, 15 January 1880

16   Josephine E. Butler, *Josephine E. Butler: An Autobiographical Memoir*, George W. Johnson and Lucy A. Johnson, eds. (Bristol: J. W. Arrowsmith, 1909), p. 27

17   Josephine Butler, *The Constitution Violated* (Edinburgh: Edmondson & Douglas, 1871), pp. 37–38

18   'The Home Secretary and the Case of Elizabeth Burley', *Derby Daily Telegraph*, 1881, p. 2

19   Ibid.

20   Ibid.

CHAPTER NINE: SOILED DOVES AND JAILBIRDS; SEX FOR SALE IN THE LAND OF THE FREE

1   Charles R. Mack and Ilona S. Mack, ed., *Like A Sponge Thrown Into Water: Francis Lieber's European Travel Journal of 1844–1845* (Columbia: University of South Carolina Press, 2002), p. 7

2   A. Roger Ekirch, 'Bound for America: A Profile of British Convicts Transported to the Colonies, 1718–1775', *The William an Mary Quarterly*, 42.2 (1985), pp. 184–200, p. 188

3   Ibid., p. 185

4   Ibid.

5   Daniel Defoe, *Moll Flanders* (London: W. Chetwood, 1722)

6   Jennifer Lodine-Chaffey, 'From Newgate to the New World: A Study of London's Transported Female Convicts 1718–1775', *ScholarWorks at University of Montana* (2006), p. 80

7   Ibid.

8   *Virginia Gazette*, 30 May 1751, p. 3; Benjamin Franklin, *The Papers of Benjamin Franklin*, Leonard W. Labaree et al., eds., Vol. 4 (New Haven: Yale University Press, 1961), pp. 131–33

9   Edward Jewett Wheeler and Frank Crane, 'Organized Vice as a Vested Interest', *Current Opinion*, 52 (1912), p. 292

10   Alexy Simmons, 'Red Light Ladies in the American West: Entrepreneurs and Companions', *Australian Journal of Historical Archaeology*, 7 (1989), pp. 63–69

11   Judith Kelleher Schafer, *Brothels, Depravity, and Abandoned Women* (Baton Rouge: Louisiana State University Press, 2009), p. 1

12   George Anthony Peffer, 'Forbidden Families: Emigration Experiences of Chinese Women under the Page Law, 1875–1882', *Journal of American Ethnic History*, 6.1 (1986), pp. 28–46, p. 28

13   Mary E. Odem, *Delinquent Daughters: Protecting and Policing Adolescent Female Sexuality In the United States, 1885–1920* (Chapel Hill; London: University of North Carolina Press, 1995), p. 10

14   Ibid., p. 122

15   Pamela D. Arceneaux, *Guidebooks to Sin: The Blue Books of Storyville, New Orleans* (New Orleans: Historic New Orleans Collection, 2017), p. 106

16   Brian Wallis, *The Mysterious Monsieur Bellocq* (New York: International Center of Photography, 2004), p. 10

17   *Blue Book* (New Orleans: *c.* 1905)

18   Billy Struve, *Blue Book* (New Orleans: 1905)

19   Jelly Roll Morton, *Mamie Desmond's Blues* (Washington: U.S Archive of Folk Song, 1938)

20   Alan Lomax, *Mister Jelly Roll: The Fortunes of Jelly Roll Morton, New Orleans Creole and Inventor of Jazz* (New York: Duell, Sloan and Pearce, 1950), p. 21

21   Thomas David Brothers, *Louis Armstrong in His Own Words* (Oxford: Oxford University Press, 1999), p. 30

CHAPTER TEN: MAISONS DE TOLÉRANCE; SEX AND THE BELLE ÉPOQUE

1   Alphonse Boudard, *Madame de Saint-Suplice* (Paris: Gallimard, 1998)

2   Henri Calet, *La Belle Lurette* (Paris: Gallimard, 1979), p. 168

3   *Le Crapouillot*, May 1939, pp. 12–13, as cited in Luc Sante, *The Other Paris: An Illustrated Journey Through a City's Poor and Bohemian Past* (London: Faber & Faber, 2017)

4   Sylvain Bonmariage, *Gagneuses! Chronique de l'amour venal* (Paris: La clé d'or, 1951)

5   William Acton, *Prostitution*, Peter Frye, ed. (London: MacGibben & Kie, 1968), pp. 97–107

6   Anonymous, *The Pretty Women of Paris* (Ware: Wordsworth Editions, 1996), pp. 66, 106, 133, 73, 121, 61

7   'Rapport: Au sujet du cafes de la Cigarette, 12 December 1879, BM2 24, APP', quoted in Andrew Israel Ross, 'Serving Sex: Playing With Prostitution in the *Brasseries À Femmes* of Late Nineteenth-Century Paris', *Journal of the History of Sexuality*, 24.2 (2015), pp. 288–313

8   Charles Castle, *La Belle Otero: The Last Great Courtesan* (London: Michael Joseph, 1981), p. 66

CHAPTER ELEVEN: THE PROPHYLACTIC DICTATORSHIP; SEX IN WARTIME

1   Lord Kitchener, 'Lord Kitchener's Advice: The True Character of a British Soldier', *King's Own Royal Regiment Museum Lancaster*, 2016, <http://www.kingsownmuseum.com/ko0418-12.htm> (accessed 8 May 2020)

2   Quoted in K. Craig Gibson, 'Sex and Soldiering
     in France and Flanders: The British Expeditionary
     Force Along the Western Front, 1914–1919',
     International History Review, 23.3 (2001), pp. 535–79

3   Mary Louise Roberts, *What Soldiers Do: Sex and
     the American GI In World War II* (Chicago: University
     of Chicago Press, 2013), p. 160

4   Thomas John Mitchell and Georgie May Smith,
     *History of The Great War Based on Official Documents:
     Medical Services: Casualties and Medical Statistics
     of the Great War* (London: Her Majesty's Stationary
     Office, 1931), p. 74

5   Maren Röger and Emmanuel Debruyne, 'From
     Control to Terror: German Prostitution Policies in
     Eastern and Western European Territories During
     Both World Wars', *Gender & History*, 28.3 (2016),
     pp. 687–708, p. 690

6   Ibid., p. 692

7   Ibid., p. 693

8   Quoted in Carl Henry Chrislock, *Watchdog of Loyalty:
     The Minnesota Commission of Public Safety During
     World War I* (St. Paul: Minnesota Historical Society
     Press, 1991), p. 237

9   Clare Makepeace, 'Punters and Their Prostitutes:
     British Soldiers, Masculinity and *Maisons Tolérées*
     in the First World War', in John H. Arnold and
     Sean Brady, eds., *What is Masculinity? Genders and
     Sexualities in History* (London: Palgrave Macmillan,
     2011), p. 419

10   Albert S. Bowen, *The Medical Department of
     the United States Army in the World War. Vol. 4,
     Activities Concerning Mobilization Camps and
     Ports of Embarkation* (Washington: Government
     Printing Office, 1928), p. 411

11   George Coppard, *With a Machine Gun to Cambrai:
     The Tale of a Young Tommy in Kitchener's Army
     1914–1918* (London: Her Majesty's Printing Office,
     1969), p. 56

12   John Boyd Coates, Ebbe Curtis Hoff, Leonard Dudley
     Heaton and Phebe Margaret Hoff, *Preventive Medicine
     in World War II* (Washington: Office of the Surgeon
     General, 1960), p. 197

13   Maren Röger and Emmanuel Debruyne, 'From
     Control to Terror: German Prostitution Policies in
     Eastern and Western European Territories During
     Both World Wars', *Gender & History*, 28.3 (2016),
     pp. 687–708, p. 699

14   Ibid.

15   Christa Schulz, *Frauen in Konzentrationslagern:
     Bergen-Belsen, Ravensbrück* (Bremen: Edition
     Temmen, 1994); Robert Sommer, *Das KZ-Bordell:
     sexuelle Zwangsarbeit in nationalsozialistischen
     Konzentrationslagern* (Paderborn: Ferdinand
     Schöningh, 2010)

16   Maren Röger and Emmanuel Debruyne, 'From
     Control to Terror: German Prostitution Policies
     in Eastern and Western European Territories
     During Both World Wars', *Gender & History*,
     28.3 (2016), pp. 687–708, p. 72.

CONCLUSION: THE FIGHT BACK

1   Lilian Mathieu, 'An Unlikely Mobilization:
     The Occupation of Saint-Nizier Church by the
     Prostitutes of Lyon', *Revue Française De Sociologie*,
     42.3 (2001), pp. 107–31

2   *Le Figaro*, 12 June 1975

3   C. Jaget, ed., *Prostitutes, Our Life* (Bristol: Falling
     Wall Press, 1980) p. 36

4   Eurydice Aroney, 'The 1975 French Sex Workers'
     Revolt: A Narrative of Influence', *Sexualities*, 23.1–2
     (2018), pp. 64–80, p. 69

5   Susan Stryker, *Transgender History: The Roots
     of Todays' Revolution* (Berkeley: Seal Press, 2008),
     p. 67

6   One of the earliest recorded examples of an
     organized sex worker protest is the 1886 march
     of the brothel workers of El Paso to a city council
     meeting to protest a new tax against them. There
     was also collective action in China in 1926 when sex
     workers in Xifen district of Guangzhou went on strike
     to protest a new police order that they all report to
     the district office to have their licence photographs
     retaken, at a cost of 1.4 yuan each. The loss in tax
     revenue caused by the strike meant the new orders
     were quickly overturned. See Elizabeth J. Remick,
     *Regulating Prostitution in China: Gender and Local
     Statebuilding, 1900–1937* (Stanford: Stanford
     University Press, 2014), p. 97. In June of 1942, sex
     workers in Honolulu, Hawaii, went on strike and
     picketed outside the police headquarters for almost
     three weeks. Eventually, both the military police and
     the Honolulu police agreed to let the sex workers live
     and work outside a brothel and to be seen in public.
     See Beth Bailey and David Farber, 'Hotel Street:
     Prostitution and the Politics of War', *Radical History
     Review*, 52, (1992), pp. 54–77.

7   '"What of Us?" Ask Magdalenes Who Crowd Church',
     San Francisco Chronicle, 1917, p. 1

8   Ibid.

9   Ibid.

10   'World Charter for Prostitutes' Rights, 1985',
     (Amsterdam: International Committee for
     Prostitutes' Rights (ICPR), 1985) <https://walnet.org/
     csis/groups/icpr_charter.html> (accessed
     4 October 2020)

11   Other groups who support the full decriminalization
     of sex work include Amnesty International,
     World Health Organization, UNAIDS, International
     Labour Organization, the Global Alliance Against
     Trafficking in Women, the Global Network of Sex
     Work Projects, the Global Commission on
     HIV and the Law, Human Rights Watch,
     the Open Society Foundations and
     Anti-Slavery International.

12   Prostitution Law Review Committee,
     *The Impact of the Prostitution Reform Act on
     the Health and Safety Practices of Sex Workers*
     (Otago: University of Otago, 2006)

Arceneaux, Pamela D., *Guidebooks To Sin: The Blue Books Of Storyville, New Orleans* (New Orleans: Historic New Orleans Collection, 2017)

Archer, Caroline, *Tart Cards* (New York: Mark Batty, 2003)

Aroney, Eurydice, 'The 1975 French Sex Workers' Revolt: A Narrative of Influence', *Sexualities*, 23.1–2 (2018), pp. 64–80

Assante, Julia, 'The Kar.Kid/Arimtu, Prostitute or Single Woman? A Critical Review of the Evidence', *Ugarit-Forschungen*, 30 (1998), pp. 5–96

Bailey, Beth and David Farber, 'Hotel Street: Prostitution and the Politics of War', *Radical History Review*, 52, (1992), pp. 54–77

Blair, Cynthia M., *I've Got To Make My Livin': Black Women's Sex Work In Turn-of-the-Century Chicago* (Chicago: University of Chicago Press, 2010)

Brackett, John K., 'The Florentine Onesta and the Control of Prostitution, 1403–1680', *The Sixteenth Century Journal*, 24.2 (1993), pp. 273–300

Budin, Stephanie Lynn, *The Myth Of Sacred Prostitution in Antiquity* (Cambridge: Cambridge University Press, 2008)

Caslin, Samantha and Julia Laite, *Wolfenden's Women: Prostitution in Post-War Britain* (London: Palgrave Macmillan, 2020)

Chateauvert, Melinda, *Sex Workers Unite! A History of the Movement From Stonewall To Slutwalk* (Boston: Beacon Press, 2013)

Cruickshank, Dan, *The Secret History of Georgian London* (London: Random House, 2009)

Drinot, Paulo, *The Sexual Question: A History of Prostitution in Peru, 1850s–1950s* (Cambridge; New York: Cambridge University Press, 2020)

Faraone, Christopher A. and Laura K. McClure, *Prostitutes and Courtesans in the Ancient World* (Madison: University of Wisconsin Press, 2006)

Friedlander, Lee and John Szarkowski, *E.J. Bellocq: Storyville Portraits; Photographs From the New Orleans Red-Light District* (New York: Museum of Modern Art, 1970)

Ghirardo, Diane Yvonne, 'The Topography of Prostitution in Renaissance Ferrara', *Journal of the Society of Architectural Historians*, 60.4 (2001), pp. 402–3

Gibson, Craig, 'Sex and Soldiering in France and Flanders: The British Expeditionary Force Along the Western Front, 1914–1919', *International History Review*, 23.3 (2001), pp. 535–79

Henderson, Tony, *Disorderly Women in Eighteenth-Century London: Prostitution and Control in the Metropolis, 1730–1830* (London: Longman, 1999)

Henriot, Christian, *Prostitution and Sexuality in Shanghai: A Social History, 1849–1949* (Cambridge: Cambridge University Press, 2001)

Karras, Ruth Mazo, *Common Women: Prostitution and Sexuality in Medieval England* (New York: Oxford University Press, 1996)

Kinnell, Hilary, *Violence and Sex Work in Britain* (Cullompton; Portland: Willan, 2006)

Laite, Julia, *Common Prostitutes and Ordinary Citizens: Commercial Sex in London, 1885–1960* (London: Palgrave Macmillan, 2012)

Lerner, Gerda, 'The Origin of Prostitution in Ancient Mesopotamia', *Signs*, 11.2 (1986), pp. 236–54

Levin-Richardson, Sarah, *The Brothel of Pompeii: Sex, Class and Gender at the Margins of Roman Society* (Cambridge: Cambridge University Press, 2019)

Makepeace, Clare, 'Punters and Their Prostitutes: British Soldiers, Masculinity and Maisons Tolérées in the First World War', in John H. Arnold and Sean Brady, eds., *What is Masculinity? Genders and Sexualities in History* (London: Palgrave Macmillan, 2011), p. 419

Mathieu, Lilian, 'An Unlikely Mobilization: The Occupation of Saint-Nizier Church by the Prostitutes of Lyon', *Revue Française De Sociologie*, 42.3 (2001), pp. 107–31

Murphy, Catherine, 'Sex Workers' Rights Are Human Rights', *Amnesty International* (2015)

Murray, Dian, 'One Woman's Rise to Power: Cheng I's Wife and the Pirates', *Historical Reflections / Réflexions Historiques*, 8.3 (1981), pp. 147–61

Norton, Rictor, *Mother Clap's Molly House: Gay Subculture in England, 1700–1830* (London: GMP, 1992)

Remick, Elizabeth J., *Regulating Prostitution in China: Gender and Local Statebuilding, 1900–1937* (Stanford: Stanford University Press, 2014)

Roberts, Mary Louise, *What Soldiers Do: Sex and the American GI In World War II* (Chicago: University of Chicago Press, 2013)

Rodriguez Garcia, Magaly, Lex Heerma van Voss and Elise van Nederveen Meerkerk, *Selling Sex in the City: A Global History of Prostitution, 1600s–2000s* (Leiden; Boston: Brill, 2017)

Röger, Maren, and Emmanuel Debruyne, 'From Control to Terror: German Prostitution Policies in Eastern and Western European Territories During Both World Wars', *Gender & History*, 28.3 (2016), pp. 687–708

Rose, Al, *Storyville, New Orleans* (Tuscaloosa: University of Alabama Press, 1974)

Ross, Andrew Israel, 'Serving Sex: Playing With Prostitution in the Brasseries À Femmes of Late Nineteenth-Century Paris', *Journal of the History of Sexuality*, 24.2 (2015), pp. 288–313

Rubenhold, Hallie, *The Five: The Untold Lives of the Women Killed by Jack the Ripper* (London: Doubleday, 2019)

Sanders, Teela, Jane Pitcher and Maggie O'Neill, *Prostitution: Sex Work, Policy and Politics* (Los Angeles; London: SAGE, 2009)

Seigle, Cecilia Segawa, *Yoshiwara, The Glittering World of the Japanese Courtesan* (Honolulu: University of Hawaii Press, 1993)

Simmons, Alexy, 'Red Light Ladies in the American West: Entrepreneurs and Companions', *Australian Journal of Historical Archaeology*, 7 (1989), pp. 63–69

Smith, Molly, and Juno Mac, *Revolting Prostitutes: The Fight For Sex Workers' Rights* (London; Brooklyn: Verso, 2018)

Stryker, Susan, *Transgender History: The Roots of Todays' Revolution* (Berkeley: Seal Press, 2008)

Torri, Maria Costanza, 'Abuse of Lower Castes in South India: The Institution of Devadasi', *Journal of International Women's Studies*, 11.2 (2009), pp. 31–48

Van Dyke, Paul A., 'Floating Brothels and the Canton Flower Boats: 1750–1930', *Revista De Cultura*, 37 (2011), pp. 112–42

Walkowitz, Judith R., *Prostitution and Victorian Society: Women, Class and the State* (Cambridge; New York: Cambridge University Press, 1980)

1 Chronicle/Alamy Stock Photo, 2 Museum purchase with funds provided by Wellesley College Friends of Art/Bridgeman Images, 4 Image by E.J. Bellocq © Lee Friedlander, courtesy Fraenkel Gallery, San Francisco, 6 Stefano Bianchetti/Corbis via Getty Images, 8l adoc-photos/Corbis via Getty Images, 8r MeijiShowa/Alamy Stock Photo, 9l Sepia Times/Universal Images Group via Getty Images, 9r Margaret Bourke-White/The LIFE Picture Collection via Getty Images, 11 Bettmann/Getty, 12 Lawrence Alma-Tadema, *The Women of Amphissa*, 1887, Oil on canvas. Acquired by the Clark, 1978. The Clark Art Institute, 1978.12., 14 Fine Art Images/Heritage Images/Getty Images, 16l, 16c The Israel Museum, Jerusalem, 16r Private Collection, 17 The Metropolitan Museum of Art, New York, 19a CM Dixon/Heritage Images/Getty Images, 19b Matteo Omied/Alamy Stock Photo, 19c CM Dixon/Heritage Images/Getty Images, 19d www.BibleLandPictures.com/Alamy Stock Photo, 19e DeAgostini/Getty Images, 19f www.BibleLandPictures.com/Alamy Stock Photo, 19g DEA / A. DAGLI ORTI/De Agostini via Getty Images, 19h Bridgeman Images, 19i CM Dixon/Print Collector/Getty Images, 20 Lawrence Alma-Tadema, *The Women of Amphissa*, 1887, Oil on canvas. Acquired by the Clark, 1978. The Clark Art Institute, 1978.12., 21, Edwin Long, *The Babylonian Marriage Market*, 1875, 22 Granger/Shutterstock, 25 Private Collection, 26 The J Paul Getty Museum, Los Angeles, 28 © Marie-Lan Nguyen/Wikimedia Commons/CC-BY 2.5, 30 incamerastock / Alamy Stock Photo, 31l The J Paul Getty Museum, Los Angeles, 31c SSPL/Getty Images, 31r Chronicle/Alamy Stock Photo, 32al The Metropolitan Museum of Art, New York, 32ar Antikensammlung, Berlin, 32cl ©The Trustees of the British Museum, 32cr The Metropolitan Museum of Art, New York, 32bl ©The Trustees of the British Museum, 32br The J Paul Getty Museum, Los Angeles, 33al Marie-Lan Nguyen, 33ar ©The Trustees of the British Museum, 33cl Private Collection, 33cr The J Paul Getty Museum, Los Angeles, 33bl Gianni Dagli Orti/Shutterstock, 33br Azoor Photo Collection/Alamy Stock Photo, 34–35 The Metropolitan Museum of Art, New York, 36 Fine Art Images/Heritage Images/Getty Images, 37 Matteo Omied/Alamy Stock Photo, 38, 40–41 Bibliothèque Nationale de France, Paris, 42l Casa del Centenario, Pompeii, 42r Lupanar Brothel, Pompeii, 43l National Archaeological Museum, Naples, 43r Terme Suburbane, Pompeii, 45 Fotografica Foglia/Electa/Mondadori Portfolio via Getty Images, 46 Acquired by Henry Walters with the Massarenti Collection, 1902, The Walters Art Museum, Baltimore, 48 © The Trustees of the British Museum, 50l Album/Alamy Stock Photo, 50c Dea/A. Dagli orti/Getty, 50r Fine Art Images/Heritage Images via Getty Images, 51l *Des cleres et nobles femmes, De claris mulieribus*, Giovanni Boccaccio, *c.* 1400, 51c Spencer Collection, The New York Public Library, New York, 51r Département des Manuscrits. Français 5054, Bibliothèque Nationale de France, 53al © The Trustees of the British Museum, 53ar, 53bl Rijksmuseum, Amsterdam, 53br ©The Trustees of the British Museum, 54l Medievalists.net, 54c, 54cr Bibliothèque Nationale de France, Paris, 55l Hulton Archive/Getty Images, 55c Fine Art Images/Heritage Images/Getty Images, 55r Bibliothèque nationale de France. Bibliothèque de l'Arsenal, 56l Fine Art Images/Heritage Images/Getty Images, 56r Peter Horree/Alamy Stock Photo, 57l Acquired by Henry Walters with the Massarenti Collection, 1902, The Walters Art Museum, Baltimore, 57r Imagno/Getty Images, 58 Art Images/Heritage Images/Getty Images, 60 Asar Studios/Alamy Stock Photo, 62l Rijksmuseum, Amsterdam, 62r Bibliothèque Nationale de France, Paris, 63l Estate of Randolph Gunter, 1962, The Metropolitan Museum of Art, New York, 63c Bibliothèque Nationale de France, Paris, 63r Rijksmuseum, Amsterdam, 64–65 The Walters Art Museum, Baltimore, 66a Irene Lewisohn Bequest, 1973, The Metropolitan Museum of Art, New York, 66b, 66c, 69 Album/Alamy Stock Photo, 70l Salomè, Moretto da Brescia, 1537, 70c Peter Horree/Alamy Stock Photo, 70r Alfredo Dagli Orti/Shutterstock, 71l Heritage Image Partnership Ltd/Alamy Stock Photo, 71c Rubens Alarcon/Alamy Stock Photo, 71r The Picture Art Collection/Alamy Stock Photo, 72 Rijksmuseum, Amsterdam, 75al National Gallery of Art, Washington D.C., 75ac *Olympia Mancini*, Pierre Mignard, *c.* 1673, 75ar Photo 12/Alamy Stock Photo, 75cl The Picture Art Collection/Alamy Stock Photo, 75c The J Paul Getty Museum, Los Angeles, 75cr The Picture Art Collection/Alamy Stock Photo, 75bl ©Philip Mould Ltd, London/Bridgeman Images, 75bc IanDagnall Computing/Alamy Stock Photo, 75br The Philadelphia Museum of Art, Philadelphia, 76 Wellcome Library, London, 78 DeAgostini/Getty Images, 80 The Metropolitan Museum of Art, New York, 83al Samuel M. Nickerson Fund, The Art Institute Chicago, 83ac Honululu Museum of Art, 83ar J Marshall, Tribaleye Images/Alamy Stock Photo, 83cl, 83c DeAgostini/Getty Images, 83cr Sepia Times/Universal Images Group via Getty Images, 83bl, 83bc Fine Art Images/Heritage Images/Getty Images, 83br Dea/A. Dagli Orti/Getty Images, 84–85 from the Shagan collection, 86–87 The Metropolitan Museum of Art, New York, 88–89 J. E. De Becker, *The Nightless City: or The History of the Yoshiwara Yūkwaku*, 1905, 90–93 The Metropolitan Museum of Art, New York, 94–95 Miyagawa Isshō, *Spring Pastimes*, 1750, 96a CPA Media Pte Ltd/Alamy Stock Photo, 96b AB Historic/Alamy Stock Photo, 97 MeijiShowa/Alamy Stock Photo, 99–101 J. E. De Becker, *The Nightless City: or The History of the Yoshiwara Yūkwaku*, 1905, 102 Philip Dawe, *The Macaroni, a Real Character at the Late Masquerade*, 1773, 104 Yale Center for British Art, Paul Mellon Collection, 107 ©The Trustees of the British Museum, 108–109 The Picture Art Collection/Alamy Stock Photo, 110a *Harris's List of Covent Garden Ladies*, 1773, 110b Guildhall Library & Art Gallery/Heritage Images/Getty Images, 112–113 ©The Trustees of the British Museum, 114l Wellcome Library, London, 114c Courtesy of The Lewis Walpole Library, Yale University, 114r The History Collection/Alamy Stock Photo, 115l Historic Collection/Alamy Stock Photo, 115c Philip Dawe, *The Macaroni, a Real Character at the Late Masquerade*, 1773, 115r ©The Trustees of the British Museum, 117 Alpha Stock/Alamy Stock Photo, 118 Wellcome Library, London, 119 ©The Trustees of the British Museum, 120–121 Wellcome Library, London, 122 Reproduced by courtesy of the Essex Record Office, 124 Private Collection, 126 Eileen Tweedy/Shutterstock, 128 Courtesy of the Peabody Essex Museum, 129 © British Library Board. All Rights Reserved/Bridgeman Images, 130 Zip Lexing/Alamy Stock Photo, 132–133 Private Collection, 135 Wellcome Library, London, 136l CPA Media Pte Ltd/Alamy Stock Photo, 136r Henry Mayhew, *London Labour and the London Poor*, Vol. 4, 136l, 137l Chronicle/Alamy Stock Photo, 136r Division of Rare and Manuscript Collections, Cornell University Library, 138l CPA Media Pte Ltd/Alamy Stock Photo, 138r Pictures from History/Bridgeman Images, 139l Chronicle/Alamy Stock Photo, 139r Private Collection, 140 Bridgeman Images, 142 Minneapolis Institute of Art, Minneapolis, 144–145 Chronicle/Alamy Stock Photo, 146–147 Look and Learn/Peter Jackson Collection/Bridgeman Images, 148 Jean Giraudeau, *The Syphilitic Diseases with Comparative Examination of their Various Healing Methods*, 1841, 150l, 150c Wellcome Library, London, 150r Nizhny Novgorod Fair Government, 151l Wellcome Library, London, 151c Look and Learn/Peter Jackson Collection/Bridgeman Images, 151r Wellcome Library, London, 152–153 Painters/Alamy Stock Photo, 154l History collection 2016/Alamy Stock Photo, 154r Notice of a public meeting issued by Josephine Butler during the Pontefract by-election, 1872, 155l, 155cl Charles Washington Shirley Deakin, *The Contagious Diseases Acts*, 1871, 155cr *Report for the Ladies' National Association for the Repeal of the Contagious Diseases Acts*, 1871, 155r Wellcome Library, London, 156–157 Chronicle/Alamy Stock Photo, 159 Heritage Image Partnership Ltd/Alamy Stock Photo, 160 Museum purchase with funds provided by Wellesley College Friends of Art/Bridgeman Images, 162 Bettmann/Getty Images, 164 Metropolitan Museum of Art, New York, 167a H Coll 298.35, George G. Cantwell Photographs, UW 12871, University of Washington Special Collections, 167b PH Coll 306.19, Larss and Duclos Photographs, UW 34431, University of Washington Special Collections, 168 University of Kentucky Archives, 169 Rumsey Collection, 170 Library of Congress Prints and Photographs, Washington D.C., 172–173 The Historic New Orleans Collection, 1950.57.17, 175 The Historic New Orleans Collection, HQ146.N6 W55, 176–177 Image by E.J. Bellocq ©Lee Friedlander, courtesy Fraenkel Gallery, San Francisco, 178l Library of Congress Prints and Photographs, Washington D.C., 178r The Historic New Orleans Collection, 1969.19.6, 179l Hulton Archive/Getty Images, 179r The Historic New Orleans Collection, MSS 520, 92-48-L.205, 180–181 The Historic New Orleans Collection, 1969.19.4, 182al The Historic New Orleans Collection, 1969.19.9, 182ar The Historic New Orleans Collection, 1969.19.7, 182bl The Historic New Orleans Collection, 1969.19.9, 182br The Historic New Orleans Collection, 1969.19.9, 184 ©Archives Charmet/Bridgeman Images, 186–187 Courtesy Nicole Canet, Galerie Au Bonheur du Jour, Paris, 188al, 188acl Private Collection, 188acr adoc-photos/Corbis via Getty Images, 188al, 188 (bottom row) Private Collection, 189–195 Paris Musées/Musée Carnavalet - Histoire de Paris, 197 Alexandre Jean Baptiste Parent-Duchatelet, *Distribution of Prostitutes in each of the Forty-eight Quarters of Paris*, 1836, 198 Ville de Paris / BHVP, 199 Ville de Paris/Bibliothèque Marguerite Durand, 200 Paris Musées/Musée Carnavalet - Histoire de Paris, 202al PVDE / Bridgeman Images, 202ar Bridgeman Images, 202b Bourgeron/Bridgeman Images, 203 Collection Bourgeron/Bridgeman Images, 204–205 Imagno/Getty Images, 207 Private Collection, 208 Ville de Paris/Bibliothèque Forney, 209 PR Archive/Alamy Stock Photo, 210–211 Paris Musées/Musée Carnavalet - Histoire de Paris, 212l Universal History Archive/UIG/Shutterstock, 212c Metropolitan Museum of Art, New York, 212r Chronicle/Alamy Stock Photo, 213l Henry Guttmann Collection/Hulton Archive/Getty Images, 213c, 213r Apic/Getty Images, 214 ©Estate Brassaï - RMN-Grand Palais, 216 Wellcome Library, London, 218 ©Corbis via Getty Images, 220l The King's Own Royal Regiment Museum, Lancaster, 220r Austrian Archives/Imagno/Getty Images, 221 Chronicle/Alamy Stock Photo, 222 Private Collection, 223 adoc-photos/Getty Images, 224–225 The Miriam and Ira D. Wallach Division of Art, Prints and Photographs, New York Public Library, 227 Private Collection, 228 Wellcome Library, London, 229 David Pollack/Corbis via Getty Images, 230l Jack Birns/The LIFE Picture Collection via Getty Images, 230r © IWM SE 5226, 231 Sammlung KZ Mauthausen (Bild 192), 232–233 Bundesarchiv, Koblenz, 234 Private Collection, 235a FLHC 93/Alamy Stock Photo, 235b The History Collection/Alamy Stock Photo, 236al ©Hulton-Deutsch Collection/CORBIS/Corbis via Getty Images, 236ar Bettmann/Getty Images, 236cl, 236cr ©Hulton-Deutsch Collection/CORBIS/Corbis via Getty Images, 236bl Ralph Morse/The LIFE Picture Collection via Getty Images, 236br Three Lions/Getty Images, 238 AFP via Getty Images, 240 Alain Voloch/Gamma-Rapho via Getty Images, 241l Jerry Engel/New York Post Archives /©NYP Holdings, Inc. via Getty Images, 241r Leonard Fink Photographs, The LGBT Community Center National History Archive, 242 Sutton Hibbert/Shutterstock, 243 Dangerous Minds, 245 John Locher/AP/Shutterstock **Endpapers** The Print Collector/Getty Images, **Cover** Adoc-photos/Corbis via Getty Images

ACKNOWLEDGMENTS

Kate Lister would like to thank Professor Andrew R. George for his invaluable help in locating Shamhat in the various translations of the *Epic of Gilgamesh*.

Tristan de Lancey, Jane Laing, Phoebe Lindsley, Isabel Jessop and Rachel Heley at Thames & Hudson.

The author and the publisher would also like to thank Wellcome Collection for their help in making this publication possible.

ABOUT THE AUTHOR

Kate Lister is a lecturer in the School of Arts and Communication at Leeds Trinity University. Kate researches the history of sex work and curates the online research project Whores of Yore, an interdisciplinary digital archive for the study of historical sexuality. She regularly writes about the history of sexuality for *inews* and the Wellcome Trust. Kate won the Sexual Freedom Publicist of the Year Award in 2017 and is the author of *The Curious History of Sex*.

P. 1 Victorian courtesans (left to right) Baby Thornhill, Clara Rousby and Lizzy Dickson, *c*. 1870.

P. 2–4 E. J. Bellocq, portraits of sex workers in Storyville, New Orleans, *c*. 1910.

P. 6 Fortune Louis Meaulle, *Discovery of a Victim of Jack the Ripper in London*, 1888.

P. 238 Sex workers following their arrest in Paris, 12 December 1960, for demonstrating against the regulation of their profession.

COVER A representation of a scene in a French brothel, *c*. 1900. Photo by adoc-photos/Corbis via Getty Images.

First published in the United Kingdom in 2021 by Thames & Hudson Ltd, 181A High Holborn, London WC1V 7QX

First published in the United States of America in 2021 by Thames & Hudson Inc, 500 Fifth Avenue, New York, New York, 10110

Harlots, Whores & Hackabouts © 2021 Thames & Hudson Ltd, London

Text © 2021 Kate Lister

For image copyright information see p. 253.

Designed by Anıl Aykan and Sara Ozvaldic at Barnbrook

British Library Cataloguing-in-Publication Data. A catalogue record for this book is available from the British Library.

Library of Congress Control Number: 2021933185

ISBN 978-0-500-25244-4

Printed in Singapore by 1010 Printing International Ltd

Be the first to know about our new releases, exclusive content and author events by visiting
thamesandhudson.com
thamesandhudsonusa.com
thamesandhudson.com.au

MIX
Paper from
responsible sources
FSC
www.fsc.org
FSC® C016973